For Jessie Ann,
with many thanks
for your support of my work.

Sister
9/08

THE NEW MIDDLE AGES

BONNIE WHEELER, *Series Editor*

The New Middle Ages is a series dedicated to pluridisciplinary studies of medieval cultures, with particular emphasis on recuperating women's history and on feminist and gender analyses. This peer-reviewed series includes both scholarly monographs and essay collections.

PUBLISHED BY PALGRAVE:

THE MEDIEVAL POETICS
OF THE RELIQUARY

ENSHRINEMENT, INSCRIPTION,
PERFORMANCE

Seeta Chaganti

THE MEDIEVAL POETICS OF THE RELIQUARY
Copyright © Seeta Chaganti, 2008.

All rights reserved.

First published in 2008 by
PALGRAVE MACMILLAN®
in the US—a division of St. Martin's Press LLC,
175 Fifth Avenue, New York, NY 10010.

Where this book is distributed in the UK, Europe and the rest of the world,
this is by Palgrave Macmillan, a division of Macmillan Publishers Limited,
registered in England, company number 785998, of Houndmills,
Basingstoke, Hampshire RG21 6XS.

Palgrave Macmillan is the global academic imprint of the above companies
and has companies and representatives throughout the world.

Palgrave® and Macmillan® are registered trademarks in the United States,
the United Kingdom, Europe and other countries.

ISBN-13: 978–0–230–60466–7
ISBN-10: 0–230–60466–8

Library of Congress Cataloging-in-Publication Data

Chaganti, Seeta.
   The medieval poetics of the reliquary : enshrinement, inscription,
performance / Seeta Chaganti.
      p. cm.—(The new Middle Ages)
      ISBN 0–230–60466–8 (alk. paper)
      1. English literature—Middle English, 1100–1500—History and
criticism. 2. Reliquaries, Medieval. 3. Poetics. 4. Chaucer, Geoffrey,
d. 1400. Book of the Duchesse. 5. Saint Erkenwald (Middle English
poem) 6. Ludus Coventriae. 7. Pearl (Middle English poem)
8. Sacred space in literature. 9. Inscriptions in literature.
10. Performance in literature. I. Title.

PR255.C48 2008
820.9'382—dc22   2008003513

A catalogue record of the book is available from the British Library.

Design by Newgen Imaging Systems (P) Ltd., Chennai, India.

First edition: October 2008

10 9 8 7 6 5 4 3 2 1

Printed in the United States of America.

To Sara Chaganti

CONTENTS

ILLUSTRATIONS

ACKNOWLEDGMENTS

From its inception as a dissertation to its emergence as a book under the innovative stewardship of Bonnie Wheeler at Palgrave Macmillan, this project has benefited from a number of generous allies. Penn Szittya, who first encouraged me to become a medievalist, deserves special acknowledgment here. Lee Patterson and R. Howard Bloch provided rigorous and insightful readings of my dissertation at Yale University. Other thoughtful interlocutors from this time include Jill Campbell, Jenny Davidson, Elizabeth Fowler, Roberta Frank, Matt Giancarlo, Kevis Goodman, Amy Hungerford, Kathryn Kerby-Fulton, Laura King, Traugott Lawler, Bobby Meyer-Lee, Annabel Patterson, Nina Prytula, Fred Robinson, George Shuffelton, Emily Steiner, and Tracey Tomlinson. At the University of California, Davis, I have had the good fortune to be surrounded by wonderful colleagues who have commented on versions of this project and provided numerous other forms of support. I thank Emily Albu, Joan Cadden, Lucy Corin, Fran Dolan, Margie Ferguson, Beth Freeman, Noah Guynn, Richard Levin, Lisa Materson, Colin Milburn, Marijane Osborn, Winfried Schleiner, David van Leer, Ray Waddington, and Claire Waters. I am grateful as well to the university for providing grants and other forms of financial support for the research, writing, and publication of this book. A circle of friends and colleagues beyond my own campus have also made valuable contributions to this project—my thanks go especially to Elizabeth Allen, Katy Breen, Glenn Davis, Andrea Denny-Brown, Bob Epstein, Lianna Farber, Kathy Lavezzo, Peggy McCracken, Chris Nealon, Susie Phillips, Masha Raskolnikov, Cathy Sanok, Jane Tolmie, Kathryn Vulic, and Meg Worley. I thank William Kuskin and Maura Nolan as well for carefully reading portions of the manuscript and providing me with helpful advice and critique. Jessica Brantley, Becky Krug, and Beth Robertson read earlier versions of the manuscript in its entirety; I am so grateful for their time, and for the perceptiveness of their comments.

I have received intellectual, creative, and emotional sustenance from other sources as well. I thank Carolyn Melville, Cara Rains, Pamela

Trokanski, and the dancers of the Pamela Trokanski Dance Workshop, in Davis, California, for welcoming me into their community. They have given me opportunities—crucial for this book—to speak in nonverbal languages and to be a performer. Joshua Clover, Carol Clover, Marcos Karnezos, James Guiry, my sister Sara Chaganti, and my parents Raju and Seeta R. Chaganti are all deeply beloved family, without whom I could not have completed this project. Sara Chaganti, to whom I have dedicated this book, inspires me with her unique ability to enfold compassion and insight within each other.

For permission to adapt material from an earlier essay published in *New Medieval Literatures*, vol. 7 (2005), I thank Oxford University Press. Sharron Wood provided clear-eyed and clear-headed copyediting. Finally, Clare Brown and the staff of Lambeth Palace Library, London, offered courteous assistance in obtaining the image of the Cross of Bromholm, which appears on the cover of this volume with the kind permission of the Trustees of Lambath Palace Library.

INTRODUCTION

At every moment in the Middle Ages, the veneration of relics formed a ubiquitous and essential component of devotional practice. Medieval reliquaries were artifacts designed to contain these sacred bodily vestiges. Reliquaries ranged enormously in shape and nature, from caskets and portable disks (figures Intr.1 and Intr.2), to objects shaped like body parts held up in ceremonial processions (figure Intr.3), to large and elaborate altarpieces decorated with busts containing relics (figure Intr.4), to architecturally inspired artifacts constructed of metalwork and windows (figure Intr.5). Even entire architectural spaces were sometimes designed to convey the formal features of the reliquary, as was the case of the Sainte-Chapelle, which Louis IX conceived of as a grandly magnified reliquary shrine. This important structure wielded influence by continuing to serve as a model for royal building projects even in late-medieval England, the main focus of this study.[1] The device of building as reliquary also persisted into the late Middle Ages, as evidenced in this period's various correspondences between architectural and metalwork ornamentation.[2] By inhabiting spaces that both echoed and contained reliquaries, late-medieval devotional life embraced and was embraced by the aesthetics of these enshrining artifacts. Enshrinement as an aesthetic principle united memorial objects of different scales and functions, including reliquaries, shrines, tombs, and chapels. Speaking of one form could imply the features and structures of others as well.[3]

Throughout the Middle Ages, communities of the faithful encountered reliquaries and other enshrining structures in a variety of devotional performances, including processions as well as liturgical and para-liturgical ceremonies. But while on the one hand these objects were designed to be viewed through the instantaneous apprehension of visual spectacle, on the other hand their decorative programs often incorporated written inscription into their iconography. Written inscription could take the form, as it famously does on the Anglo-Saxon Brussels Cross, of a declaration about the object's maker or patron. It could also indicate the reliquary's contents, as in a fifteenth-century French umbilical-cord

Figure Intr.1 Reliquary decorated with scenes from the childhood of Christ and the life of the Virgin, first half of the fourteenth century. Copper with gilding, engraving, and champlevé enamel; 20.2 x 24.1 x 10.1 cm. Musée national du Moyen Âge–Thermes de Cluny, Paris, France.

Source: Photo by Gerard Blot. Réunion des Musées Nationaux/Art Resource, New York.

Figure Intr.2 Disk Reliquary: Virgin and Child surrounded by the four Cardinal Virtues, ca. 1146–74. Godefroid de Huy, the Netherlands. Champlevé enamel ongilt copper; the reverse, with vernis brun; 17.70 x 17.20 cm. The Cleveland Museum of Art.

Source: © The Cleveland Museum of Art, purchase from J. H. Wade Fund, 1926.428.

Figure Intr.3 Reliquary Arm, ca. 1230. German, made in Lorraine. Silver over oak; hand: bronze gilt; appliqué plaques: silver-gilt, niello, and cabochon stones; 64.8 x 16.5 x 10.2 cm. The Cloisters Collection, 1947 (47.101.33). The Cloisters, New York.

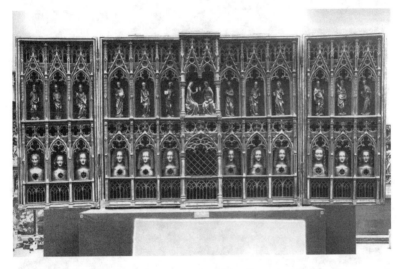

Figure Intr.4 Winged Altarpiece, ca. 1350. Cistercian Abbey, Marienstatt, Germany.

Source: Foto Marburg/Art Resource, New York.

Figure Intr.5 Monstrance-reliquary, ca. 1320–40. Venice. Gilded, engraved, openwork copper, cast iron, and glass; 33 x 11 cm. Musée national du Moyen Âge–Thermes de Cluny, Paris, France.

Source: Photo by Franck Raux. Réunion des Musées nationaux/Art Resource, New York.

reliquary (figure Intr.6), or it could participate in the visual iconography's narrative of scriptural history, as in the twelfth-century Stavelot triptych (figure Intr.7).

Reliquaries and shrines investigated the interaction between the modes of inscription and performance. We tend to think of written inscription as a mode of communication that is silent and inward-turning, a system of marks referring to their internal differences in order to produce meaning. We tend to think of performance practice, on the other hand, as voiced, turned outward, and engaged with the world around it.[4] But reliquaries and shrines powerfully integrated written inscription with the culture of performance. Seen within their appropriate contexts of devotional activity, these objects offered a model of representational practice to medieval culture. The reliquary performatively contacted and contributed to a reality exterior to itself through its implication in ceremony and vocal utterance, while it simultaneously encapsulated a system of self-reference formed by its silent instances of written inscription. This study will argue that the reliquary offered a model of representational practice in which inscription and performance existed dialectically: while seeming to oscillate between these two modes, the reliquary in fact merged the two possibilities by allowing each to frame and enable the other. This model produced the formal mechanism for a late-medieval English poetics—what this book will term the poetics of enshrinement. In some ways, such a perspective on the components of artistic representation reflects recent discourses in media theory, which similarly investigates the relationship within different media between a poststructuralist "play of signs" and the "real, effective presence of media in our culture."[5] Keeping this theoretical development in mind will help to remind us of the ways in which our perspective on medieval life and thought is unavoidably shaped by our absorption of subsequent discourses and patterns of perception. But within this larger context, I aim to build the case that the medieval world spoke in its own languages about representational phenomena that we might most effectively understand through the terms of performativity and inscriptionality. The medieval terminologies that define such phenomena, I shall argue, differ mainly in that they were often primarily visual and artifact-based.

A few preliminary examples will illustrate how performance and inscription encountered each other in the reliquary. First is a twelfth-century phylactery, inscribed with the words "Esfigiem XP(ist)I dum trans sis pronus adora non tamen effigiem sed quem designat honora" [Revere the image of Christ by bowing before it when you pass by it; but in doing this make sure you do not worship the image but rather Him

Figure Intr.6 Reliquary-statue of the Umbilicus of Christ, 1407. From the collegiate church of Notre-Dame-en-Vaux (Châlons-sur-Marne). Openwork silver with gilding, engraving, and repoussé; 33.4 x 18.9 x 17.2 cm. Musée national du Moyen Âge–Thermes de Cluny, Paris, France.

Source: Photo by Gerard Blot. Réunion des Musées nationaux/Art Resource, New York.

Figure Intr.7 The Stavelot Triptych, twelfth century and earlier. Full view, wings open, small panel doors open. The Pierpont Morgan Library. Purchase; J.P. Morgan (1867–1943); 1910. AZ001.

Source: Reproduced by permission of The Pierpont Morgan Library, NY.

Figure Intr.8 Phylactery (obverse), ca. 1165. Circle of Godefrois de Claire. Lorraine, Maas area. Copper and enamel; engraved champlevé enamel, with gilding; 22.8 x 23 cm. The State Hermitage Museum, St. Petersburg. Inv. No. F-171.

Source: The State Hermitage Museum, St. Petersburg.

whom it represents] (figure Intr.8).[6] As Herbert Kessler points out, this directive comments upon the complex nature of the act of seeing, and of understanding the representational content of the image.[7] In addition, the inscription gestures simultaneously toward the object's implication in an act of ceremonial performance (the spectator's bowing and passing before it), and its use of written characters to generate meaning through differences articulated between its signs ("effigiem" vs. Christ). The phylactery's sacred qualities articulate themselves specifically through the object's participation in scenes of veneration, ceremony, and prayer. As we shall see, such scenes rely on voiced expression and the performance-based,

Figure Intr.9　Phylactery (reverse), ca. 1165. Circle of Godefrois de Claire. Lorraine, Maas area. Copper and enamel; engraved champlevé enamel, with gilding; 22.8 x 23 cm. The State Hermitage Museum, St. Petersburg. Inv. No. F-171.

Source: The State Hermitage Museum, St. Petersburg.

and performative, gestures of spoken utterance. At the same time, these sacred aspects of the phylactery also ask to be read through the interpretive apparatus of the inscription, which organizes itself rhetorically around the concept of difference—between image and deity. The reverse of this phylactery displays an additional inscription that reinforces the object's investment in using difference to create its meaning through writing: "Nec Deus est nec homo, qu[a]m presens cernis imago, / Sed Deus est homo quem sacra figura(t) imago" [It is neither God nor man, the present image you discern, but it is God and man whom the sacred image represents] (figure Intr.9).[8] In this case as well, writing as a silent and visual mode constructs the play of difference among signs—*deus, homo*—of which the viewer must be aware in the object's representational act. This inscription's dual terms reveal oppositions functioning at increasingly deep levels, eventually resulting in a kind of self-fragmentation through the inscriptional characters. The inscription draws a distinction between God and man, but in addition, the terms *neither* and *both*, meant to designate the relationship between the surface duality of God and man, are themselves juxtaposed in a paradoxical framework. Thus the mystical quality of the relationship between the two terms produces itself through a fundamental semantic instability. The object points toward the way that written words, in Hillis Miller's terms, are "like a dehiscent seedpod...inaugurally productive," and "always already broken open, divided within themselves."[9]

Inscription and performance enshrine each other in this object. The inscriptional mode of signification described here always exists within an interactive, performance-based scene of prayer or liturgical ceremony. But viewing the object in another light, we see that the acts of differentiation inherent within the written inscription—God and man, neither and both—provide a conceptual frame for the occasion of veneration. They exert a constitutive and anterior force. The interaction among the object's many forms of representation—text, image, enshrining shape—all contribute to the constitution of a sacred experience through the object's inscriptional features existing in a dialectical relationship to its performance context.

A second example specifies how inscription participates in the object's visual or ceremonial capacity, while also functioning as a self-referential mode of representation within the performance context. The fifteenth-century reliquary of the umbilical cord of Christ consists of an impressive statue of a seated Madonna, whose child has a midsection compartment—framed with the inscription "De Umbilico Domini Jesu Christi"—for the cord relic (figure Intr.6). The lettering of this inscription indicates that this part of the reliquary is a later addition; however, inventory records state that the original object had the same inscription around the relic.[10] The object's means of interacting with an audience and participating in a ceremonial context are clear from its structure. As leveled by mother and child, the gazes collaborate with the visual impact of the umbilical-cord compartment. The statue's imposing features, its use of jewels and architectural motifs, suggest its interactive power in a situation with a venerating viewer. Its original use of polychromy, now faded, allows us to imagine further this object's resonant potential in its encounters with viewers during a ceremonial or devotional occasion of worship. Its features played an important role in the devotional performance surrounding it.

But again, the object also makes use of inscription. In our first example, the inscription on the phylactery's reverse placed itself formally in the enclosed center of the object. Here, however, the inscribed characters create a frame for the sacred relic within. As Jeffrey Hamburger has argued, frames in medieval visual culture often indicate self-awareness about representational acts. Frames, as he puts it, "can be viewed as one of the principal means by which all images, not only medieval images, qualify and comment on their status as representations."[11] Poststructuralist theory also sees framing as a means of commentary on representation and epistemology: "the limit of the frame or border of the context," as Jacques Derrida writes, "always entails a clause of non-closure. The outside penetrates and thus determines the inside." Thus the frame's gesture toward the processes of representation and contextualization subverts the boundaries between interior and exterior. And for Derrida, written inscription in particular as a framing device ("that which marks the limit of a corpus or context") is both constitutive and self-effacing.[12]

The umbilical-cord reliquary suggests that these definitions of the frame obtain at physical and conceptual levels in the Middle Ages. The framing inscription on the umbilical-cord reliquary uses its status as both writing and visual object to comment upon the reliquary's representational work. The inscription forms a self-containing circle. Its deictic act of reference to the holy object spatially turns inward rather than outward. The inscription thus suggests that the act of representing an object such as the umbilical cord in language is an act that turns inward and gestures toward itself. The physical positioning of the glass within the lettered border reinforces this idea. The indeterminate visibility of the object behind the glass leaves the reader of the inscription with only the words, chaining themselves to each other and forming their own visual and verbal coil. The viewer's task of negotiating between representation and sacred presence occurs within the object's own negotiations between text and materiality. By interacting with each other, the letters point out a sacred object that might be physically inside the frame. But this sacred physicality might also be internal to the letters as signs, something that they construct and that inheres within them. This is not, however, an oversimplified and debased rendition of the word made flesh. In addition, the inscription here distinguishes itself from *carmina figurata*, shaped poems that explicitly produced visual images.[13] Instead, the framing inscription of the umbilical cord connects itself to the sacred object through the concept of inward-turning forms. The relic itself is so inscrutable that the reliquary visually designates its center as an inward-turning circle of written language.

As a replacement of an earlier inscription, the golden signs function as a reminder of that past inscription. They both emphasize the importance of inscription as a component of the reliquary, and also demonstrate the constitutive nature of material inscription. Looking at the object as modified inhibits in one sense our ability to make positivist pronouncements about its participation in medieval scenes of worship. But the very fact of one inscription's replacement with the other shows how written inscription's perpetual self-reference through time allows it to function as a vestigial object. The replaced inscription emblematizes all inscriptions' capacity to gesture backward in time as it also gestures toward and constitutes itself with a perpetual sense of anteriority.[14] This reliquary captures an external world in its gaze and simultaneously generates a reality and mystical presence made of self-reference through its inscriptions. It thus reveals another way in which the dynamics of performative interaction dialectically coexist with a silent and inward-turning inscriptional act as two complementary modes of representation in the reliquary.

Because this reliquary's inscription both points to its own past and surrounds its relic physically, it also exemplifies an important convergence in this project between the concepts of anteriority and exteriority. Reliquaries are memorial objects, and so theories of the work of memory and memorial can provide important ways for us to understand them, as well as their interactions with literary figuration. When Derrida takes on the work of mourning in his meditations for Paul de Man, he elaborates on de Man's questions about the nature and existence of anteriority. For de Man, the historical past itself is less compelling, and less real, than anteriority as a location for "for[m],...fiction and figures."[15] Derrida extends this argument to suggest that anteriority also functions as exteriority. He ends his "Art of Memories" by asking if memory without anteriority would in fact be a spatial experience, arguing that the "exteriority of the sign" helps to create spatially organized relationships among different forms of memory, and can replace anteriority itself.[16] I would join other medievalists in balking at the idea of denying the historical past altogether; nevertheless, the reimagining of anteriority through the form of exteriority, and as a space of figuration, will play an important role in my invocations of anteriority throughout this study. Furthermore, like the reliquary of the umbilicus, which stages dynamic intersections between its exteriorizing and interiorizing impulses, Derrida's conceptions of mourning and the memorial trace also usefully challenge the boundaries between interior and exterior space.[17]

The physical structures of reliquaries in general reflect a dialectical relationship that they themselves create between interiority and exteriority. In their strategies for enshrining their sacred contents, reliquaries, as

Caroline Walker Bynum suggests, undermined easy distinctions between interior and exterior categories of space.[18] Cynthia Hahn also describes the arm reliquary in particular as engaging in a "metaphoric" relationship with the body part (not necessarily an arm) that it contained, so that the container comes to dictate and reshape the meaning of what it contains.[19] And in Julia Lupton's important formulation, "By conflating the reliquary and the relic, the container and the contained, this topology of an encased encasement maps the opposition between inside and outside as the indeterminate product of a single surface folded on itself."[20] When, throughout this book, I refer to enshrinement as a physical and spatial practice, I refer not simply to acts of enclosure, but instead to the more complex effect whereby contained and containing are interchangeable, and the borders between them are indeterminate even as the containing act continues to articulate itself in the object's physical features.[21] The myriad enfoldings of the Stavelot triptych—a reliquary within a reliquary that the next chapter will discuss in more detail—illustrate this definition of enshrinement (figure Intr.7). This physical conflation of inside and outside mirrors the reliquary's conceptual intersection between the interiorized mode of inscription and the exteriorized mode of performance. As objects of enshrinement, reliquaries thus make visible a model of representational practice at work in medieval culture.[22]

This coexistence of representational modes within devotional objects provided a visual language for defining acts of representation in late-medieval English poetry. Making this kind of claim necessitates the simultaneous use of historicist methodology and critical theoretical discourses.[23] It takes up Theresa Coletti's important suggestion to see the historicized study of the Middle Ages as "a point where the medieval and the modern intersect."[24] Readers and writers of poetry in the medieval world viewed language as staging constant interactions between what modern critical discourses would classify as its performative and its inscriptional aspects. But the results of these interactions—even when depicted in these critical terms—firmly ground themselves within the relevant contexts of specifically medieval literary, intellectual, and devotional cultures.

As the remainder of the book will demonstrate, the dialectical framing of inscription and performance took different forms, and had different implications, in different late-medieval texts. At some moments, inscription and performance together produce the possibility of an absent presence in a text's representation of a holy figure. At other moments, performance and performativity explain the relationship between the textual and visual. Poetic texts perform themselves as inscriptional objects. And on still other occasions, the reliquary itself, as inscriptional and performative object, stands as a method of describing cognitive process. It is a way of conceiving of a space that the mind creates for engaging in acts of poetic figuration.

As performance, the medieval ceremonial spectacle formed itself through linguistic utterances, but also potentially existed as a miraculous event that transcended its human constitution in language. The possibility of this world exterior to language exists in Derrida's description of the "event." This is a term that he problematizes but that, as this study will argue, exists in medieval experiences of devotion and poetic representation.[25] The Middle Ages leave open the possibility of the event as devotional phenomenon. It exists outside language and is not constituted by it. Language in medieval perspectives had both a performative, constitutive capacity and the ability to interact with realities outside it. Medieval poetic language conceived of devotional events as both anterior to the performance of language and as existing through it.

Inscription, in turn, took on a self-conscious materiality in ceremonial artifacts, one that can aid in our thinking about the inscribed characters of a poem on a page. Poetry on the page also exerted significative and even performative force as material inscription. As Katherine O'Brien O'Keeffe has suggested in a study of early medieval manuscript practices, "writing is language made spatial," and medieval manuscripts contained a number of marking features—such as "pointing"—that existed on a border between verbal and nonverbal, emphasizing the importance of visuality in verbal expression.[26] If performance itself exists at a fulcrum between representation and reality, then the inscriptional features of artifacts showcase the potential for all written inscription to constitute realities at both visual and verbal levels. Through inscription and performance, I suggest here the construction of a poetics based on sources derived from other elements of the culture, following Emily Steiner's assertion that "a culture's understanding of textuality is revealed both in its literature's reflexive moments and in its material texts or ritual objects."[27] The poetics of enshrinement uses material inscription, performance, and their mutual framing—their conflation of interior and exterior space—to lend a defining form to medieval poetic acts of representation.

Chapter 1 begins with an account of the performance contexts of reliquaries and shrines, and then moves on to their incorporation of written inscription. Using visual evidence from various moments in the Middle Ages, it argues that reliquaries offer to their audiences a mode of representation integrating voiced, public performance and silent, self-referential inscription. The chapter then moves to the *Book of the Duchess* in order to begin investigating the connection between the representational practices of objects and those of poetic texts. In its allusions to contemporary artifact cultures, the *Book of the Duchess* exemplifies texts that draw upon devotional idioms even within the context of a secularized program. It thus provides a point of departure for demonstrating how a variety of differently conceived poetic texts participate in a poetics dictated by devotional tradition. In framing inscription and performance within each other, the *Book of the Duchess* provides one example of how a poetics of enshrinement might work. The narrative sequence of the Black Knight's introduction into the dream, and his inset lyric, are a self-enfolding triptych that defines its form through the culture of enshrining objects.

Working from this initial demonstration of the poetics of enshrinement, chapter 2 claims that reliquaries, shrines, and the ceremonies in which they participate constitute a model of representational practice for the late-medieval alliterative poem *Saint Erkenwald*. This text's components turn upon enshrinement (the mysterious pagan judge's enclosure within layers of decoration, iconography, and architecture), inscription (the illegible writing that itself forms a layer of enshrinement around the body), and ceremonial performance (the High Mass, baptism, procession, and periodic references to an audience of worshippers who witness every utterance and gesture in the poem). *Saint Erkenwald* has lent itself effectively to a broad range of historicist readings because of its suggestive interactions with contemporary political and theological contexts. I focus on a different cross-section of medieval history: the context of relic translation, veneration, and enshrinement in fourteenth- and fifteenth-century England. Through this context, the poem depicts its pagan judge as both inscriptional and performance object, in order to conceive of him as a miraculous absent presence.

Chapter 3 moves away from narrative poetry to ask how the poetics of enshrinement functions when the language of poetry is performed on stage. In chapter 3, the play of the N-Town *Assumption of Mary* demonstrates how performance in this period moved the body or object between states of interiorized and exteriorized expression in the act of representing it. The N-Town *Assumption*, this chapter argues, generates an imagined Marian artifact of enshrinement on stage, one rendered impossible by the body's disappearance in the Assumption narrative. This play's idealized Marian artifact constructs itself of both language and image. Using the conventions of spectacle, the *Assumption* implicates the Marian body in the reliquary's dynamic conflation of container and contained. But the play also draws upon its formal features as poetry to emphasize its identity as written inscription. Like other contemporary artifacts, the *Assumption*'s impossible reliquary is made of inscriptional signs—patterned and self-enfolding verses—as well as iconographic and spectacular ones.

Chapter 4 focuses on poetic form in the alliterative dream vision *Pearl*. The poetics of enshrinement allow *Pearl* to transcend analogical relationships between poem and artifact—a relationship often ascribed to the poem and used to describe it. *Pearl's* inscriptional and performative elements frame each other, and in this dynamic lie its strategies for moving beyond the level of its own comparison to beautiful objects. *Pearl* instead performs itself as inscriptional object, and ultimately produces a devotional event, a vision at once interior and exterior to the experience of reading the poem. This chapter also uses the format of the dream vision in particular to explore what kind of seeing the poetics of enshrinement requires. It suggests that in *Pearl*, this poetics does not ask the reader to visualize objects directly, but rather to see in a peripheral, indirect way, emblematized by the pale daytime moon in the dreamer's vision.

The artifacts in the language of *Saint Erkenwald*, the *Assumption* play, and *Pearl* all reflect the reliquary's own uses of inscriptional signs. The false reliquaries of the *Pardoner's Tale*, however, are missing their inscriptions. Chapter 5 argues that poetic metaphor, in late-medieval English thought, is a process in which the mind constructs its own reliquary, where it enacts figuration's necessary transformations and juxtapositions. The *Pardoner's Tale* erases physical inscription from the reliquaries it depicts; rather than experimenting with the possibilities of its own language as material inscription, the tale instead transfers the representational model of the reliquary to a site of cognition: the reliquary of the mind. This reading explains why the text so famously discards the need for belief in the authenticity of the actual relic. And in the reliquary of the mind, metaphor becomes a performative act, ultimately existing as exterior to the mental space that seemed to enclose it.

The book concludes by turning toward lyric. While the late-medieval English lyric tradition occupies a somewhat vexed status, subordinated to the great legacies of narrative poetry from this period, lyric in a broader sense becomes a defining mode in thinking about poetry beyond the Middle Ages. For this reason, the conclusion investigates how the poetics of enshrinement might function specifically as a lyric poetics, not only in the Middle Ages but also at contemporary experimental moments that are temporally distant from but conceptually resonant with the nuances of lyric voice in medieval texts. The conclusion examines lyrics within the contexts of sermons and other kinds of documents, as well as returning to chapter 1's discussion of the *Book of the Duchess's* inset lyrics. It suggests finally that the dialectical enshrinement of inscription and performance is inherent to the lyric "I" itself.

CHAPTER 1

THE POETICS OF ENSHRINEMENT

As the phylactery and umbilicus statue suggested in the last chapter, the physical features of the medieval reliquary often drew attention to and commented upon its representational strategies. Reading other such devotional objects, as well as the cultural traditions informing them, can help us to elaborate further on the reliquary's inscriptional and performative strategies, and ultimately to establish an artifact-based language about representation. As Chaucer's *Book of the Duchess* will demonstrate, the ways that inscription and performance enshrine each other in the reliquary provide a formal mechanism for understanding the representational strategies of poetic language. The *Book of the Duchess* provides an initiating instance of the poetics of enshrinement at work.

Through the reliquary, the relationship between visual object and verbal text moves beyond analogical comparison; instead, we find in the reliquary a visual and material language that gives form to acts of poetic representation. Wendy Steiner has shown that making arguments about visual and verbal expression inevitably requires a somewhat complicated dance around the concept of analogy. On the one hand, analogical comparisons are difficult to avoid in such arguments, and in pre-Romantic discussions they traditionally provide a foundation for thinking about the "reality claims" of the two fields. But on the other hand, as Steiner points out, such arguments have developed as needing also to generate a separate term in the analogy—an aesthetic concept that unites the two forms beyond their chronological or thematic context.[1] In one sense, enshrinement functions as such a term in the case of this study. As a principle of complex enclosure, an integration of container and contained, it provides aesthetic and even epistemological structure in a number of areas of medieval life. These range from visual art to poetry to devotional perceptions of the incarnation body, in which, for example, the faithful consume Christ in order to be incorporated into him, undermining the boundaries between container and contained.[2] But I wish also to revise slightly Steiner's technique of invoking this kind of additional term beyond the analogy or ratio. The particular enshrining dialectic of inscription and performance, which this study will demonstrate is central to the functioning of poetic language in the late Middle Ages, makes itself visible and explicit through the material features of the reliquary. This dialectic of enshrinement thus is not simply an independent transitional term in an analogy here. It is instead a language that fully reveals itself only in visual objects, and that shapes and defines medieval perceptions of literary expression.

Reliquaries as Performance Objects

To refer to a reliquary as a performance object is to acknowledge the role that its ceremonial and spectacular context played in determining its meaning and use to medieval viewers. Through the late Middle Ages, worshippers generally did not encounter reliquaries and shrines as isolated artistic objects. Rather, reliquaries formed part of processions and liturgical and para-liturgical ceremonies. They also played roles in more intimate forms of devotional practice. This section will argue that the ceremonial practices associated with enshrined relics often examined representational process itself. Ceremonies and spectacles accomplished this by sustaining active questions about the relationship between an object, such as the cross, and its symbolic representation. Within the context of performance, the iconographic form of a reliquary asked these questions through its physical acts of juxtaposition and substitution between sacred objects and their representations. Furthermore, these performances, through their uses of prayer and audience interaction, also reveal themselves as performative occasions. The language incorporated into them is not only descriptive, but also constitutive of the ceremony. The sacred spectacle surrounding the reliquary comments on processes of representation in part by speaking aspects of those spectacles into being.[3]

In both the early and late Middle Ages, the reliquary explored models of representational practice through its implication in performance. Early medieval traditions of pilgrimage narrative suggest that enclosure and spectacle contributed to the holy object's examination of its own representational processes. Specifically, enclosure informed the relationship between the symbol of the cross and the authentic cross in the late antique and early medieval period. Early accounts of the cross borrow from the language of figuration when they juxtapose the object with, or enclose it within, a form of its representation. For example, in the *Historia Ecclesiastica Tripartita*'s summary of Eusebius's dream scene in the *Vita*

Constantini, "Christus apparuit cum signo, quod vidit in caelo, iussitque, ut fieret eius signi figuratio, quae foret auxilium" [Christ appeared to him with a sign, which he saw in the sky, and commanded that he make a form/replica of that sign, which would be as a help].[4] Pilgrimage narratives develop these references to acts of juxtaposition and substitution, and expand upon the language of signs and figuration invoked in the *Historia*'s account. A pilgrim's account of Golgotha from the sixth century illustrates the decorated enclosures created for the cross and the place of Christ's Passion:

> In the midst of the city is the basilica of Constantine. At the entrance to the basilica, on the left hand, is a chamber where the cross of the Lord is kept. Beyond this, as one enters the church of the Holy Constantine, there is a large apse on the western side, wherein the three crosses were found. There is a raised altar made of pure silver and gold, and nine columns which support that altar....And from hence you enter into Golgotha. There is here a large hall, on the place where our Lord was crucified. Round about it, on the hill itself, are railings of silver....It has a silver door at which the Cross of our Lord is displayed, all covered with ornaments of gold and jewels, with the open sky above it....Beyond this, to the west, you enter the [church of the] Holy Resurrection, wherein is the sepulchre of our Lord....[5]

Here again, juxtaposition and substitution organize the space of the basilica. But this description emphasizes the fact that the site in its entirety is based on a series of enclosures experienced as ceremonial procession. In this procession, one experiences the True Cross coffered within its jeweled reliquary and appearing as unenclosed under the open sky. The account of Golgotha displays a series of spectacles of representation, different ways of designating the cross through physical signs existing both in juxtaposition to and enclosing each other. Tracing the particular invocations of the cross in this scenario reveals a number of the representational mechanisms surrounding the devotional object. First of all, the arrangement of the different cross objects implies a kind of ceremonial spectacle both staged for and involving the viewer, as the pilgrim enters one space after another, and sees one spectacle after another. In this sense, the act of representing the cross, of enabling these jeweled symbols to gesture toward the True Cross, relies upon an aesthetic of kinesthetic or progressive spectacle, not simply an object itself devoid of context or temporality. Second, physical acts of enclosure reinforce the connection between the object itself and its jeweled copies. By the fifth century, the True Cross had in fact been moved to Constantinople, and the cross in the Holy Land was a substitute. Nevertheless, pilgrims visiting Jerusalem believed that the substitute cross implied an authenticity of its own. In 417, the emperor Theodosius enshrined the silver cross at Jerusalem in gold and precious stones, and pilgrims worshipped this cross as the true one.[6] The decorated cross image worshipped as though it were the True Cross creates the possibility of a meaningful object within. The connection between the replica and the original in this system of nonverbal signs occurs through enclosure specifically as a component of spectacle and performed occasion.

Jeffrey Hamburger has described devotion itself in its broadest sense in the terms of performance, and the reliquary integrated itself into the performance-based elements of devotion.[7] Liturgical dramas, for instance, mention the incorporation of relic objects into the representation of scriptural narrative. An example exists in a fifteenth-century account of an Easter play from Magdeburg. After playing out the scene of the visit to the Sepulchre, the archbishop proclaims "Surrexit Dominus," and relics at the altar are revealed as part of the spectacle: "deponet velamen de reliquiis in altari."[8] Furthermore, Lisa Ciresi's study of a high medieval reliquary shrine from Cologne Cathedral suggests that "the relics, as well as the shrine, were very much part of the altar ensemble and were instruments that aided the liturgical dialogue that was focused on the sacrificial corpus Christi."[9] Later in the Middle Ages, processions in Salisbury Cathedral passed underneath an elevated reliquary.[10] In addition, Eleanor Townsend points out that fifteenth-century written evidence, such as the *Tale of Beryn* and the account of Margaret of Anjou's visit to Canterbury, details a carefully organized processional ceremony, structured around "subsidiary relics and shrines" as well as the great shrine of Saint Thomas.[11] Various traditions thus indicate the specific role that reliquaries and shrines played in religious performances. As devotional objects they were part of the ceremonial act.

The reliquary and shrine's placement within ceremonial contexts also implicates it in the complex interactions among the spectacle, the audience, and their own acts of worship. All the examples above emphasize that these spectacles made of both objects and people contained an important interactive element with the audience. Through the audience's participation, their own acts of prayer, we see performance move into the realm of performativity. Ciresi argues that the physical ability of certain reliquaries to be opened created a "gateway into the sacred space of the shrine and allowed a direct interactive experience. The supplicants could now *see* and in an entirely new way commune with the relics as the holy presence of those enshrined was made visible to the earthly realm beyond the golden walls of its Heavenly City."[12] And as Ogden notes, the performers of the liturgical drama at Magdeburg placed themselves "physically out in the midst of a congregation."[13] The history of liturgical drama, he further maintains, constantly challenged boundaries among audience, worshipper, and spectator.[14] Thus the acts of prayer and veneration located themselves everywhere in the spectacle—in the audience, in the performance, and in the interaction between the two.

In this sense, then, prayer as a ceremonial context for the reliquary had a performative function as well as being part of the spectacular performance. In a study of Augustine in the postmodern age, John D. Caputo argues that "a prayer is a performative act—the very act of directing one's words to God *is* the prayer—with a unique reflexivity, so that to pray for the prayer itself, to pray that one be able to pray, is already to pray."[15] Prayer does not simply concern the authenticity of belief; it also reveals the epistemological structures that belief creates.[16] As an act of worship and prayer, the viewer's encounter with the reliquary shrine in a performance context is not only a witnessing of spectacle, but also a constitutive act that participates in bringing the reliquary's very spirituality and presence into being.

Thinking about worship performatively (and not just as performance), however, leads us toward questions about what might lie beyond the dynamics of performativity; what possibility is there for an existence temporally and spatially outside the one generated in the linguistic performative? Poststructuralist theory has taken up this question in its re-formulation of the concept of "event." Rather than thinking of performative speech acts as constituting an event, Derrida, for instance, refines the definition of the term "event" to see it instead as something potentially existing as anterior to the performative, but as extremely elusive because of the inescapability of language as performative:

> As long as I am to speak performatively, I have to do this under certain conditions, conventions, conventional conditions. I have the ability to do this and to produce the event by speaking. That is, I can or I may master the situation by taking into account these conventions. I may open the session, for instance. I may say "yes" when I get married, and so on. But because I have mastery of the situation, my very mastery is a limitation of the eventness of the event. I neutralize the eventness of the event precisely because of the performativity.[17]

The present study, meanwhile, claims that in the intersection of medieval literature and the culture of shrines and reliquaries, this possibility of the performance as event—unanticipated, exterior to the performative—did in fact exist, and that it was often intimately juxtaposed with, but still separate from, performative speech acts. This point will receive more concrete elaboration in chapter 2, but it appears briefly here in order to

gesture toward another way in which the reliquary, through its implication in performance traditions, interacted with a world exterior to it. The
reliquary's participation in the event exterior to language coexisted with
its participation in prayer as a self-constituting and performative act.

The reliquary as performance object embodies this dynamic physically,
subverting the viewer's notions of interior and exterior space in the
ceremonial encounter. Its ability both to exist within a self-constitutive
act of prayer, and to reach outward to a material and ceremonial world,
is mirrored in its own capacity to explore the relationship between
interiority and exteriority. The Stavelot triptych, for example, uses its
enfolding form to gesture inward to itself and outward to its ceremonial
setting (figure Intr.7). This triptych, as an important object of pilgrimage
commissioned by Abbot Wibald, would have been centrally located and
displayed in the nave of the cathedral; thus everything that follows about
this object must be understood in the context of its participation in ceremony, performance, and spectacle.[18] Like others from the same period,
the Stavelot triptych was exhibited as folded closed during most of the
year, but opened for viewing on certain feast days.[19] Its iconographic
program, and the relationships among its components, were manipulated and altered by folding and unfolding the piece according to the
ceremonial context. The triptych's visual structures of enclosure, within
the context of its role in performance, thus became an important way
of experiencing it as an object of veneration. Its own hinges and folds
represent the complexity of its relationship to its ceremonial setting. The
act of venerating the object produces the ceremonial performance even
as that context enfolds the object.

This piece's negotiation of its own spatiality also explicates enshrinement and framing as terms central to this study. The presence of the
smaller Byzantine reliquary triptychs at the center in one sense stages a
clear aesthetic translation, with the larger winged Mosan piece basing
itself upon the originating items in the center (figure 1.1). In another
sense, though, the shape of the Mosan triptych frame itself gestures back
toward, and symbolically situates itself as part of, the established Eastern
tradition that created and disseminated reliquaries of this particular
shape and style. In other words, the specific triptych form that characterizes the enclosed Byzantine object reappears in the larger piece as a
means of organizing and framing the Western iconographic and decorative material. The triptych-within-triptych format suggests a model of
enshrinement dictating that what encloses is also enclosed. As the Stavelot
triptych arranges its imagery to fold together a sacred past, present, and
future, it also uses enshrinement as a device to complicate the relationship
between the originating form and the newer work that draws upon it. To

Figure 1.1 The Stavelot Triptych, twelfth century and earlier. Detail of full view, wings open, small panel doors open. The Pierpont Morgan Library. Purchase; J.P. Morgan (1867–1943); 1910. AZ001.

enshrine something is thus to enter it into a dialectical spatial dynamic of container and contained. This effect of the simultaneously contained and containing informs my definition throughout this project of enshrinement as a material practice of devotion. In addition, the Stavelot triptych demonstrates the correspondence between framing and enshrining in its formal features: for this object, to frame is to enshrine, and vice versa. I will often invoke the terms of framing to explicate the dynamics of enshrinement; as this and other reliquary objects show, these are two deeply related aesthetic impulses.

In the late Middle Ages, the focus of this study, reliquary shrines as performance objects continued to investigate representational process through their performative engagements with their viewers. As we have seen, devotional ceremonies are a form of spectacle that draws on participation from audience, performers, and objects as part of the performance. The characteristics of late-medieval shrines also reveal other kinds of epistemological potential in shrines as performance objects. Involvement in liturgical or para-liturgical performance implied not only the enactment of the performance, but also the performance's capacity to refer to its means of representing its subject. A relevant development of late-medieval English devotional culture here was the simultaneous existence of image shrines and more traditional relic shrines, which contained physical vestiges of the dead. Increasingly personalized relationships with saints encouraged the increased artistic production of saints' images.[20] Toward the end of the Middle Ages, certain forms of devotional object that once primarily housed relics, such as winged altarpieces, began to tend toward featuring images and statuary. Donald L. Ehresmann has shown that while there was historically a close association between the desire to display relics and the development of winged altarpieces in the later Middle Ages, some of these objects instead privileged their decorative images through their physical structures. These altarpieces exemplify the increasing complexity involved in the devotional object's negotiation between relic and image in the late Middle Ages. As is the case with the reliquary triptych, the physical manipulation that the wings allowed in liturgical ceremony emphasizes the role of the performance context in this negotiation.[21]

But the traditional relic shrine also still existed in the late Middle Ages, and it made use of images in order to examine its own means of representing the sacred body. Some relic shrines received additional embellishment in the thirteenth through the fifteenth centuries. There was a broad trend in the thirteenth and fourteenth centuries in particular toward expanding and reconstructing the eastern ends of churches in order to showcase relics.[22] Visual evidence in England for the use of relics and shrines in the later Middle Ages is especially scarce due to iconoclastic activities after the fifteenth century.[23] As Sarah Stanbury has argued, the emergence in the late Middle Ages of these debates and controversies over the visual reception of devotional images and objects had significant impact on medieval writers in various genres.[24] Within the context of this charged environment, image production intensified in certain ways. The shrine of Saint Erkenwald, for instance, has associated with it contracts with London goldsmiths for 1339 and 1401.[25] (Chapter 2 will discuss this relic shrine in further detail, through its relationship to the poetic text of *Saint Erkenwald.*) The various forms of work done on the Erkenwald shrine emphasize the reliquary's strategy of juxtaposing the body with its artistic representation in order to demonstrate to viewers their mutual constitution of sacred presence.[26] The object of veneration and ceremony generates presence through the enclosed body's visual discourse with the image.[27] New images purchased for Erkenwald's shrine in 1401 would have cast into relief for viewers the shrine's habitual engagement in the dual materialities of body and artifact, and created a dynamic space for the viewer to consider the relationship between relic and image.

Image shrines, meanwhile, sought to perform the same function as those housing a holy object, exploring the nature of representation while participating in performance and ceremony.[28] Several well-known image shrines existed in this period, such as the famous Marian shrine of Little Walsingham (further discussed in chapter 3), as well as the image shrines of Saint Katherine. In the late Middle Ages, Katherine Lewis maintains, "a cult image of Saint Katherine would have performed the same function as a relic."[29] Eamon Duffy corroborates this point, adding that "it was the multiplication of images in the later Middle Ages that made possible the multiplication of shrines."[30] Little Walsingham in particular demonstrates that fragments and an aesthetics of enclosure inform the image shrine as much as they do the traditional relic shrine. As Gail McMurray Gibson has described, the pilgrimage center included a stone chapel that in turn enclosed the replica of the holy wooden house. The image shrine implicitly involved itself in a continuing discourse concerning not only the appropriateness of relic veneration itself but also the representational strategies underlying devotional objects. The layers of enclosure in the shrine at Little Walsingham suggest that enshrinement itself constitutes presence, in the relic's absence. This site demonstrates enshrinement's role in the act of substituting iconographic image for bodily matter. Furthermore, in image shrines, enshrining iconography also created a space for performative, constitutive acts intended to approach the divine. The evidence around Little Walsingham in particular emphasizes the components of choreography and spectacle involved in the veneration of the image shrine. As late as 1512 Erasmus described the pilgrims to this shrine as forming a procession, and it was favored with a number of royal visits and state pilgrimages throughout its late-medieval history.[31] Within the framework of the shrine's status as an object of performance and spectacle, the viewer's interaction with the image of divinity constituted its presence.

Thus in Ricardian and Henrician England, the relic cult had developed a distinctive character. It was aware of and dependent upon the concept of the relic to define its invocations of holy presence through images, which were often simply treated as relics. Relics remained the fundamental means of establishing *praesentia* even in their physical absence.[32] The image shrine used the reliquary's mechanisms of enshrinement and vestigiality to establish its own uses of signs, as well as the reliquary's spatiality. And the balance between images and relics as privileged components of a devotional artifact shifted back and forth with complexity. Furthermore, the presence of both image and relic shrines, as well as the functions of other devotional artifacts, such as altarpieces, suggests that the medieval audience's understanding of the object's representational work took place specifically through the conventions of ceremony and spectacle, as well as through the performative interaction between worshipper and object. In these ways, late-medieval perspectives on semiosis and representation (and their implications for other systems of language as well) were interconnected with a dominant and diverse culture of performance.

As an object generally encountered within the performance contexts of procession, ceremony, and liturgy, the medieval reliquary engaged in various relationships with the world around it. Instances of late-medieval embellishments to relic shrines indicate the period's particular interest in juxtaposing image and body and allowing acts of spectatorship to negotiate this juxtaposition. The reliquary also participated in the performative act of prayer, constituting representational spaces in its interaction with the worshipper. But in addition, the inscriptional and iconographic marks that appeared on the reliquary dictated the nature of these representational spaces. This fact necessitates a turn toward this other aspect of the reliquary as an object that investigated representational practice.

Reliquaries as Inscriptional Objects

As the introduction to this volume suggests, the inscriptional features of the reliquary function in the inward-turned, self-referential manner of all written inscription. The ceremonial context of the reliquary partly creates, through acts of prayer and worship, a means of performative self-constitution. This constitutive function finds another manifestation in the reliquary's own inscribed letters. But unlike the voiced utterance of prayer that both surrounded and interacted with the devotional object, inscriptions draw attention to a different quality of language. They are a silent statement existing in the midst of the ceremonial event, a use of linguistic signifiers that is visual rather than uttered. As Eric Jager has argued, medieval literate culture offered a context for this connection between the inscriptional and the unuttered in its metaphoric construct of the "book of the heart." Through such metaphors, inscribed characters functioned as embodied expressions of interiority and self-reference.[33] The inscription of institutional documents possessed, as Emily Steiner has argued, a material instrumentality of its own.[34] In both artifacts and manuscripts, inscription complicated language's relationship to performance and asserted the multidimensional materiality of visual sign systems.

The eleventh-century Charlemagne "A" (Figure 1.2) exemplifies the reliquary's particular use of inscriptionality. This object, housed in the abbey treasury of Conques, is thought originally to have represented an alpha (its base and angels are later additions), thus gesturing toward Christ's apocalyptic self-designation as alpha and omega. Amy Remensnyder argues that over the course of its history, however, it came to signify the letter *A* as part of an alphabet referring to Charlemagne's foundation of several monasteries.[35] While not carved into metal, as other reliquary inscriptions are, this object in many ways embodies the inscriptionality associated with reliquaries. It is at once deeply connected to the history and context from which it springs, and at the same time emblematic of inscription's system of difference and self-fragmentation through its displacement from its alphabetic context into a category of visual object.

In the "A" reliquary, the materiality of the letter translates between one sign system and another. This reliquary participates in a number of different sign systems, and in particular undermines distinctions between verbal and iconographic signs. It is an extreme subversion of the distinction between language and object. In his reading of the semiotic structures surrounding Charlemagne, including both the "A" reliquary and the *Chanson de Roland*, Eugene Vance posits a "semiotics of the reliquary" at work in Carolingian strategies of asserting power. Vance sees this reliquary as a "secondary semiotic program dialectically declaring the spiritual glory of the saint's body reassembled in heaven."[36] Its embodiment of the letter allows it to function both as inscriptional character and as a nonverbal object conveying the integrity of the sacred body.

The "A" reliquary's broader historical and cultural context also elaborates upon the object's negotiations among different sign systems. On the one hand, the reliquary demonstrates clearly a familiar and accepted view

Figure 1.2 So-called reliquary letter "A" of Charlemagne, before 1107 and with later additions. Workshop of Abbot Begon III. Two angels with censers. Gold, gilded silver, enamel, filigree; h. 42.5 cm. Treasury, Abbey Ste. Foy, Conques, France.

Source: Photo by Erich Lessing/Art Resource, New York.

of the incarnational potential of language, achieved through the recip-
rocal legitimation process of reliquary and sacred relic. The word can
become a thing through belief in scriptural doctrine, and this is staged
in a sense by the artifact reflecting the shape of the letter—embodying a
semiotic component—and at the same time possessing another material
reality as an artifact of sacred bodily matter. The reliquary thus indicates
and also performs the possibility of Christ as alpha and omega. On the
other hand, however, the letter reliquary not only signifies Christ in this
way, but also becomes part of a monastic alphabet. It forms part of a legendary alphabet, a chronicle tradition that depicted Charlemagne giving
such letter reliquaries to the monasteries he visited as a form of legitimation. As part of this monastic alphabet, as opposed to a sacred one, the
"A" reliquary constructs itself out of its relationality, its interaction with
other such complex signs.

As letter and object, the "A" reliquary foregrounds the intersection
between verbal and visual signification at work in the poetic tradition of
the Charlemagne narrative. Like a tomb inscription, it exists at an intersection of language and object.[37] Legible as a letter of the alphabet, the "A"
reliquary at the same time participates in a visual system of signification,
an iconography pointing toward the enshrinement of the holy object,
and the ceremonial processes surrounding such enshrinement. As an
object associated with a legendary Charlemagne narrative, however, the
"A" reliquary participates in the representational strategies of this narrative's other manifestations as well. In poetry especially, the culture of the
Charlemagne narrative elaborates on inscriptionality and the relationship
between visual objects and words. The *Chanson de Roland*, for instance,
describes Charlemagne confronting what Vance calls "the sublime cal-
ligraphy of Roland's final swordblows" ("He came beneath two trees and
knew it was / Roland who struck those blows on the three rocks..."). As
Vance puts it, Roland is "the first iconographer and sculptor of his own
sanctuary," so that these inscriptions become part of the chronicling project.[38] They narrate—in both a verbal and nonverbal capacity—Roland's
fate. Thus the conception of letters as objects possessing a separate iconographic legibility is both incorporated into, and potentially reflective of,
the poetic project that chronicles and memorializes. The manuscript and
textual history of the *Chanson de Roland* reinforces this point as well.
James A. Rushing argues that during the development of this narrative
tradition, the text moves increasingly into the realm of the "interface":
between song and book, oral and literate, vernacular and Latinate. And
"at that interface...the *Roland* material is illustrated." The manuscript
becomes a decorated object when the story tradition moves across these
communicative divides.[39] This tradition's capacity as interface produces

a space in which visual and verbal forms of representation interact with each other. It suggests poetic Charlemagne narratives as embodying a culture of such interactions, in which an object like the "A" reliquary plays a particularly dynamic role through its complex use of the concrete inscribed character.

In addition to its negotiation between letter and object, another important aspect of inscriptionality is its silence. Inscribed characters have a tomblike memorial quality through which they articulate themselves voicelessly. The "A" reliquary's physical shape and nature suggest, for example, that we might investigate its relationship to the Hegelian A as pyramid and tomb, and the Derridean excursus upon this figure. Derrida posits linguistic sign as the material witness of a silent, invisible bodily vestige:

> [the letter *a* in *différance*] is offered by a mute mark, by a tacit monument, I would even say by a pyramid, thinking not only of the form of the letter when it is printed as a capital but also of the text of Hegel's *Encyclopaedia* in which the body of the sign is compared to the Egyptian Pyramid. The *a* of *différance*, thus, is not heard; it remains silent, secret, and discreet as a tomb: *oikesis*.[40]

In one sense, Derrida's invocation of the word "*oikesis*" marks a point of ideological disjuncture between poststructuralism and the Middle Ages, since the development of this term has tended to stress an essential absence at the center, whereas the reliquary object relies upon presence. At the same time, the term also acknowledges enshrinement as an act that informs signification. *A* is an object of enshrinement here—enclosed by the rest of the word and yet also an enclosing tomb that casts the whole word into a silent form of signification. The tomb as a visual structure of enshrinement allows *différance* to constitute its meaning. For Derrida, the associations of tomb and pyramid emphasize the element of linguistic signification that depends upon the silent, the visual, the entombing and entombed—the signifying mechanism of language revealed through its identity as inscription.

The "A" reliquary's silent inscriptionality, however, exists within the setting of performance. One point that a letter-shaped reliquary makes particularly obvious is that reliquaries like it might participate in ceremonies involving spoken language, but their own means of signification within these are not aural. The letter reliquary embodies this vision of silent language, of the association between tomb and textuality, both hidden and manifest. But a reliquary such as Charlemagne's "A" speaks its silent codes of both iconography and inscription through the engine of ceremonial declaration and performance. The Last Judgment tympanum at Conques, for instance, depicts a procession involving a prelate leading a bearded monarch and two men, one of whom carries a shrine-like container. Amy Remensnyder argues that this scene participates in fixing the meaning of "royal generosity" as legitimation for the monastery, and is connected to the phenomenon of Charlemagne's reliquary distribution, the dissemination of different letters as memorial objects throughout his domain.[41] The object itself functions as the voiceless center of these activities. If it engages in the devotional ceremony's performative acts, it must do so silently, with its own version of signification, and thus it demonstrates the possibility that this particular kind of silence was one component of performance practice. Theodore Lerud points out the need to complicate the late-medieval definition of performance, arguing that "both elaborate visual *tableaux* and religious plays were seen as quick images, to be considered in the same general category as painted or sculpted images."[42] In an earlier medieval context, the "A" reliquary establishes that performance shifted not only between the static and kinesthetic, but also between the voiced and the silent.

If the "A" reliquary in one sense represents inscription framed by performance, in another sense it also emphasizes inscription's role as a framing context for ceremony. Attending to the inscriptional element of the medieval reliquary requires acknowledging that inscription and performance ultimately surround each other. As we saw earlier, encounters with reliquaries and shrines often took the form of performed spectacles that involved speech, sound, and movement in the re-creation of important scriptural moments, and the "A" reliquary is no exception in its involvement with spectacle. But this object also uses its inscriptionality to contextualize its historical and ceremonial function. Specifically, the "A" reliquary's commemorative self-constitution engages it in a kind of historicized *différance*: its identity is constructed in the object's relational interaction with Charlemagne's already-constructed legacy of the monastic alphabet, in which the reliquary signifies even as it is fragmented from its original signification. This historicized form of inscriptional *différance*—an integration of difference and anteriority—establishes the reliquary's ceremonial and memorializing meaning. Its act of legitimation as part of both sacred and monastic alphabets is entirely dictated by its status as inscriptional mark. The object's embodiment of inscriptionality thus creates the framing terms for the ceremony.

The medieval reliquary existed not only as a devotional object, but also as an object that investigated processes of representation and interactions among sign systems through its inscriptional components. It created a perspective on signification that saw the silent interaction of inscribed signs both enclosing and enclosed by the voiced performance of ceremony. The remainder of this chapter will suggest that this model offered itself as a way of understanding poetic language as well. Reliquaries, shrines, and other related devotional objects reveal to us a medieval poetics based upon an immediate context of material culture.

Relics and Poetics

A couple of points about the cultural work of performance and material inscription in the Middle Ages will clarify the specific ways that these features of artifacts interacted with literary texts. The resulting poetics of enshrinement positions itself as an alternative to more traditional perceptions of a rhetorical poetics for the Middle Ages.[43] Even medieval writings that style themselves as poetics, such as Geoffrey of Vinsauf's and John of Garland's, do not consistently communicate through their exemplary format a medieval understanding of representational practice. Geoffrey of Vinsauf, for instance, makes several interesting comments that might lead us toward a theorization of poetic temporality, with his reliance on metaphors of planning and structure, progress, beginning and ending. Ultimately, however, we find ourselves confronted more conspicuously with a theory of composition than with a theory of representation.[44] At the same time, Geoffrey's work emphasizes that, even as a theory of composition, medieval poetics drew on the imagery of visual and material objects. As Jody Enders has shown, authors of classical discourses on poetic composition and their medieval inheritors thought about compositional process in terms of vision and imagination, " 'reading' from their own pictorial scripts" and translating *visiones* in their "memory theatres" into language.[45] If these visually based phenomena contributed to compositional theory and practice, then it is also worth considering how specific elements of visual culture (inscription and performance) contributed to the medieval understanding of poetic language's representational function.

Performance underlies representational discourse in medieval culture as a whole. Paul Zumthor has argued, for instance, that all medieval poetry participated in what we would call theatre.[46] John Ganim has demonstrated that theatricality and performance can function as effective underlying metaphors for the textual workings of the *Canterbury Tales*. As he suggests, instances of popular and civic performance and procession may have informed not only the events, but also the very structure and representational strategies of Chaucer's tales.[47] At a more general level, Carol Symes has argued that performance in the Middle Ages did not limit itself to the textual conventions of script and playbook; we have imposed "critical tasks fashioned in later years" upon our definitions of dramatic performance in this earlier period. Instead, performance functions as a mode of representation in the culture, one that transcends the boundaries of traditional theatrical textuality. "The study of medieval drama," Symes suggests, "is not the study of rarefied literary monuments but the study of a vital performative element within the surrounding culture."[48] Through this perspective, drama and performance become available as a cultural aesthetic with pervasive influence, rather than as the discrete literary or artistic genre that other historical periods understand it to be.[49] The components of medieval performance and spectacle form an aesthetic that is not simply about the occasion of a literal performance, and not necessarily connected only to the affective elements of staged plays or ceremonies.

Middle English usage itself also reflected the prevalence of performance as an organizing principle of culture. One notable example of such usage is the performance-related term *pagent*, which, as Jessica Brantley points out, fluctuates compellingly between the narrative and the visual. In the fifteenth century it designated both a narrative representation and, as the *Middle English Dictionary* describes it, "an ornamental hanging for a room." Brantley also cites A.S.G. Edwards's argument that the term could refer to manuscript illustration, and usefully develops the correspondence between pageant and *pagina*.[50] This evidence implies that performance as a concept could inhere in artistic representations outside the boundaries of theatrical presentations themselves. Performance as a medieval cultural phenomenon locates itself more ubiquitously than in the physical act of staging a drama or a procession; in its medieval sense, it also comprises a set of aesthetic principles that can undergird a number of forms of artistic expression.

Inscription, meanwhile, also informs numerous aspects of medieval cultural expression. Emily Steiner's work on medieval "documentary culture" represents one of the most explicit engagements with the culturally constitutive force of inscribed characters on a page. The specific materiality of written documents is both instrumental in its own terms and, equally importantly, "a means of articulating the strategies and ambitions of…literary making."[51] As Katherine O'Brien O'Keeffe has shown, medieval inscriptional practices shaped the development of literacy not simply through the fact that these practices involved writing words on a page. Instead, the material nature of this writing, its uses of "pointing" and its shifting of thought from temporal into spatial modes, calls attention to a culture not just of writing but of material inscription.[52] Written inscription's visual features (in the context of Latin verse during the Old English period), patterns, and contrasts could play an important role in signification itself.[53] Ardis Butterfield, in addition, argues that later medieval music manuscripts in particular reveal the "medieval understanding of categories of composition" specifically through "modes of inscription," the material and visual features of the manuscript.[54]

Inscriptions in other forms held other kinds of signifying and even constitutive potential. In the high Middle Ages, for instance, written inscriptions on church portals and other architectural elements began to name into existence the architectural feature's role in the ceremonial space.[55] Furthermore, an example of a Carolingian altar inscription demonstrates especially powerfully the complexity and importance of inscription's role in medieval devotional and aesthetic culture. Verses run around a ninth-century Milan altar, stating:

> This dear, beautiful ark gleams on the outside with a shining
> Decoration of metals; ornamented, it shines with gems.
> Inside, this gift is rich with sacred bones,
> Shining more with that treasure than with decorated metal.
> The good, famous priest Angilbert offered this work
> In honor of the blessed Ambrose who rests in
> This temple. He anxiously dedicated it to God,
> Through whom, in time, he will dwell in the peaks of the shining seat.
> Seek, highest father, to have mercy on your son;
> With your mercy, God, he will carry off the sublime gift.[56]

These verses emphasize inscription's function as a means of naming patrons and narrating their spiritual relationships to the objects they commission and donate. But in addition, the passage here explicitly engages the inscribed characters in the dialectic of interiority and exteriority central to the aesthetics of shrines. Its exterior metalwork, "decorated" by the inscription itself, shares the language of "shining" with the treasure inside it. While the inscription claims to constitute the object's meaning by physically framing it and narrating its creation, this constitutive force in turn finds itself encompassed and eclipsed by the presence of the relics themselves ("shining more"), whose luminosity the inscription names. Through its interaction with the relics, the inscription turns in upon itself. The Milan altar's inscriptions exemplify the work of all inscriptions: the engraved words frame and contextualize the sacred object, but in naming the object's encompassing brightness their act of signification folds in upon itself, conflating inside and outside. Like performance, material inscription such as this played a suggestive and important role in acts of artistic expression throughout medieval culture.

As a site of convergence between inscription and performance, the reliquary becomes a locus from which to examine the relationship between these two terms in other expressive forms. One such form is the written text. As a method of inquiry, the use of visual art to understand verbal text elaborates on some existing discourses in art historical study. Jeffrey Hamburger has recently posed a series of important questions about the relationship between medieval visual art and the verbal traditions of theological discourse:

> In what ways could medieval art be construed as argumentative in structure as well as function? Are any of the modes of representation that can be identified in medieval art analogous to any of those found in texts, and in what ways did images function as vehicles, not merely vessels, of meaning and signification?[57]

This passage recognizes the potential for the visual and plastic arts to "function as vehicles," to investigate processes of representation rather than simply to serve an illustrative purpose. A number of other medieval art historians have also thought about how visual objects in the Middle Ages could be read, and how the experience of reading an object might have been more a matter of sustained comprehension than immediate apprehension.[58] This perspective has been applied to various objects, from reliquaries to tomb architecture, and it helps us to see how an object can speak to the viewer in its own nonverbal language about its strategies of representation.[59] Hamburger suggests that "exegesis and other genres of theological discourse shed light on the form, as well as the content and function, of medieval images."[60] If medieval written traditions can illuminate discourses about representation inherent in the visual arts, then it is equally possible that the enshrining object's visual language about representational practice also describes some of the mechanisms at work in texts.[61] The reliquary in particular uses its inscriptional and performance-based features to comment upon its own processes of "meaning and signification," and it also constitutes languages for characterizing this process at work in other expressive forms.

Before turning toward the poetics of enshrinement as located in the reliquary's integration of inscription and performance, it seems important to spend a moment on some medieval semiotic perspectives concerning the relationship between visual and verbal. Visual objects themselves join other cultural forces in exploring connections between words and objects. In one sense, the concept of incarnational language makes it possible to think about words and objects in terms of each other throughout medieval culture. The organizing principle of the Word made Flesh had always provided a means of understanding the concrete potential of language. Studies of medieval cultural productions have identified an "incarnational aesthetic" at work in medieval performance and writing, an aesthetic that acknowledges this potential of the word's interaction with the material world through devices such as shaped poetry or the spectacle of Christ on the stage.[62] At the same time, Augustinian theology complicated this conception of incarnational language and expression through its various meditations on the postlapsarian state of language, whether in the *City of God*'s discussion of the loss of originary and unifying language, or in *On True Religion*, in which Augustine platonically contrasts poetry as the ideal art with the earthly practice of poetic writing. Actual "verse is beautiful as exhibiting the faint traces of the beauty which the art of poetry keeps steadfastly and unchangeably." Poetic meter in its ideal form has a godliness of proportion that actual poetic language (rather than meter) necessarily compromises in some ways.[63] Thus, on the one hand, the possibility of incarnational language and aesthetics always exists in medieval thinking about the relationship between an idealized conception of language and the world. Within this context, on the other hand, the ways that this interaction works itself out depend upon particular instances of cultural practice in which the relationship between sign and object is constantly examined and renegotiated, particularly in poetry.[64]

Another means of understanding the postlapsarian relationship between sign and object—also based in Augustinian writing—inheres in the *vestigium* (footprint). For Augustine, every sign is also a thing. A word, as a sign, might not exist in the same category of thing as a log or a sheep, to use Augustine's examples in *De Doctrina Christiana*, because its signifying function has a different kind of potential. It is still, however, a thing in this world. And it shares this status with other signs whose physicality Augustine considers obvious and concrete, like the footprint of an animal. In *De Doctrina Christiana* II.ii's designation of this sign (*vestigium*), we realize that a sign can convey meaning through the operation of vestigiality, being something that has been left behind to indicate a past presence.[65] Augustine maintains a distinction between the example of the footprint as a natural sign and language as made of up conventional signs, whose connection to what they signify is arbitrary. But his conception of sign as thing at the same time raises some important questions about how to characterize the physicality of the verbal sign, the nature of its status in the physical world, particularly once it has lost its original incarnational potential. In identifying the vestigiality of the verbal sign, we see a way to understand its materiality.

The reliquary provides concrete elaboration upon vestigiality's implications. For the reliquary, the vestige was the central component that both dictated the meaning of the object and was subject to various forms of interpretation and translation by the iconography, inscription, and performance practice surrounding it. Housed within a reliquary, the relic's identity as decomposing matter is transformed into something eternal and frozen by artifice, an unchanging memorial—as Bernard of Angers understood reliquaries—to the saint.[66] And from the early Middle Ages, the relic embodied for its viewers a paradox of fragmentation coexisting with the integrity that the saint's vestige recalls.[67] The relic as enshrined vestige gestured always toward its present, concrete reality and its implication in a historical narrative, upon which the embellishment and ceremonial setting of the reliquary might elaborate. In its vestigial capacity, the relic influenced the work of the devotional image as well. Hans Belting argues that images and relics in the West were in some ways mutually constitutive of meaning; they "explained each other."[68] Late antique and early medieval theology established the capacity of the image to imply "both appearance and presence," so that the image fore-grounded itself as both representational act and, through its association with the relic, generator of presence. Belting describes a shift between Christ images and cross signs as playing out a larger debate about the nature of the image as human depiction; its ability to make a person visible and present.[69] In the interactions among relics, reliquaries, images, and signs, vestigiality emerges as a powerful force that recalls what is past while producing presence.

Thus, the reliquary reveals that underlying its own integration of inscription and performance is *vestigium*'s ability to bridge the distance between artifacts and verbal signs. Hamburger has pointed out that *vestigium* "nicely captures an ambiguity that commentators and mystics exploited to the hilt." It is both a "ghostly vestige or trace" and a physical imprint.[70] As the physical relic—and its interaction with the reliquary—makes clear, *vestigium* accommodates these different resonances because it implies a simultaneous physicality in past and present. In developing its poetics of enshrinement, this study will at various moments examine poetry's conception of language as trace.[71] As inflected by the mechanics of vestige and trace, poetic language's signifying acts find form in the material signifying practices of the relic enshrined within its reliquary.

A Late-Medieval English Context

Language's ability to reflect the relic's vestigiality, and thus to investigate interactions between visual and material signs, might exist in a number of historical instances. Why focus, then, on the late Middle Ages as possessing its own version of a poetics of enshrinement? The answer to this question lies in late-medieval England's self-conscious exploration of vernacular poetics, and the dynamic coexistence of this exploration with a tradition of highly varied modes of ecclesiastical and popular performance, which featured in particular the late-fourteenth-century rise of cycle drama.[72] Clearly, other medieval cultures also contained some of these elements, but in the English late Middle Ages, both of these aspects of cultural production were especially taken up with investigations of representational practice itself, whether through popular vernacular spectacle, or through this period's interest in Ockhamist and other philosophical debates about epistemology and signification, often articulated through the vehicle of vernacular poetic expression.[73] By the fourteenth century, poets were as interested as grammarians were in the ambiguity of signs, and in language's relationship to reality.[74]

A brief examination of the *Book of the Duchess* here will provide an initial example of how one might read through a poetics of enshrinement, as situated in late-fourteenth-century England. Given the complexity of this poetics' network of terms, an initial demonstration of its features through a familiar text might serve as a useful strategy for orientation. As the introduction suggested, both the *Book of the Duchess*, and its companion dream vision the *House of Fame*, provide useful starting points, in part because both suggest that even relatively secularized artistic expressions still reflected a consciousness of devotional practices and material traditions.

The two texts use the culture of reliquaries and shrines to consider representational practice.[75] In the *Book of the Duchess*, the narrator finds himself in a "chambre,"

> Ful wel depeynted, and with glas
> Were al the wyndowes wel yglased
> Ful clere, and nat an hoole ycrased,
> That to beholde hyt was gret joye.
> For hooly al the story of Troye
> Was in the glasynge ywrought thus...
> And alle the walles with colours fyne
> Were peynted, bothe text and glose,
> Of al the Romaunce of the Rose.[76]

Like the Sainte-Chapelle, this dreamed space embellishes and inscribes all its different surfaces with narrative. In both the real chamber of the palatine chapel and the dreamed chamber of the poem, different categories of sign systems—visual and verbal—interact to contain, ultimately, the physicality of death and the desire for memorial.[77] The *House of Fame* places its dreamer

> [w]ithyn a temple ymad of glas,
> In which ther were moo ymages

Of gold, stondynge in sondry stages,
And moo ryche tabernacles,
And with perre moo pynacles,
And moo curiouse portreytures,
And queynte maner of figures
Of olde werk, then I saugh ever....
But as I romed up and doun
I fond that on a wall ther was
Thus writen on a table of bras:
"I wol now synge, if I kan,
The armes also and the man...."
                (ll. 120–27; 140–44)

In the manner of many late-medieval reliquary shrines and memorial artifacts, this structure incorporates glass, metalwork, jewels, iconographic
images, and a variety of levels of enclosure with its "tabernacle" alcoves
(figures Intr.4 and Intr.5). Within both enclosed spaces, inscriptions and
decorations create fluidity between visual and verbal forms of representation. The wholeness of the window is the wholeness of the story. Chaucer
uses ambiguous and multivalent words such as "graven," "ywroght," and
"peynted, bothe text and glose" to describe what he sees, and he shifts
between accounts of written inscription on the one hand and ekphrastic descriptions of pictures or statues on the other.[78] The inscriptional
features of the enshrining space thus examine their own status as both
language and objects.

This exploration of representational process is intimately linked to
the late-medieval interest in vernacular expression. The scenes in the
Chaucerian dream visions use the shrine as a space to engage in the task of
translating classical material into the vernacular. We generally understand
late-medieval English vernacularity to refer not to a particular language but
instead to a system of linguistic functioning, a pattern of interactions among
various linguistic currencies and contexts. And this interaction among
different languages inevitably called attention to the issues surrounding
representational practice more broadly.[79] The *House of Fame*'s couplet, "I wol
now synge, if I kan, / The armes also and the man" famously makes a pun-
ning reference to the Virgilian "arma virumque cano." In this translation
pun, we see an examination of language's status as an object of both material inscription and sound, a close look at its ways of conveying meaning
through its simultaneous interlocking with and differentiation from other
systems of signification ("kan" and "cano"). Playing with the properties
of inscription, this vision of the shrine juxtaposes and interweaves various
forms of signification. For this reason it becomes an especially appropriate
space in which translation can occur, as it does in Chaucer's two scenes.

The intersection of the semiotics of the shrine and the rise of self-conscious vernacularity thus provides one reason for focusing on the poetics of enshrinement as a late-medieval English aesthetic phenomenon. This argument will not attempt to treat the issue of vernacularity exhaustively; a number of other recent studies have engaged in that important work.[80] Pointing out the general context of poetic vernacularity at the outset, however, allows us to recognize this period in English literary and cultural history as one with an interest in relationships among different sign systems as articulated through poetry. Inscriptionality functions as an important way of articulating this interest.

But if the Chaucerian dream visions use inscriptionality to make their points, how do these poems, as examples for this study, also interact with performance traditions? The answer to this question lies in their identity as dream visions, for dream conventions offer a set of terms to characterize the worlds that poetic language performs.[81] In the late Middle Ages, the genre of the dream vision provided a vehicle for considering performative acts of speaking worlds into being.[82] A.C. Spearing observes that a medieval dream poem "is a poem which has more fully realized its own existence as a poem" because of the attention it draws to its beginning and end through the framing presence of its dreamer/narrator; "its status is that of an imaginative fiction....[I]t is not a work of nature but a work of art."[83] The late-medieval dream vision explores how realities constitute themselves and relate to each other within the frame of language. These questions manifest themselves in the Chaucerian dreams through the language each uses to categorize and identify dreams in relation to reality. The *House of Fame*'s dreamer is particularly obsessed with this aspect of visions. Are they generated internally, a landscape of "complexions" and "reflexions," or externally, by "spirites" (ll. 21–22, 41)? Where do they locate themselves in relation to consciousness and the world?[84] Peter Brown sees the late-medieval "literary dream" as "the meeting place of [self and society], being at once intensively private and expansively public, providing a means whereby the outer world can be read through the inner."[85] Here the dream becomes a location that both articulates and undermines borders among different conceptions of realities. Brown reads the medieval dream as opening up the possibility for a state of "altered consciousness."[86] Steven Kruger perceives a sensitivity to "betweenness" in late-medieval dream vision culture, suggesting again the dream's capacity for negotiation between different worlds and different forms of reality. Dreams in the Middle Ages, Kruger argues, were "able to navigate that middle realm where connections between the corporeal and incorporeal are forged."[87] Kathryn Lynch argues that later dream literature increasingly foregrounds the structure of infinite enclosure as a gesture toward the medieval traditions on which it draws; her representative example is *A Midsummer Night's Dream.* Lynch's argument also suggests that the dream's performative engagement with reality is behind the early modern affinity between dreams and dramatic performance. In discussing *A Midsummer Night's Dream,* she states, "the confusions among dream, vision, and 'reality' become an important part of the drama's meaning, similar to the layers of artifice dramatized by the doubling of roles and plots—confusions which make us ask just where the 'play' begins and ends."[88] In these different cases, the dream vision investigates the nature of worlds created through artistic expression. The epistemology of dreams intersects with that of performance, implicating the Chaucerian texts in questions about performance and performativity by virtue of their very genre.

The *Book of the Duchess* at first appears to articulate its various dream worlds through the privileging of inscriptionality. The layers of inset narratives in the dream are typically textually based, from the book that puts the dreamer to sleep, to the knight's poetic form of complaint appearing at an inner level of the dream. This latter example establishes itself in the poem as inscriptional object. While a complaint holds the potential to be a musical or oral performance, this one is "a maner song, / Withoute noote, withoute song" (ll. 471–72). It occupies the realms of both voice and silence—it is a strange songless song—and we therefore encounter it at least in part as an inscribed entity on the page, drawing attention to itself by its formal separation from the couplet structure. As this kind of inscriptional object, the complaint reinforces the poem's sense of the dream worlds' layers as constructions of writing.

In the context of the scene as a whole, however, the knight's complaint is not simply inscription, but instead forms a moment in which inscription and performance enshrine each other. In one sense, the knight's body as performing vehicle surrounds the complaint, framing it as a piece of static text set off from the rest of the poem. We see the knight make a "dedly sorwful soun" (l. 462), a bodily and voiced expression of sorrow that may or may not be articulate, just before the inclusion of the short lyric. After the lyric, the narrator provides a detailed description of the knight's bodily action. Blood drains "doun to hys herte" (l. 491), causing "his hewe" to "chaunge and wexe grene / And pale" (ll. 497–98). In this narrative progression, the knight's bodily actions, as a voiced and physical performance of his sorrow, surround and motivate the complaint lyric. The poem's moments of bodily performance enclose the inscriptional entity.[89] Through the dream vision's interactions among different worlds, the knight becomes an embodied and performed reality framing a textual one.

Shifting our perspective on this same section, however, reveals that the scene also contains its performing body within two marks of silence, and through this act of framing the nature of the body, and its status within the dream, changes. After describing the knight's bodily pallor, the narrator states that he "spak noght" (l. 503). This statement resonates with the reference to the song that is at best problematically voiced: a "maner song" that is without note and without song. Thus emphases on reticence—the refusal to sing and ultimately to speak—precede and follow the description of the expressive body, making a narrative frame for this body. The pallor of the knight's body, as the blood rushes to his heart, also anticipates his account of himself as a "whit wal or table" (l. 780). With this later simile, the knight makes of his body an object to be inscribed—"redy to cacche and take / Al that men wil theryn make," or on which to "portreye or peynte" (ll. 781–83).[90] *Table* here probably signifies "tablet"; however, Vincent Gillespie has also discussed the late-medieval tradition of painted tables, especially alabaster ones, as popular church decorations in England. These surfaces sometimes displayed a combination of image and text.[91] The "whit...table" thus potentially signals an inscriptional as well as a decorative space; it is for both poetic making and painting. In this context, the earlier description of the knight's pale body also makes itself available as an object of inscription, and its enclosure within references to compromised speech reinforces this possibility. His song's connection to voicedness becomes increasingly attenuated in the poem's suggestion that the song locates itself as inscription on the knight's body. The references to the knight's difficulties with voice narratively frame, in the sequence of verses, the object of his body. These lines suggest that his body not only performs the look and sound of sorrow, but also becomes a field on which silent characters of sorrow inscribe themselves. Thus while references to bodily performance surround the lyric itself, the scene also offers the possibility that allusions to silence might frame and reshape that same performing body as an object of silent inscriptionality. In these two different views of the scene, inscription and performance frame each other. The poetics of enshrinement allows us to see the dream vision as two interlocked triptychs that enfold inscription and performance within each other.

This poetics thus provides a particular shape for understanding the relationship between voice and silence in the medieval poetic text. In a chapter on "Memory and the Book," Mary Carruthers explores the interaction between *painture* and *parole*, arguing that, "The author is a 'painter,' not only in that the letters he composes with have shapes themselves, but in that his words paint pictures in the minds of his readers." At the same time, as she says, "visual forms in a book 'speak,'" and the relationship between literate knowledge and memory dictates that images not be silent.[92] In the example of the *House of Fame*, Carruthers argues, "all the voices, the *parole*, of human beings are described as rising from earth to Fame's house, where they assume the shape of those who spoke them," to illustrate "the traditional medieval understanding of what words are" and how they do their representational work.[93] This medieval understanding was complex. It included not only the materialization of the speaker or concept spoken, but also the different possibilities of the inscribed word itself, the different ways that it might function as material trace. The poetics of enshrinement offers a visual and material form for this understanding. It encloses voice and silent inscription within each other, revealing and concealing each, through the culturally specific representational modes of performance and inscription.

CHAPTER 2

SILENT INSCRIPTION, SPOKEN CEREMONY: *SAINT ERKENWALD* AND THE ENSHRINED JUDGE

Through its form, content, and implicit dialogue with contemporary ceremonial practices, the Middle English *Saint Erkenwald* reveals a poetics of enshrinement underlying late-medieval literate culture. *Saint Erkenwald* depicts the interaction between the English saint and a reanimated pagan dignitary, who speaks from a tomb embellished with golden inscriptions. After some opening comments about the establishment of Christianity in the British Isles, the poet alludes to the conversion history of a number of formerly pagan temples in seventh-century England, which have become Christian churches. One such structure is Saint Paul's, which when the poem begins is undergoing further renovations. In the process of digging a new foundation, the workmen come upon a splendid tomb, garnished with marble gargoyles and embellished with a border of beautiful but indecipherable golden letters. The lid is pried open, and the assembled crowd presses forward to see what is inside. The tomb contains the perfectly preserved body of what seems to be an ancient king, attired in gold, pearls, and miniver, crowned and holding a scepter. Learned clerks consult the chronicles, but no one can figure out who this enigmatic figure is, and the people become troubled and anxious. The eponymous protagonist—a bishop during his lifetime—hurries to London to investigate the mysterious tomb. Erkenwald, through a ceremony of the Mass, a prayer, and even a symbolic baptism of tears, then brings about two consecutive miracles. First is the reanimation of the corpse, who identifies himself as a pagan judge from a distant time, one whose soul is caught in Limbo. Second is the body's instantaneous disintegration as the soul is allowed to proceed to heaven when one of Erkenwald's tears falls on the body, thereby baptizing it. The poem ends with a joyous procession.

Saint Erkenwald's entombed body draws upon both the imagery and representational practices of shrines, tombs, and their contexts. The narrative turns on enshrinement (the body's enclosure within layers of decoration, iconography, and architecture); inscription (the illegible writing that frames the body); and ceremonial performance (the High Mass, baptism, and procession that Erkenwald orchestrates). This chapter argues that the interaction between Erkenwald and the judge integrates performance practice and inscription, two modes of expression whose connection derives from the culture of shrines, tombs, and reliquaries. In the poem, these two modes frame each other to represent the judge as a presence that is both of this world and separate from it. The mechanics of the encounter between judge and saint become legible through the cultural context of devotional artifacts. But equally importantly, the poetic representation of the judge generated in this encounter reveals its strategies through the dialectics of inscription and performance. The silence of inscription as it turns in on itself, and the voiced, public, and world-creating properties of the performative, interdependently form in *Saint Erkenwald* a poetics of enshrinement.

Saint Erkenwald emphasizes an important general point in the study of devotional practice's connections to literature: even texts that concern themselves with aspects of secular culture are still fundamentally informed by surrounding material cultures of devotion. This is not to say that they require a kind of Robertsonian interpretive practice.[1] Rather, their form and imagery often indicate a consciousness of spiritual practices that might lie outside the specific literary or secular agenda of the text. As Stanbury argues, Chaucer, for instance, uses the conventions of ritual and sacrament in his secular writings to cross boundaries among the religious, the political, and the domestic.[2] Like the Chaucerian dream visions we have examined, with their tabernacle imagery and their spaces decorated with an ecclesiastical aesthetic, *Saint Erkenwald* demonstrates how medieval artistic productions formulate sacred and secular as a continuum, and not two dichotomous categories. One secularized field of inquiry for *Saint Erkenwald*, as Monika Otter has argued, is historical discourse. Otter states that this poem is primarily concerned with its relationship to historical narrative. Specifically, the genre of the saint's *inventio*, mirrored in this poem through the discovery of the pagan judge, provides some important tools with which to understand the nature of historical discourse in the Middle Ages, and the deceptively complex relationship that medieval writers and thinkers envisioned between themselves and their historical past.[3] But the poem's examination of this discourse structures itself around devotional conventions. The invocation of renovation locates the imagistic framework for this political discourse in the material traditions of the shrine. The secular and the sacred become interlocking territories through the material practices associated with the latter.

Furthermore, the poem interweaves secular and sacred by displacing acts such as translation and tomb construction onto the pagan judge in the poem, and away from Erkenwald as saintly figure.[4] The saint's hagiographic tradition includes numerous accounts of bodily translation, reburial, and miracles surrounding the site of his own shrine. Erkenwald had an active relic cult lasting from the late seventh century until the end of the Middle Ages, a cult that focused on his bodily remains and objects that he touched or used. Erkenwald's funeral pall, for example, was reported by his twelfth-century chronicler Arcoid to have survived a major fire, and the litter on which he was carried during an illness was worshipped as a relic that performed miracles of healing.[5] Through hagiographic narrative, Erkenwald's body and shrine associated themselves with miraculous integrity. The displacement of this shrine tradition onto various activities surrounding the judge's tomb indicates the poetic text's movement between sacred and secular realms through the channel of shrine culture. While it was certainly the case that the historical and enshrined Erkenwald maintained an identity as the "saint of London" as much as the textual Erkenwald in the poem, the latter's depiction outside the tomb rather than in it allows him to become a politicized and nationalist figure in more explicit terms. He intertwines himself in a historically localized and secularized assertion of the importance of New Troy. The body of the non-Christian judge, on the other hand, occupies a dynamic of sacred enshrinement that is far more complex. By transferring a tradition of Christian shrine imagery away from the sacred figure of Erkenwald, displacing it onto a pagan body in order to emphasize Erkenwald's political resonances, the poem destabilizes the boundaries between sacred and secular. It shows how questions of politicized historiography might articulate themselves through the language of devotional and liturgical objects.[6]

This shifting of sacred matter creates a doubling effect between saint and pagan judge, and in this way as well their relationship represents an oscillation between spiritual and non-spiritual. An image of Saint Erkenwald appears in an early-fifteenth-century French book of hours made for the English knight Sir William Porter (figure 2.1).[7] Erkenwald is reading a book, which suggests the same impulse toward acts of decipherment and reading that the mysterious letters in the poem invoke. In addition, his placement in a cloister-like setting and the ornate inscribed

Figure 2.1 Pierpont Morgan Library MS M 105, fol. 57, fifteenth century. Hours of William Porter. The Pierpont Morgan Library, New York. Gift: J.P. Morgan (1867–1943); 1924.

Source: Reproduced by permission of The Pierpont Morgan Library, New York.

border further contribute to this sense of Erkenwald's enclosure, like that of the poem's pagan judge, inside both golden girding and a border of words. By shifting the themes of enclosure, decipherment, wisdom, and power from the saint to the judge, the poem imagines a fictional mirror image of the saint, as defined by the latter's hagiographic and historical tradition.[8] In his doubling capacity, the judge undermines the boundary between devotional tradition and a more secular discourse of fictional construction. The poet draws upon both fields to generate a narrative of the judge. When these two characters mirror each other, passing between each other various sacred and secular associations, they make available to the poem an important possibility for literary texts. A poetic text existing outside the boundaries of liturgical or devotional practice, and even posing some secular questions, can still draw upon the representational strategies of these realms. This possibility will be instrumental throughout the following reading of *Saint Erkenwald*. In this reading, *Saint Erkenwald* uses the shrine's dialectic of inscription and performance to define and shape its own strategies of representation.

Poem and Performance

Contemporary traditions of performance and ceremony underlie *Saint Erkenwald*'s depictions of both the saint and the judge. By identifying the interaction between these two characters as a moment of spectacle, we see the process by which the poem represents the judge. This process depends upon voice, utterance, translation, and audience. *Saint Erkenwald* frequently designates Erkenwald as the instigator of ceremonial occasions, but it also imagines the judge as both person and performance. The interaction between saint and judge creates an event that defines the judge's absent presence.

The poem's background suggests connections to liturgical and paraliturgical practice. According to Gordon Whatley, for instance, the feast of the Invention of the Cross occurred during Saint Erkenwald's spring octave, so that "Erkenwald's offices and masses formed a frame around the Invention liturgy."[9] Thus *Saint Erkenwald* existed for its audience as part of a broader devotional tradition of spectacle focusing on the revelation and deciphering of a sacred object. The liturgy's defining formal quality as integrating narrative progression and the implicit stasis of the repeated ceremony finds a parallel in the poem as well. Bruce Holsinger has described the temporality of liturgy (drawing upon Levinas) as "a means of discerning and living the past in its impossible totality within the present even as the lineaments of that past remain unknowable, incomprehensible, overwhelming."[10] Liturgy moves toward the past even as it acknowledges the present's separation from it. The temporality of the ceremonial and liturgical traditions over which Erkenwald presides is also the temporality of the poem. *Saint Erkenwald* simultaneously focuses on contemporaneity and historical recursiveness. It invokes the appellation "New Troy" as a way to situate itself as continuous with historical tradition, and at the same time acknowledges the complications of the "lineaments of that past" by compulsively returning to renovation and change. Ruth Nissé sees in the poem a related dichotomy of both "the desire for cultural continuity, and the fragmentary, uncertain nature of history itself." *Saint Erkenwald* "recasts an oft-told tale to tell an entirely new story."[11] In addition to the political resonances Nissé describes here, *Saint Erkenwald*'s complex sense of temporality also refers to structures of devotion, and to the dichotomous understanding of time to which medieval audiences were habituated through liturgical practice.

The saint's participation in the Mass and related ceremonies calls forth a number of traditions of devotional performance in the late Middle Ages. Erkenwald incorporates his interaction with the pagan tomb, for instance, into a regulated moment of ecclesiastical spectacle and vocal expression. Erkenwald structures his quest for the body's identity around his involvement in the Mass:

> Þe byscop hym shope solemply to synge þe heghe masse;
> Þe prelate in pontificals was prestly atyride.
> Manerly wyt his ministres þe masse he begynnes,
> Of Spiritus Domini for His spede on sutile wise,
> Wyt queme questis of þe quere wyt ful quaynt notes.
> Mony a gay grete lorde was gedrid to herken hit
> (As þe rekenest of þe reame repairen thider ofte),
> Tille cessyd was þe seruice and sayde þe later ende.
> Þen heldyt fro þe autere alle þe heghe gynge—
> Þe prelate passide on þe playn, þer plied to hym lordes;
> As riche reuestid as he was he rayked to þe toumbe,
> Men vncloside hym þe cloister wyt clustrede keies,
> Bot pyne wos wyt þe grete prece þat passyd hym after.
> The byschop come to þe burynes him barones besyde,
> Þe maire wyt mony maȝti men and macers before hym.[12]

The bishop, accompanied by the prelate and a ceremonial retinue, initiates the Mass. His presence in turn generates a procession toward the pagan's tomb. Around the narrative time of this entire ceremonial occasion appear musical intonations and choreographed gestures and motion. The "queme questis" as a voiced element of the Mass alliterates with both "quere" and "quaynt" (the latter describing the musical notes). The

poem thus uses repeated sounds to emphasize the vocality of the singing choir as a precursor to the procession. The canon then proclaims the
story of the tomb when the procession reaches it (ll. 146–58). At other
moments as well, the poem takes care to characterize Erkenwald's own
actions as public, voiced, and oriented toward an audience. His appeal to
the corpse happens in front of an audience of "lordes" (l. 146), and when
the pagan judge does speak, the poem reminds the readers of the presence of this audience, who are rendered "as stile as the ston" (l. 219) in
shock, contrasting with the singing heard earlier. In these ways, the saint's
encounter with the judge establishes itself within a context of spectacle,
and a dynamic contrast between sound and silence.

Saint Erkenwald's references to performance, however, do not limit
themselves to the saint's actions. The poem defines the judge not only as a
bounded material object, but also as an occasion of performance and performative self-constitution. In the above simile, "as stile as the ston," the
transfer of stone's materiality from the judge's tomb (and static body) to
the people looking at it makes them interactive participants in a scene of
performance blending spectacle, ceremony, and architecture. John Howe
argues for a long history of semiotic interaction between sacred shrines
and observers in defining the nature of sacred space itself. "All participants became symbols themselves," he claims, "part of the entourage of
the saints."[13] Saint Erkenwald interprets this spatiality by making its spectators part of all aspects of this scene, including the judge, and entering
them and the judge into the occasion of performance. The language of
the poem renders indeterminate the boundary between the stone tomb
and the astonished audience, so that both fill the positions of either a
material thing or an occasion of spectacle.

The mobility of this imagery, between judge and audience, casts the
judge as both an event—existing beyond the control of himself and his
spectators—and a performative self-constitution. The judge's own performance is essentially an act of speaking his identity into being. But
this performance shows that he is both an event (in the Derridean
sense described in chapter 1) and at the same time an illustration of the
self-constitutive properties of the performative:

> Þe bryȝt body in þe burynes brayed a litelle,
> And wyt a drery dreme he dryues owte wordes,
> Þurghe sum Goste-lant lyfe of hym þat al redes.
> (ll. 190–92)

The Derridean definition of the term "event" can help us to see how the
pagan judge integrates his own status as event with his performativity,

two terms Derrida himself contrasts. "For the truth to be 'made' as an event," Derrida says, "then the truth must fall on me—not be produced by me, but fall on me, or visit me."[14] He contrasts this form of happening with the more recognizably performative act of speaking something into being, and suggests that the very possibility of "event" in this pure, unanticipated form is itself problematic because of language's constitutive anteriority. The pagan judge's startling move from death into consciousness, combined with his act of constituting and making himself before his audience through his reanimated voice, integrate both the pure unexpectedness of event (for the judge as well as his audience) and the performative gesture of self-creation. The judge receives a Derridean "visitation" in the form of the "Gost-lant lyfe" that explains his reanimation. He exemplifies in many ways event theory's conception of the event as "passing through the body without the body's ability to contain, bind, or channel its energy, either physically or psychically. The force of this passage works on the body—dead or alive."[15] But within *Saint Erkenwald's* instance of event, spontaneous and unconstructed in its relationship to the body, is also the presence of a self-constituting and performative language in the judge's self-identifying speech. Through his connections to devotional traditions, the judge breaks certain language theories into their component parts, and accommodates both what is everywhere and anterior (the performativity of language) and what is impossible (event) in the terms of these theoretical discourses. Many facets of performance and the performative thus glint forth in the pagan judge's representation. The terms of performance, performativity, and event help us to understand what happens in those moments of utterance through re-animation. The judge's movement from silence into speech narrates the condition of a specifically devotional and even miraculous performativity.

While the judge encompasses event and performative language, he also functions as a silent object of performance practice in the moments before his reanimation. As a performance object (discussed in chapter 1), the entombed judge and his specific features reveal additional meanings in their juxtaposition with contemporary performance practice. In the processional context of the approach to the pagan judge's tomb, *Saint Erkenwald* also refers to the way that choreography and ceremony surrounding important church sites constructed meaning at those sites. Physical access to late-medieval shrines and reliquaries took on a more complex and choreographed quality than at other points in the Middle Ages. This historical moment becomes especially illuminating in studying devotional objects as objects of performance, and in considering these performance contexts as part of the object's signifying capacity. Pilgrims followed deliberately constructed paths through cathedrals as part of an ecclesiastical authority's attempt to control the nature of access to—and the nature of the audience's interaction with—the various relics held at major sites.[16] The choreography of devotional spectacle took other forms as well in the late Middle Ages. For example, architectural and archeological evidence suggests that during the fourteenth and fifteenth centuries, churches and cathedrals were home to a proliferation of screens and reredoses, which regulated and mediated access to shrines.[17] These discouraged the possibility of long vistas inside the church and arbitrated the ways that both pilgrims and clergy configured around a cathedral's main shrine. As Ben Nilson argues, using physical obstacles to limit access to the shrine meant that "with time it became less public and more mysterious, an inner sanctum which one could only reach by passing through successive barriers."[18] This setting suggests a controlled and ceremonial quality for the pilgrims' actual interactions with shrines; the moment of veneration became a form of spectacle in itself. On the one hand, access was necessarily mediated, but on the other, the process of this mediation constituted the object's particular devotional significance through the regulated spectacle it presented in ceremony.

This aspect of ceremonial practice suggests that the inscrutability of the pagan judge and his border of golden letters symbolize increasingly mediated and mystified means of access to shrines in English cathedrals. *Saint Erkenwald* points out that the letters surrounding the tomb cannot be deciphered:

> The sperle of þe spelunke þat sparde hit o-lofte
> Was metely made of þe marbre and menskefully planede,
> And þe bordure enbelicit wyt bryȝt gold lettres
> Bot roynyshe were þe resones þat þer on row stoden.
>
> (ll. 49–52)

The word *roynyshe* has been glossed speculatively as "runish," or "unreadable"; its specific meaning is not clear, but it does convey the sense that the words are unfamiliar in shape to the finders of the tomb, and are themselves the last remaining vestige of some more ancient language. The foreign nature of the letters implicitly raises the issue of linguistic translation. As the text describes it, "Mony clerkes in þat clos wyt crownes ful brode / Þer besiet hom a-boute noȝt to brynge hom in wordes" (ll. 55–56). The body emphasizes the need for translation in rendering legible the performance object of the shrine. Frank Grady has read the poem as reflecting a historicized and secularized consciousness about exceptional salvations, in part through the device of the golden letters: "the identity and meaning of the judge is plainly represented as a textual problem....[T]he 'roynyshe' figures are never deciphered in the poem, I would argue, because they are a figure for the poem itself, which supplies the deficiencies of chronicles and corrects the failures of memory that render the letters unreadable."[19] In the context of historiography and chronicle tradition, then, the letters point toward the poem's potential for correction and the reconstitution of historical matter. Reading them in the context of the poem's immediate material culture of the reliquary shrine and late-medieval ceremonies of access to it, however, confronts us with the material capacity of the letters. They both embellish and obscure the meaning of an enshrined object. And in this capacity, their illegibility symbolizes the mystified nature of the late-medieval shrine in English churches and cathedrals. The runes speak through their very impenetrability, their resistance to being read as language, about the nature of ceremonial encounters with shrines as decorated objects, a mystery at once challenging and suggestive.

Because they ask to be translated, the letters allow us to see how the judge makes translation itself a vital element in his identity as a performance object. As marks that seem to function decoratively rather than linguistically, the letters introduce the possibility of translation between verbal and visual or material forms of expression. Thus translation moves out of the realm of language and into that of the material. And for devotional performance culture, translation in fact had more concrete meanings. Translation meant the movement not only between languages, but also through space. *Translatio* referred to the physical movement from one place to another of a relic, as well as the narrative that described that movement.[20] And as *Saint Erkenwald* suggests, translation also implies the movement between these material and verbal realms. In its physical sense, translation was an important aspect of the ceremonies surrounding shrines, and *Saint Erkenwald*'s judge as performance object shows us the relationship between translation ceremony and the translation of signs.

Translation became a term by which ceremonies and performances changed and determined the meanings of their sacred objects, and it forms a part of the judge and Erkenwald's relationship to performance and ceremony. Even through the end of the Middle Ages, records indicate the existence of elaborate ceremonies and spectacles surrounding the act of physical translations. As the Middle Ages progressed, a number of different reasons for engineering such translations occurred, including shifting religious foundations; a desire to make what was abstractly spiritual into something concretely exchangeable; political turmoil; and competition among monasteries. Patrick Geary points out that rural monasteries of the tenth and eleventh centuries would often use the acquisition of relics to gain political support from local nobility. In addition, as relic thefts became a more urban phenomenon, the motivation behind the thefts changed from a spiritual one on behalf of a particular religious institution, to a purely economic one.[21] Narratives of relic translations often focused on the idea of recontextualizing the relics at a new site, and on the saint's ability to express an opinion, through miraculous intervention, about the translation itself. Saints were often believed to interfere with or contribute in some way to their own translations, by making their relics miraculously heavy or causing other trouble.[22] In 1349, the English monarchy participated in the translation ceremony of Saint Thomas of Hereford, and even in these later moments in the Middle Ages, translation ceremonies used liturgical elements and ecclesiastical ceremony to establish the legitimizing function of relics in their shrines.[23] In the fifteenth century, what Paul Strohm calls the "awkward odyssey" of Richard II's reburied body (both sacred and earthly) interwove itself into a narrative of monarchical legitimation and spectrality.[24] These instances all point toward the inextricability of translation's act of recasting meaning from the conventions of devotional spectacle and performance.

The hagiographic material pertaining to the historical Erkenwald illustrates that translation, in its capacity as spectacle, destabilizes categories of meaning and being. The saint's tradition suggests that translation manipulated spectacle to such an extent that it changed the viewer's sense of physical and visual categories. Relic translation in general demonstrated how the significance, purpose, or community identity of a relic could be transformed through its physical translation and its change in signifying context and ceremonial practice. Saint Erkenwald's cult bears this idea out. In 1326, for example, the shrine of Saint Erkenwald had been moved in such a way that its own altar was preserved, and that the route for censing the church went all the way around it, so that the movement of the body implicated itself in considerations about the flow of the procession and the visual spectacle it generated.[25] According to the fourth miracle of Saint Erkenwald in Arcoid's *Miraculi Sancti Erkenwaldi*, the saint's body was originally sealed inside a reliquary shaped like a steeply gabled house and resting on a platform.[26] In 1148 Erkenwald's body was translated to a silver reliquary decorated with plates depicting scenes from the saint's life and adorned with three-pound silver angels on either end, as an inventory of Saint Paul's from the mid-thirteenth century indicates.[27] The plates embossed with scenes from Erkenwald's life represented a means of both dictating and mediating the body's meaning; iconographic signs translated and transformed it for the viewer. More vividly, during the translation to the silver reliquary, the coffin containing the body was too big to fit inside a stone casing designed for it, and so the stone miraculously expanded in order to accommodate the body of the saint:

> For the sake of him who was being denied burial by the craftsman's ignorance, the opening of the stone was made larger by the right hand of [the one] who extends the heavens. When the saint was being placed inside it, the hardness of the slabs became soft, the stone forgot its natural condition and submitted to the gaze of its creator.[28]

The example of Erkenwald's miracle of *translatio* suggests in particular that translation destabilizes ontological categories through its engagement with the visual and material. Just as the poem's onlookers metaphorically metamorphose from flesh to stone, so the materials of the saint's tomb abandon their own nature and become something else in the performance and process of translation.

Translation's enactment through visual spectacle contributes to its ability to mediate among different kinds of signs. Because of their illegibility, as we have seen, the golden letters surrounding the judge function as both language and visual objects. Emily Steiner argues for a cultural perception of "material textuality" based on the intersection of poetry and the concrete and physical conventions surrounding documents in the Middle Ages.[29] Her analysis provides a useful context here for thinking about the possibilities for language and text to occupy different categories of being and employ different—sometimes nonverbal—means of signification. *Saint Erkenwald* implies that the movement between translation ceremonies and acts of linguistic translation also includes a fluidity between visual and verbal forms of expression. Erkenwald's own historical tomb displayed metalwork angels, whose construction and purchase are documented in contracts with London goldsmiths from the early 1400s.[30] The pagan judge's tomb in the poem, meanwhile, features "gargeles garnysht aboute alle of gray marbre" (l. 48). *Saint Erkenwald* relocates the familiar element of metalwork decoration in its golden inscribed letters rather than the pagan figures rendered in stone. In the same way, the text re-imagines the silver plates on the older shrine as golden inscriptions on the judge's tomb. In both instances, the inaccessibility of this language allows the letters to function in the realm of visual figures as well. They parallel visual icons and engage in visual and material forms of translation and transformation.

Performance and translation collude as vehicles for representing both saint and judge in *Saint Erkenwald*. Through his mysterious obscurity, the judge in particular illuminates translation's relationship to performance. He recalls a history of translation ceremonies embedded within various forms of para-liturgical practice, in which spectacle takes place in the midst of an interaction between visitation and voiced performativity. But as a performance object, he also generates an impulse to move between different kinds of sign systems—verbal and visual, intelligible and strange—to fix the body's meaning. The judge's tomb demonstrates that translation is part of a larger investigation of sign systems. This impulse to translate from an unknown language occurs within spectacle's indeterminacy between visual and verbal signs.[31]

Inscription and Aura

Even as the judge's tomb participates in the vocalized rituals of performance and ceremony, it also contains silent, self-referential inscription in the golden letters that are able essentially to communicate only with themselves in the poem. The manuscript image of Erkenwald (figure 2.1), presented earlier as a double to the figure of the judge, explicitly associates written language with privacy and enclosure. This association is not simply a depiction of a particular conception of reading as social practice. It also reveals the inward and enclosed quality of written inscription itself, set against the more public performance traditions surrounding the saint. In the illustration, the book exists at the center of, and seems to generate, a number of framing enclosures. Written words here create the enclosure of self-reference. The inscriptionality of enshrining objects, this second part of the chapter argues, is the other half of the poem's representational apparatus. Like performance, it occupies in different ways the provinces of both the judge and the saint.

The process by which the poem represents the judge requires negotiation between performance and inscriptionality. As stated earlier, the judge exists not only as an object, but also as an interactive moment of performance and spectacle, delineated by gesture, voice, and ceremony. But inscription also functions as part of this negotiation. It is both enshrining instrument and linguistic signifier to the audience. The inscriptions on the judge's tomb allow the moment of performance to exist as its own self-constituted reality, what V.A. Kolve refers to, in the context of dramatic spectacle, as a "world set apart."[32] The notion of being in the physical world and also separate from it finds explication as well in art historical studies of devotional objects. Jeffrey Hamburger, for instance, has argued that the medieval West's concept of the *imago* in visual representation "always had a...power...that resided in its indeterminacy: it was at once material and immaterial, an idea and a thing."[33] Through its interaction with performance, inscription acknowledges the absences and indeterminacies within the experience of physical presence.

Evidence revealing some specifics about late-medieval devotional life will provide a concrete illustration of these ideas about inscriptionality. This devotional context will ultimately assist in demonstrating how inscription and performance intersect in *Saint Erkenwald*. Cultural evidence suggests that in practice, moments of interactivity with devotional objects involved not only performance—generated through both spectator and spectacle—but also varied uses of written inscription. Like the pagan judge, the devotional object was also an occasion performing itself, both in the world and separate from it, and generating an indeterminate space between spectator and spectacle. Medieval art attempted to create a fulcrum between the seen and the unseen, as Herbert Kessler describes it, in its interaction with the viewer.[34] In particular late-medieval instances, as we shall see, this fulcrum involved the use of written inscriptions as part of the performance.

The inscribed Bromholm cross card allows us to reconstruct a performative moment involving this separate representational space (figure 2.2). A vellum card, stitched and then pasted into a fifteenth-century book of hours at Lambeth Palace Library (Lambeth MS 545, folio 185r.), it displays an image of the Bromholm cross relic (in the shape of a patriarchal cross and encased in decorative metalwork, indicated by gilt edging). The image of the relic is superimposed upon a partial hymn text and collect. The textual material was probably meant for recitation in front of the cross, and it has been conjectured that the card exemplifies a type of souvenir produced by the priory and available to pilgrims. Francis Wormald likens it to modern cards and pictures sold at pilgrimage sites. In addition, the depiction of the cross in the Lambeth Palace manuscript is embellished with the inscriptions "This cros þat here peyntyd is" down one side and "Signe of þe cros of Bromholm is" down the other.[35] The vellum artifact forms an intersection of visual and verbal signs representing the cross. Its inscriptions explicitly refer to a multilayered act of representation, through both its reference to the mimetic act of painting and the referential force of the "signe." These framing inscriptions, like the pagan judge's golden letters, occupy a silent and self-reflexive category that differs from the prayers to be read aloud. They also serve, like the judge's letters, as a visual mechanism of enclosure. If *Saint Erkenwald*'s golden letters draw attention through their illegibility to the act of representing the judge, these inscriptions also draw attention to this act through the spectrum they delimit between painting and signs. The judge's inscriptions integrate the categories of verbal and visual by both insisting on their status as letters and refusing to be read (hence the clerks' frustration). The Bromholm card uses its inscribed border to articulate this same integration by juxtaposing

Figure 2.2 Lambeth Palace Library MS 545, fol. 185r., fifteenth century. The Cross of Bromholm. Lambeth Palace Library.

the visual representational strategy of painting with the slightly more ambiguous "signe."

The card explores these verbal and nonverbal modes of representation while using its texts to lead viewers through a ceremonial veneration of the object. As Thomas Lentes argues, in describing a ceremony of prayer before an altarpiece, "Neither the act of looking at the picture nor the act of gazing should be isolated; the complete choreography during the prayer in front of the picture must be considered." He maintains that elements of liturgical gesture and performance play an important role even in acts of private prayer and encounters with religious objects.[36] The regulation and choreography dictating the encounters with the Bromholm relic thus involved what was essentially a small scene of performance. These recitations of verse devotions both participated in and represented the holy spectacle through the network of trajectories created among cross relic, worshipper, and card with verse and image. The scene of performance-based interaction between worshipper and relic investigates the process of representing the holy object. In the moment of holding the card up to the cross, words become iconic and enshrining inscription, and poetry becomes performance in its intonation.[37] During this interaction, language functions as both its conventional semiotic system and as iconographic object on the card. Through the occasion of performance that this object produces, the cross image finds itself enshrined within two forms of written language: the progressive temporality of a poetic prayer, and the cyclical framing commentary about the cross's means of representation, circling between painting and sign. The complete choreography of this veneration therefore involves an interweaving of static and temporalized expression in the representation of the cross.

But in addition, this self-awareness about representational acts, and the spectrum of representational practice created between written inscription and painting, ultimately contribute to a complex sense of what the relic's own presence entailed. Caroline Walker Bynum has suggested that in the interaction between the devotional image of the Gregorymass and the actual ceremony of the Mass, "the exact nature of [real] presence was less an established formula than a living and demanding problem to Christians."[38] A devotional image, that is, does not merely denote devotional content; it actively involves itself in an investigation of the means of representing this content. Medieval viewers experienced presence as a vehicle for considering the nature of authenticity and representation. The Bromholm cross exists not simply as an object but rather at a point of confluence between word and image, specifically through the interactions among relic, card, and viewer in the moment of ceremonial performance. Here the investigative conventions of ceremonial iconography enclose the object's presence even as they themselves are enclosed by that presence. The cross, negotiating with its depiction, exists in an enshrining space of performance, one that defines itself, in Bynum and Kessler's terms, as both seen and unseen, "a seeing of considerable ambiguity."[39]

As a copy held up before the original, the Bromholm card shows in other ways as well how the particular aura of the devotional object derives from the interaction among original, copy, and audience. Reading this artifact alongside texts that treat artistic aura and reproduction will help to clarify this point. It will also isolate the particular role that inscription plays in this dynamic for the Bromholm card. In Don DeLillo's *White Noise*, the protagonist and his colleague take a trip to "the most photographed barn in America":

> "We're not here to capture an image, we're here to maintain one. Every photograph reinforces the aura. Can you feel it, Jack? An accumulation of nameless energies."
>
> There was an extended silence. The man in the booth sold postcards and slides.
>
> "Being here is a kind of spiritual surrender. We see only what the others see. The thousands who were here in the past, those who will come in the future. We've agreed to be part of a collective perception. This literally colors our vision. A religious experience in a way, like all tourism."
>
> Another silence ensued.
>
> "They are taking pictures of taking pictures," he said.[40]

The passage's revisiting and revision of Benjaminian aura speak in many ways to the medieval performance object's modes of representation.[41] The existence of the Bromholm "postcard" (and related artifacts such as Fitzwilliam Museum MS 55, folio 57v.), and its claims to participation in the viewer's performative experience of the actual object, suggests that questions of reproducibility and aura were at stake for medieval audiences within the context of a larger belief in the primacy of the relic. "The Work of Art in the Age of Mechanical Reproduction" characterizes aura as "a unique phenomenon of distance however close it may be," specifically tied to premodern conceptions of "cult value." For Benjamin, the history of art hinges upon a moment that distinguishes early forms of copying from "mechanical reproduction," which changes our definitions of authenticity in art, so that "instead of being based on ritual, it begins to be based on another practice—politics."[42] In the course of defining the modern, Benjamin sees acts of reproduction as "detach[ing] the reproduced object from the domain of tradition" and from a kind of original "presence."[43] Art in this context is designed for the mechanism of reproducibility, and it problematizes aura.

Considering the Bromholm ceremony alongside Benjamin's articulation reveals how inscription negotiates relationships of reproducibility. In the case of the Bromholm cross, the frame of the letters connects the object to its reproduction by pointing out various aspects of the act of artistic reproduction. The card suggests that its relationship to the actual cross takes place simultaneously through the voiced, externalized ceremony of prayer and the self-referential mechanics of written inscription. It employs a system of written signs instrumentalized by a discourse about difference carried on within its own signifying system. This system inheres in the ambiguous differentiation, for instance, between the words "painting" and "sign." In this difference we discern the card's claim to function both as an instance of mimesis or even artificiality, and as a more indeterminate mark or token—the "sign." The card's inscription also introduces problems of deferral and anteriority into the relationship between itself and the cross. On the one hand, the relic itself would appear to possess a kind of ideal anteriority, a status as original. But on the other, the inscriptions as a physical frame around the cross's representation emphasize the extent to which the card's engagement in language and writing constitutes and frames the devotional experience as a whole. The inscriptional frame brings into being the copy and its multilayered relationship to the original. By functioning as both language and visual image on the page, the inscriptions explicate the act of reproducing the cross. This act involves translation not only into different media, but also into different signifying systems. Looking at the card is a kind of "taking pictures of taking pictures." The card spells out the process of replication for the viewer by inscriptional means, which are visual and verbal.

But while we might see inscription as a framing commentary on the act of replication, the framing context of performance plays an equally important role in devotional activity. Performance generates presence through the interaction between cross and copy. As the devotional practices of late-medieval English churches in general, and the Erkenwald cult in particular, suggested, miraculous presence exists not simply in the artifact itself, but in the performance occasion of which it is a part. The Bromholm cross card makes inscription a part of a constitutive occasion of performance, the moment when cross and card are held up to each other. Locating the auratic at this moment requires acknowledging a perceptual space in the midst of cross, card, and viewer.[44] This perceptual space of performance does not simply capture the divine, but instead, as we saw earlier, examines the translation between verbal and visual marks in the process of representation. Benjamin's essay suggests that discourse concerning the representational act is fundamentally linked to the conventions of performance. He uses the example of film acting, as opposed to stage acting, to describe film as the "work of art designed for reproducibility." Unlike the response of a stage audience, which involves an interaction with the personal presence of the actor, the film audience's identification with the actor is really an "identification with the camera. Consequently, the audience takes the position of the camera; its approach is that of testing. This is not the approach to which cult values may be exposed."[45]

By framing inscription and performance within each other, the Bromholm card usefully complicates the Benjaminian opposition between the modern audience and the cultic audience. The scene of worship of the Bromholm relic can be read as an instance in which the audience, while not exactly taking the position of the camera, does engage in a consciousness of representational means, mediation, and mechanism. This investigation takes place for the viewer specifically through the dialectical enshrinement of the card's inscriptional and performative aspects. As an object that layers frames of language and affective image, the Bromholm cross card is a particularly appropriate vehicle for characterizing this dialectic. The frame of inscription contributes to a dynamics of reproducibility, a way of speaking the reproduction into being through its visual and verbal engagement with the object. The frame of performance creates another kind of space in which to experience presence through the investigation of representational process.

Inscription, Performance, and the Absent Presence

The Bromholm cross card's dialectic of inscription and performance sheds light on *Saint Erkenwald*. The card suggests that performative gesture and inscriptional aesthetics frame and contextualize each other to create for the judge a state of absent presence. As we saw earlier, the poem triangulates among judge, Erkenwald, and audience in depicting a scene of ceremonial spectacle. It also uses its allusions to both performance and hagiographic convention to suggest a phenomenon of mirroring, and thus perhaps replication, between Erkenwald and the judge. The model of the Bromholm cross card reveals that the quality of the auratic might similarly locate itself in the interaction between saint and judge. The shared device of mirroring allows us to read the scene of performance in *Saint Erkenwald* through the one that the Bromholm card creates. In both cases replication and repetition are themselves part of the occasion of performance. And in both cases this performance of replication determines meaning and identity for the miraculous object. At the same time, the effect of replication asks viewers to consider what is contained in the perceptual space between the two mirror images.

As an object that is both inscriptional and performance-based, the Bromholm card in fact deals in the realms of absence as well as presence. In poststructuralist terms, written inscription gestures toward a broader system of iterability in which the absence of the original inheres.[46] This formulation might seem incompatible in some ways with the medieval worldview; however, the poignant souvenir-like quality of this card, its ability to be removed from the sacred site, provides a culturally specific context for perceiving the deeper absences potentially underlying its inscriptional marks. We might understand *Saint Erkenwald* in similar terms. The act of representing the judge in the poem renders him both present and absent, at once present as a ceremonial spectacle and at the same time associated with the distancing, silencing, and mediating qualities of an undecipherable written language. His abrupt disappearance at the end in one sense reinforces this perception. But perhaps more telling is the poem's reference to the condition of disintegration threatening him as the state of being "moght-freten" ("moth-eaten") at line 86. The line refers to his ceremonial garb, and alludes to his appropriateness as public spectacle. At the same time, however, this phrase has traditional associations with the world of books, manuscripts, and writing on the material page through the Anglo-Saxon paradox/riddle "Moþþe word fraet" [The moth eats words], in which the moth, a thief in the darkness ("þeof in þystro"), does not grow any wiser for the words he has swallowed ("forswealg"). Such riddles were part of the vernacular and nationalist alliterative tradition with which this poem takes pains to ally itself.[47] This riddle in particular uses the concept of the "moth-eaten" to draw attention to the physicality of the word on the page, as well as its self-consumption in the riddle's verbal game; the moth as word devours words. Through both this specific image and the border of letters around him, the poem constructs the judge from the silence, self-reference, and even self-obfuscation and self-cancellation of written inscription, as much as from the performative contexts that allow him to reach toward his audience. The judge's absent presence occurs through the interaction of inscription and performance.[48]

The specific form of this interaction emerges as enshrinement, a mutual framing expressed through inscription and performance's temporalities. *Saint Erkenwald's* alliterative language, for instance, participates in this dialectic. Alliteration makes the poem into an inscriptional object by drawing attention to its identity as a set of marks that constitute meaning through their relationship to each other. As a poetic technique,

alliteration calls upon the voiced aspect of language, but it also emphasizes its inscriptional character, the silent visual reference that takes place
between one letter and another. Particularly in this visual and material
sense, alliteration reinforces a pattern of vestigiality: letters are repeated
in pagan and Christian names, so that the past not only prefigures the
present, but it also leaves behind pieces—letters, like statues and buildings—which are adapted in the present and incorporated into newly
cleansed Christian structures and words.[49] The poem uses the narrative
capacities of material objects and the material capacities of letters and
language to demonstrate the trope of vestigiality, the *reliquiae*, that which
is left behind.[50] The inscriptional aspect of alliteration thus provides a
defining temporality for the poem; the recursive return to what has been
left behind. But the performance traditions underlying *Saint Erkenwald*
also instigate this temporality. By alluding to a contemporary culture
of shrine production, *Saint Erkenwald* articulates an exterior and anterior mechanism for articulating vestigiality. In the culture on which it
draws, bodies from the past are enshrined and ceremonialized as a way
of making them present. Thus in one sense, *Saint Erkenwald*'s formal use
of alliteration provides a framing temporality for the poem. It uses the
reproducibility of written inscription to constitute a form of time that
shifts past into present. And yet, as a narrative of memorial ceremony,
Saint Erkenwald also encloses its inscriptional play within a particular
ceremonial temporality.

The form of the speech containing Erkenwald's prayer for guidance,
and his subsequent act of baptism, also enshrine inscription and performance within each other to represent the miraculous event. The text's
miracle of baptism, like its earlier miracle of reanimation, functions in
the problematic poststructuralist sense of the term "event." Like the
reanimation, the baptism closely examines the possibility of a truth that
is unexpected rather than already linguistically constituted. As Jennifer
Sisk argues, the poem deeply complicates the nature of Erkenwald's own
agency in his sacramental actions.[51]

> "Oure lorde lene," quoþ þat lede, "þat þou lyfe hades,
> By Goddes leue, as longe as I my3t lacche water
> And cast vpon þi faire cors and carpe þes wordes,
> 'I folwe þe in þe Fader nome and His fre Childes,
> And of þe gracious Holy Goste' and not one grue lenger;
> Þen þof þou droppyd doun dede hit daungerde me lasse."
> Wyt þat word þat he warpyd þe wete of eghen
> And teres trillyd adoun and on þe toumbe lighten,
> And one felle on his face and þe freke syked.
>
> (ll. 315–23)

In this passage, Erkenwald wishes that he might perform the ceremony of baptism by embedding the ceremony's identifying utterances within his own statement of desire. But in the process of expressing this desire, he weeps tears that ultimately fulfill a baptizing function when they land on the pagan judge and allow his soul to be released from Limbo. The framing speech contributes to the performative efficacy of the embedded speech, as the tears shift from the level of emotional expression of desire to that of ceremonial action. Because the structural pattern of the speech within a speech also enables a moment of performative utterance, it has various implications for thinking about the mutual enclosure of performance and inscriptionality in poetic language. The internal speech about a hypothetical ceremony of baptism both contains itself within the larger conditional framework of Erkenwald's utterance, and at the same time moves outside it when we realize with surprise—along with Erkenwald—that the force of this speech is not simply the representation of an act, but also a participation in the act itself. And as Gordon Whatley has pointed out, this act is specifically a ceremonial performance: *Saint Erkenwald* here elaborates on earlier versions of the virtuous pagan tradition, highlighting the role of the sacraments in the pagan's salvation.[52] The ceremonial act exists as a devotional event—exterior and anterior to its constitution in language. This anteriority, however, is visible through the device of the speech within a speech, a formal feature dependent on the poem's status as written inscription. Speech within speech moves between a temporalized and spatialized sense of poetic language. As we have seen, this movement into spatiality is specifically connected to the inscribing of poetry on the page.[53] This particular moment's expression in poetic language, and its form of self-containment, create an enshrining space in which spectacle interacts with writing. The result is an event both uncontainable and at the same time contained within an inscribed boundary.

As a moment of poetic inscription, this scene in *Saint Erkenwald* stages the conflation of interior and exterior inherent to speech and writing. According to the Derridean model, "writing is at the same time more exterior to speech, not being its 'image' or its 'symbol,' and more interior to speech, which is already in itself a writing."[54] Bruce Holsinger provides an important gloss upon this idea as well, one that locates a sacramental point of contact between poststructuralism and the medieval:

> As Derrida writes [on Rousseau], "In the last pages of the chapter 'On Script,' the critique, the appreciative presentation, and the history of writing, *declares* the absolute exteriority of writing but *describes* the

interiority of the principle of writing to language. The sickness of the outside...is in the heart of the living word, as its principle of effacement and its relationship to its own death" (313). Derrida's language here approaches the sacramental: if writing's exteriority to melodic language is the fallacy that sustains Rousseau's project, it remains nevertheless true that writing, that "scriptive contagion," is always already enshrined or consecrated in spoken language, the "living word" that must exist in intimate relation with the inscribed rem(a)inder of its own death.[55]

Saint Erkenwald's imagery, syntax, and devotional context collaborate to demonstrate how the vocal utterances of performances and the silence of writing—emphasized here by the golden letters' strangeness and the poem's own formal qualities—perpetually enshrine and are enshrined within each other in the act of representation.

If the mutual enshrinement of inscription and performance requires an oscillation between interiority and exteriority, then *Saint Erkenwald*'s engagement with devotional culture makes this structural possibility available. The poem uses the judge's tomb and body as an emblem of the reliquary's conflation of inside and outside. At the level of the poem's explicit narrative, for example, exist many self-enfolding layers of enclosure, establishing the role of enshrinement in the text's imagery. On the one hand, the poem is explicitly concerned with breaking down structures of enclosure and removing them. The mayor, for instance, "bede vnlouke þe lidde and lay hit beside" (l. 65). But on the other hand, within this narrative context of unearthing and opening, the poem's imagery insists upon a more pervasive aesthetic of enshrinement. The judge's body has a "gurdille of golde" that "bigripide his mydelle" (l. 80), and the poet invokes the word "bordures" to describe the fur trimming of the corpse's mantle (l. 82). The judge's body therefore presents itself as decoratively encircled at a number of different levels. He is an object of enshrinement, and this structural feature of his also causes him to be a spectacle before an audience. When the tomb is opened, the Londoners see the body:

> Al wyt glisnande golde his gowne wos hemmyd,
> Wyt mony a precious perle picchit þer-on,
> And a gurdille of golde bigripide his mydelle,
> A meche mantel on-lofte wyt menyuer furrit
> (Þe clothe of camelyn ful clene wyt cumly bordures),
> And on his coyfe wos kest a coroun ful riche
> And a semely septure sett in his honde.
> Als wemles were his wedes wyt-outen any tecche

Oþir of moulynge oþir of motes oþir moght-freten,
And als bryȝt of hor blee in blysnande hewes
As þai had ȝepely in þat ȝorde been ȝisturady shapen.
And als freshe hym þe face and þe fleshe nakyde
Bi his eres and bi his hondes þat openly shewid
Wyt ronke rode, as þe rose....

(ll. 78–91)

The body of the judge in *Saint Erkenwald* becomes an artifact that is at once relic and reliquary—it is both organic matter and enclosing aesthetic object. The language used to describe the pagan's clothes and body discourages the reader from making clear distinctions between the two. The word "blee" in line 87, used here to refer to the judge's unnaturally perfect appearance, often means "complexion," with connotations of face and skin, as it does later at line 342 of the poem; it is a word that denotes the organic body and at the same time its aesthetic preservation. The flawless youthfulness of the judge's face seems of a piece in this passage with the untarnished garments and adornments that enclose it. His many layers of enclosure, including inscription, present the judge to his audience as a performance object. These layers undermine the distinction between container and contained, interior and exterior. Through its different aspects, the judge's description recalls the reliquary's special ability to conflate these terms. In its conflation of interior and exterior, the reliquary's physical structure is both a metaphor for its means of conveying meaning, and the instrument that makes this meaning possible. When *Saint Erkenwald*'s language draws attention to the portrayal of the judge as object of enshrinement, it illuminates poetic language's own processes of representation, its use of dialectical containment.

Saint Erkenwald narrates the process by which inscription and performance enshrine each other to create a space for presence. This presence is of this world and set apart from it, interactive and self-referential. The argument of this chapter offers a foundation from which to explore the poetics of enshrinement through other examples of poetic language and representation. The various instances of reproducibility in this chapter—from judge and saint, to cross and inscribed card, to alliteration's repeated signs—all showcase the poetics of enshrinement's dependence upon textual iterability; the possibility of reproduction and the accommodation of absence as well as presence. But understanding the poetics of enshrinement fully also requires a closer look at the ways in which poetic language itself can function performatively. What happens, for instance, in the realm of dramatic poetry, where the performance of poetry might actually occlude its identity as written inscription? The next chapter will address this question to show that even in the cultural form that most intimately connects poetic language, performance, and performativity, the dialectical enshrinement of performance and inscription still obtains.

CHAPTER 3

THE N-TOWN *ASSUMPTION*'S
IMPOSSIBLE RELIQUARY

Many influential studies of medieval theatre have described themselves as counteracting—either implicitly or explicitly—a conception of theatre studies as primarily the province of the textual. As early as 1944, the argument that "if [theatre] is an offspring of literature on one side of the family tree, it is no less a descendent of painting and sculpture on the other side" was put forth as a corrective to an older conception of dramatic analysis.[1] Since then, a number of arguments in the field have refined our understanding of drama's dependence as a literary genre upon its material artistic contexts.[2] We might organize these arguments along a broad spectrum, from positivist reconstructions of dramatic performance as a material practice, to a more general imagining of the aesthetics of drama as a visual art form.[3] The argument that follows will attempt to recuperate the role of textuality in drama by focusing on the poetic features of a medieval play. But it will do so in conjunction with an awareness of dramatic utterance as a visual and spectacular phenomenon. The N-Town *Assumption of Mary*, this chapter argues, creates for its audience an idealized Marian reliquary where none exists. The play uses its language and spectacle, as well as its cultural context of anchoritic spirituality, to perform its Marian reliquary. This reliquary on the stage participates in the enshrining dynamics we have seen in actual reliquaries. But the *Assumption* also foregrounds inscriptionality, through the attention the play draws to its poetic language, as an essential component of the object of enshrinement it creates. In the N-Town *Assumption*, inscription and performance frame and enshrine each other in order to produce the impossible Marian reliquary.

The *Assumption* play uses techniques of visual spectacle to make Mary's body into a reliquary, and it also capitalizes on the poetic features of its language to bring this idealized reliquary into a state of complicated being for the audience. Medieval play texts are also poetic texts, and this reading of the *Assumption* will progressively turn its focus toward the status of the Mary play as poetry, in order to make the case that a play in the Middle Ages was not simply a play but instead a poem as multidisciplinary object—inscriptional, performative, and enshrining.[4] Charles Bernstein argues that the recitation of a poetic text is a performance that helps to "constitute and reconstitute the work itself."[5] Acknowledging the identity of the medieval play text as a poem emphasizes the extent to which its performance is a self-constitution as poetic utterance, and as poetic inscription.

Drama as Representational Practice

As a play and a poem, the *Assumption* exhibits self-awareness about its representational practices. Modern conceptions of medieval performance and theatricality often define performance in terms of the affective response it evokes in its audience, and distinguish it from concepts such as mimesis and representation. Kathleen Ashley, for instance, argues that one way to differentiate representation from performance is precisely through the notion of the response that performance triggers. For her, representation is a kind of embodiment, whereas performance is defined and measured through the response it invokes in its audience. As she argues in her discussion of dramatic representations of Saint Anne, the dramatic character's "potency as cultural symbol in the late Middle Ages was a function of her usefulness in triggering or activating ideological formations."[6] I would like to expand upon Ashley's thoughts about dramatic images and consider further the specific relationship between performance and representation. This relationship has also seen elaboration through ideas about what drama in fact represents. Jody Enders, for instance, sees medieval drama as "the variegated oral representation of ritual conflict in different social and historical contexts."[7] And O.B. Hardison uses representation as a fundamental term in the trajectory of drama's development. The shift from a *Quem quaeritis* ceremony to a Resurrection cycle play, for instance, involves crossing "over the line dividing ceremony from representation…a replica of the thing represented."[8] More recent work has called the existence of this line into question, arguing that performance could function as both an act of worship and a mimetic spectacle, but both perspectives still see representation as a defining component of medieval drama's function.[9] Lawrence M. Clopper also complicates the categories of ceremony and performance. He points out that how we understand theatre and drama as artistic and generic categories might require some reformulation when thinking about the medieval perspective on such cultural practices.[10] In both modern critical and medieval perspectives on dramatic activity, performance sustains a complex relationship to representation.

Specific Mariolatric traditions around Mary's body dictate that it contains the modes of its own representation and is contained by them. The fact and the consciousness of Mary's pregnancy on the medieval stage, for instance, employ a framing dialectic of interior and exterior to represent Mary throughout the cycle. Mary's pregnancy, not seen in the *Assumption* but always implied for its miraculous nature in all Marian plays, serves as a ubiquitous context. As Stanton Garner argues, awareness of the pregnant body on stage "subverts the integration of bodily experience, blurring the distinctions between inside and outside, myself and other, and compounding the experience of subjectivity." Garner claims that while pregnancy contributes to the phenomenological awareness of the body and "puts into play the variables that characterize embodiment as a phenomenon, it manifests them in forms that reflect its own internal and external configurations."[11] The pregnant body on the stage is always both calling attention to its phenomenological presence and shaping itself through various interactions with the signs it creates to delineate and contain itself. Gail Gibson has described the *vierges ouvrantes* that explore Mary as both container and contained (figure 3.1).[12] This type of object concretely demonstrates the idea that Mary's body, and the verbal and iconographic signs representing it, contain and are contained by each other. The signs are always both inside and outside the body; the object makes the borders of the body itself indeterminate. The *vierge ouvrante*'s gesture toward infinitude creates a charged awareness of the body, a sense that it is everywhere and nowhere in the object's structure. This model of iconographic sign containing and being contained by the body will become an important element in constituting the Marian reliquary on the stage. It will also help to bring to light the importance of the play text's inscriptional identity as part of the representational process.

In a drama, however, the audience also plays a role in the representational act. Like the devotional performance surrounding the Bromholm cross card, the interaction between audience and spectacle generates representational work. In interacting with ceremonial and dramatic performance, the medieval audience's experiential and imaginative capacities fulfilled an important function. Niklaus Largier refers to the "visionary stage" as a site for engaging the audience in a transition from liturgy to "event," invoking their visual and imaginative capacities in this process.[13] In her argument about drama as a social phenomenon, Claire Sponsler has made the point that audience responses to medieval theatre necessarily

Figure 3.1 *Vierge ouvrante* (open), ca. 1400. Wood and polychrome. Western Prussia/Germany. Inv. Cl. 12060. Musée national du Moyen Âge–Thermes de Cluny, Paris, France.

Source: Photo by Gerard Blot. Réunion des Musées nationaux/Art Resource, New York.

took diverse forms.[14] Questioning the ideologically monolithic conception of the medieval spectator's experience creates opportunities for thinking about a range of aesthetic responses as well. The vision of Mary might suggest to viewers not only the kind of complex incarnational aesthetic characteristic of depictions of Christ, but also the diverse material strategies used in art to convey her embodiment and her mediating presence. Clifford Davidson has observed that, in participating in the conventions of affective piety, "drama attempted no longer to pierce the veil of appearances through presentation of abstract and idealized forms, but rather it turned its efforts toward stimulating the *imaginations* of the beholders."[15] As Gibson puts it, "It is the truth of imagination, of imaging, which is the fundamental truth behind late medieval lay spirituality and is the shaping aesthetic for the religious drama and lyric."[16] By enabling this imaginative act on the audience's part, the play investigates processes of representation.

The Problem of the Marian Body

Through such imaginative acts, the beholder sees an ideal Marian reliquary on stage in the N-Town *Assumption*. Mary as visible on the stage enters into the complex dynamic of sacred enshrinement. Imaginative response allows the Marian figure on stage to be not only the representation of a divine presence, but also the re-creation on stage of a familiar genre of Marian artifacts that fulfilled the function of mediating and invoking an affective dynamic. The audience participates in constituting this artifact in the space between their affective experience and the aesthetic occasion on the stage. And yet it is vital to acknowledge as well that as deeply as this Marian artifact generated by the play and the audience might be desired, it is in fact an impossible and idealized artifact. Marian relics did exist; one example is the *sacra cintola* at Westminster Cathedral, a popular object of devotion in the late Middle Ages.[17] But actual bodily relics of Mary were more problematic, precisely because of the narrative of bodily assumption. The play asks its viewers to see the sacred nature of the Marian figure on stage by imagining it as an idealized Marian devotional artifact, a miraculous vestige and an integrating reliquary. This idealized artifact enshrines word and physical body within each other. It engages the poetics of enshrinement by creating a dialectical interaction between the play's spectacular elements and the inscriptional aspects of its poetry.

The possibility of an imagined reliquary requires that we consider actual Marian artifacts in both their sanctity and their scarcity. Most saints who provided a focus for medieval veneration left behind bodily relics that became part of the cult of their worship, through visits to pilgrimage sites and various forms of encounter with these sacred vestiges. Mary's cult emerged differently in the late antique and early medieval period, because the narrative of her Assumption precluded the existence of bodily relics. In the West, Marian pilgrimages as part of a tradition of Marian devotion were a relatively late development (tenth century), in part because devotional conventions in this period were so closely tied to the presence of relics.[18] In the early Christian East, meanwhile, the cult of Marian relics comprised clothing and contact relics as an acknowledgment of her bodily absence.[19] In addition, Marian altars in the early part of the Middle Ages made vivid the awareness of Mary's bodily absence through their strong associations with her physical body, her womb and breasts. Peter Damian's writings, for instance, highlight this feature of Marian devotion.[20] Furthermore, Marina Warner has described early medieval images of Mary, often attributed to Luke or various angels, which make up for the lack of bodily connection to her by focusing on other categories of object. These indicate another way in which visual and material images not derived from Mary's body took on spiritual meaning as much as the few extant bodily relics, such as drops of milk, clothing, other contact relics, or the belt referred to above.[21] Thus the absence of Marian bodily relics affected the nature of Marian veneration throughout the Middle Ages.

Traditions of devotional art substituted—in other metonymic ways as well—for this lack of actual relics. In late-medieval northern Europe, Marian worship focused largely on symbolic objects rather than bodily relics. These were venerated in a manner that drew attention to their materiality. Through these practices of veneration, Marian artifacts attempted to fix a bodily reality for her in the absence of bodily vestiges. Gibson has discussed, for example, the function of the Marian shrine at Little Walsingham, pointing out that the replica of the Virgin's house there took on the miraculous powers of Mary's actual birthplace, substituting for it as a place of healing. As an image shrine, Little Walsingham uses the defining principles of relics and *praesentia* to create another kind of devotional space.

Little Walsingham, along with other evidence of the late-medieval Marian cult, suggests that what is most striking about this particular branch of Marian devotion is the localized specificity of its materiality. As Gibson notes, a late-fourteenth-century ring is described by its owner as bearing "not the image of Mary but of Our Lady of Walsingham."[22] This attention to localization helps us to understand how the image shrine constituted itself in the absence of the relic. Late-medieval altar panels as well sometimes depict contemporary interiors as the setting for the

Virgin's death.[23] Such representational techniques further emphasize the impulse toward concretizing the Virgin's body by placing her in settings that are local and accessible to viewers. Donald Duclow characterizes these depictions as "'secularizing' the dormition—i.e., presenting it as the death of an ordinary woman in a contemporary setting."[24] The concrete reality of this particular locus of Marian worship takes on spiritual significance as an available physicality in the face of Mary's lack of bodily relics. Duclow adopts a perspective somewhat different from Gibson's, using books of hours to characterize the late-medieval impulse toward making Mary's death local and concrete. He claims that Mary's "dormition provides a model for dying." In conjunction with *ars moriendi* texts, the books of hours suggest that the elaborate physical detail surrounding Mary's death becomes a locus of identification for medieval worshippers. In this way as well, Mariolatry preoccupied itself not only with the body but also with a highly specific materiality metonymically associated with it.[25]

Furthermore, traditions of the dormition and assumption of the Virgin associated Mary's body with Christ, the realm of Passion relics, and other devotional artifacts to emphasize the potential power of the Marian body. The origin of this association locates itself in twelfth- and thirteenth-century discussions about the extent to which Mary experienced her own bodily suffering as a result of the Passion.[26] Duclow cites a late-medieval altar panel that displays Christological connections to the dormition by creating visual parallels between the scene of Mary's death and those of the Resurrection and Ascension.[27] As Stephen J. Shoemaker demonstrates, dormition legends often referred to True Cross relics, and are generally preoccupied with relic worship. He explains the allusions to cross relics and other holy bodies in earlier medieval dormition narratives as reflecting the general influence of the cult of relics, and more specifically as deployed in opposition to Jewish taboos concerning dead bodies.[28] In certain Syriac dormition narratives, the True Cross in particular is aligned with the body of the Virgin Mary; the cross and body similarly display miraculous powers.[29] True Cross relics and beliefs about the power of the Virgin's body clustered together around anti-Semitic impulses in these early accounts, but they also create a useful emphasis on the associative principle between object and body in the medieval awareness of representations of the Virgin Mary. Dormition traditions create a metonymic connection between Mary's body and Christ's as well through their frequent depictions of Mary at the tomb of her son. She engages in ceremonial practices, such as offering incense.[30] This parallel drawn between Passion relics and the awareness of Mary's assumed body suggests that the absence of Mary's bodily remains in medieval devotion resonates with Christ's lack of bodily relics. The two devotional traditions

conjure the power of the sacred body, despite its absence, through a
network of metonymic associations between bodies and objects.

   This dynamic requires in turn that we acknowledge the implications
behind thinking of material representations of Mary—whether in statuary or on stage—as substituting for her body. While the boundaries
between relic and image could be fairly fluid, Hans Belting stresses that
the correspondence between relic and image is necessarily undermined
"by the fact that the cult of saints was secondary to that of Christ and the
Virgin, who...had not left behind any bodily relics....[T]he two central
figures of Christian faith also required a visual presence, which could be
provided by images of the crucifix and the Madonna Enthroned. In this
case, however, there was a lack of reality compared to that of the image-
relic of the saints." He goes on to point out that other relics were sometimes deposited in image-artifacts of Christ and Mary, a phenomenon
that he sees as "an obvious attempt to borrow the status of a reliquary."[31]
Thus in some ways the very act of venerating Christ and Mary emphasizes the difference between the bodily presence contained in a relic and,
in its absence, the more complex and mediated signifying strategies of
a devotional image. Drama, however, complicates this distinction in
some ways. In the specific context of theatrical imagery, Sarah Beckwith
has argued that late-medieval drama addresses the issues attendant upon
understanding the bodily Christ as both absent and present. God, as she
says, is "endlessly disseminated in strenuous and difficult encounters."[32]
And as Gibson has shown, the N-Town Mary plays in particular display an "incarnational aesthetic" of their own surrounding the bodily
representation of the Virgin.[33] Gibson describes the Incarnation's cultural
role in late-medieval England as giving rise to an obsession with Mary,
because "her body had enclosed divinity, had given Godhead a human
form and likeness." The bodily reality of Mary participates in the idea of
Incarnation, so that in this way as well Mary's unique physicality, and
what Gibson terms "the particularity of religious experience," underlies
every artistic depiction of her, including theatrical ones.[34] Thus while
some devotional traditions emphasized the difference between an image
of Mary and the bodily reality of a relic, drama had particular capacities for negotiating a relationship between bodily reality and imagistic
representation.

Enshrinement as Performance in
the N-Town *Assumption*

In the N-Town *Assumption*, staging techniques, the devotional context
of anchoritism, and the use of performative utterance all collaborate to

perform Mary as an object of enshrinement.[35] In reading the various workings of performance in this play, I invoke Patrice Pavis's helpful explication of mise-en-scène. For Pavis, the act of theatrical realization does not simply involve the "conversion, translation, or reduction" of text into spectacle. Instead, mise-en-scène requires a balance between the "opposing semiotic systems" of visual and verbal communication. Pavis also draws on the dialectics of interiority and exteriority to describe the relationship between text and performance, claiming that stage direction, as a fulcrum between text and performance, might be seen to exist "beside" the dramatic text but is really "inside" it.[36] The following argument thus moves across script, stage direction, and spectacle to argue that all form part of a system not for transforming language into performance, but instead for performing the Marian object of enshrinement in a space of negotiation between visual and verbal.

From its earliest moments, the play defines Mary's body as enclosed object through both speech and stage direction. The N-Town *Assumption* introduces its attention to Mary's body with depictions of characters who not only want to destroy or desecrate it, but who in fact specifically want to undermine its potential for sacred enclosure. This framing concern in the play makes of Mary's body the powerful object that it is. The *Assumption* opens by introducing us to the power of Mary's body through the anxiety expressed over it. The bishop—the Jewish official—says menacingly, "But be that seustere ded, Mary, that fise, / We shal brenne here body and the aschis hide, / And don here all the dispith we can here devise."[37] It has been suggested that the Jews in this play, who focus only on Mary's body, reflect the inability to see her spiritual significance.[38] But it could just as easily be argued that in fact the Jews are aware that her body contains power for her followers and worshippers. This power would be compromised by preventing the body's burial and enclosure, and instead threatening it with fragmentation and the undermining of its material integrity. Mary herself raises this issue in her plea to John: "Helpe I be beryed, for yn yow my tryst is" (l. 231). Her body becomes meaningful in part through the play's impulses from the very beginning toward ceremonially containing it. Stephen Shoemaker's examination of dormition narratives reinforces the potential power of the body as sacred vestige; as cited earlier, he argues that Jews are depicted as equally aware of the body's potential power as relic or object of martyrdom.[39] In the specific instance of the *Assumption* play, the body derives this power from its ceremonial enclosure.

The play uses staging conventions and visual gestures toward liturgical practice to present Mary as an enclosed object in a number of different ways. The stage direction "*in templo*," for instance, before line 94 dictates our initial perception of Mary as being inside an enclosed and sacred space. Victor Scherb has pointed out that in the N-Town cycle, references to scaffolds and artificial structures are not always explicit or clear.[40] Nevertheless, Mary's introduction to the audience praying and speaking to God, immediately following the bishops' low-minded conversation about her death, seems to require some form of separation between the two registers. The direction "*in templo*" in this instance does suggest some visual allusion to her enclosure. Here the familiar convention of Mary in the temple takes on additional meaning through the act of physically enclosing her body within this structure before the eyes of the audience. The spectacle of her integral body finding sanctuary in the temple visually subverts the threat of burning and disappearance. As a character who shows herself to us on the stage as placed within the containing setting of a sacred space, she takes on one of the functions of a reliquary artifact. Other aspects of the play as spectacle reinforce this reading. When her spirit leaves her in the play, and her body is portrayed on the stage in its dormition, Mary displays certain additional qualities of a ceremonially enclosed relic. She is theatrically enveloped within arrangements of lights, candles, virgins, apostles, and other attendants. At this moment the play displays with particular clarity its debt to the visual traditions of liturgical ceremony. After the visit from the angel, Mary asks her "holy maydenys," "assedually wachith me be dayes and nythis." They assent, calling her "oure sengler solas, radyant in youre lythis" (ll. 169–77). Later Mary further directs her own dormition—"Now wyl I rest me in this bed that for me is rayed. / Wachith me besily with youre lampys and lithis" (ll. 298–99)—enclosing herself in light and symmetry.[41]

In the manner of a relic in a reliquary, this enclosed body performs miracles of both punishment and healing in the comic episode of the Jewish character who leaps onto Mary's *feretrum* in order to desecrate it. Mary's body causes his hands to become withered and painful:

> Allas, my body is ful of peyne!
>   I am fastened sore to this bere!
> Myn handys are ser bothe tweyne.
>   O, Peter, now prey thy God for me here.
>   (ll. 423–26)

At line 437, Peter commands the priest to venerate her corpse and acknowledge his newfound belief in Mary's divinity: "In Goddis name, go doun than, and this body honure." These acts miraculously restore the unfortunate man. Theresa Coletti uses the term "stage iconography" to characterize the particular spectacular quality of the N-Town cycle's

Marian plays.[42] In this play, stage iconography explicates visually not only Mary's divine nature but also the capacity in which the Marian body on stage becomes an enclosed relic; the dream of a powerful, healing, entombed object that cannot exist in this world.

In the dynamics of sacred enshrinement that this study lays out, however, the ability to imagine Mary as devotional artifact depends equally upon her ability to function as an enclosing object. Gibson, in tracing relationships between the N-Town Marian plays and contemporary art and architecture, points out that in a number of these other media, Mary's body appears as "mystical tabernacle for the Messiah and *tabernaculum*— holy receptacle for the Eucharist that joins the body of the Church to the body and blood of incarnate God."[43] The N-Town *Assumption* stages through Mary's body the complex potential of enshrinement by allowing this body to shift from contained to container. For instance, it draws on the convention of referring to Mary as a sacred container. At the end of the play, God refers to Mary as "Tabernacle of joye, vessel of lyf, hefnely temple" (l. 511). The source material in the *Golden Legend* is equally expansive on this point, calling her a "tabernacle of Christ," a "vessel of Christ," and a "sacred living ark."[44] Some of this language gestures toward Mary's womb as a typological manifestation of the Ark of the Covenant.[45] The play allows these familiar metaphors to become concrete and particular, however, by juxtaposing them with the visual image of Mary's soul reentering her body.

The play also uses visual and narrative framing to foreground Mary's enclosing potential, and thus her potential as an object of enshrinement, both enclosing and enclosed. After the moment when Mary's spirit departs, another scene with the Jews occurs, creating out of the beginning and the end of the play a frame around the integral and miraculous depiction of Mary's body. Once again, the focus is on the symbolic and ceremonial potential of her body, with the apostles bearing her to the sepulcher accompanied by torches. But this time, the Jews' reaction acknowledges Mary's universalized status and the way that she seems to enfold all of them. The bishop asks, anguished, "what noyse is al this? / The erthe and the eyer is ful of melodye!" (ll. 371–72). The First Prince replies that "Whatsumeuyr they be, hougely they crye!" (l. 376), indicating that Mary's body has created an experience of spirituality, a miraculous presence, that surrounds and encompasses the entire world as represented on the stage; the air is filled with it. Presumably the performance space would have been as well. At the same time, the bishop attempts to reclaim control over the sacred body by demanding again that it be brought to him (l. 396). Thus the *Assumption* sets Mary's body within scenes depicting the Jews as characters who want to degrade it.

It also uses this frame, however, to emphasize her transcendence of her own physical enclosure and her ability to occupy the space that surrounds all the characters. Sylvia Tomasch has studied the motif of framing and frame breaking in medieval dramatic and artistic production. She argues that the common forms of manipulating frames in medieval art result in a "simultaneity of vision" that undermines linear temporality and is replicated in locus and platea staging.[46] Frames complicate both time and space. When articulated through Mary's body on stage, they present a vision of the body as at once enclosed and enclosing. In this way Mary becomes an object of enshrinement.

By naming Mary as a mediator, the *Assumption* emphasizes that it is performing her as a devotional object of enshrinement. As Peter Brown has shown, one of the central purposes of the relic and shrine, from the beginning of the Middle Ages, was to fulfill a mediating function between heavenly and earthly realms. Marian devotion in the West involves a significant history of seeing her as a mediating figure between God and man, and as Theresa Coletti argues, "If the N-Town *Magi* play provides the opportunity for the dramatic representation of the Virgin's capacity as intercessor, the *Death and Assumption* play celebrates that capacity with lavish grandeur."[47] The liturgy for the Vigil of the Assumption emphasizes the intercessory aspect of Marian devotion, and it makes sense to see it as an underlying issue in the N-Town *Assumption* as well, given the strong liturgical influence that is traditionally perceived in this play.[48] The N-Town *Assumption* makes explicit reference to this mediating aspect of Mary in a number of ways: Paul calls Mary a "mene for mankind and mendere of mys," for instance (l. 280). The Mary play's conception of its central character as a mediating figure reinforces her access to the status of a devotional artifact.

The play's performance of Mary as object of enshrinement does not just occur through the mechanisms of mise-en-scène or the language of the script, however. This performance exists within a larger context for the N-Town *Assumption*, which includes other performance-based elements of devotional practice, and also other plays that represent the Virgin Mary. One such performance-inflected element is anchoritic practice. J.A. Tasioulas makes the case that the "tone" and aesthetic of the N-Town cycle in particular are reminiscent of the atmosphere created in the *Ancrene Wisse*. He also cites Joannes Vriend's speculation that "the N-Town cycle was written by someone with a practical knowledge and interest in religious communities of young women."[49] Anchoritism thus exists as an aesthetic ingredient in the play. It provides a contextual means by which to explore the play's uses of interiority and exteriority in creating the Marian artifact.

The context of anchoritic spirituality in the late Middle Ages provides a template for tracing the movement between interiorized and exteriorized forms of expression. Anchoritic tradition functions as a social version of the devotional aesthetic I have been describing as the dynamics of enshrinement. Nicholas Watson states that the imagery of anchoritic spirituality is an imagery of "enclosure or fixity—wombs, bodies, crucifixions, walls, castles."[50] Despite the fact that they gesture toward, and are produced within, an enclosed environment, however, anchorites also draw attention to dynamic transitions between interior and exterior life. As Watson says, "anchoritic works habitually return the reader to a sense of her own external conditions by recalling the anchorage."[51] Christopher Cannon also sees the anchoritic life as both creating and resolving a paradoxical relationship between community and isolation, between internal experience and awareness of the exterior life.[52] The cloister thus in some ways complicates the distinction between interiority and exteriority. While on the one hand it defines itself through motifs of enclosure, on the other it constitutes a community that requires a specific move of exteriorization on the part of the anchorite when thinking about her spiritual condition. The larger context of anchoritic spirituality converts what is interior into what is exterior while simultaneously drawing attention to the complexity of the relationship between these two terms. It emphasizes and subverts the boundaries between interior and exterior.

In subverting these boundaries, the anchoritic context draws particular attention to the ways that women's bodies always entail a vexed relationship between inner and outer. This context helps to reinforce the perception of Mary on stage as transcending and subverting her own boundaries in order to constitute her identity. Sarah Beckwith makes the important point that in anchoritic practice, and in the *Ancrene Wisse* in particular, "Interiority...is not so much the opposite of exteriority as its complex coproduct."[53] Beckwith goes on to argue that inside and outside both produce and reproduce each other, and in the process create bodily integrity.[54] For the Marian figure on stage, then, the spectacle's constant shifting between her positions as enclosed and enclosing ultimately enables the audience's perception of her as integral. We see this effect not only in the *Assumption*, but also in other Marian plays from the cycle. At the end of *The Betrayal*, for instance, the Virgin Mary makes an elaborate speech about her sorrow upon learning the fate of Christ. She returns repeatedly to imagery describing her own heart: "hert hard as ston" (l. 162); "myn hert xuld cleve on tweyn" (l. 172); "these prongys, myn herte asondyr þei do rende" (l. 176). The metaphors of violence to her own heart have several important effects. One is clearly to draw attention to the inward-turned nature of her suffering, to the heart within her. But at the same time, the tone of the passage and the escalating precision of the visual imagery depicting the injury done to her heart reveal how Mary uses this speech to enter herself into a tradition of iconography and the system of signs that represent her. The Marian figure on stage interacts with what Davidson characterizes as the audience's own cultural and imaginative awareness of images and artifacts. In this way, Mary can draw her own outlines with the emblematic figures of her suffering. The imagery oscillates between the bodily condition of interior suffering and an exteriorized expression of that suffering articulated specifically through allusions to a public, performance-based culture of images and artifacts. The speech further reinforces this effect through Mary's description of Christ: "And now þe bryth colour of his face doth fade" (l. 180). He becomes an artistic spectacle made for a public world. Mary's speech in the *Betrayal* demonstrates through dramatic spectacle the aesthetic that the anchoritic works suggest. The text represents Mary by allowing her to perform an integral self as moving interiorized and bodily experience into a public realm of recognizable imagery.

Anchoritic spirituality also speaks to dramatic tradition and spectacle through its own uses of performance conventions, in which lie the interplay of silence and speech, objects and words. Earlier in the Middle Ages, the ritual of enclosure involved the staging of a funeral mass, with the anchoritic cell referred to as a sepulcher, and singing and prayers from the choir and bishop on behalf of the recluse.[55] The condition of the anchoress constituted itself through performance and ceremony; the component of anchoritic enclosure that still turned out toward a community articulated itself in the language of performance. This act had a performative character as well, fixing the recluse's identity through the gesture and vocalization of an enacted funeral. On the one hand, the anchoress functions as a silent and entombed object of performance here, with the ceremony itself speaking her into this state of inwardness and silence. But on the other hand, as an object of performance she is still implicated, like the reliquaries and shrines we have examined, in the interactive force of the ceremony, its participants and audience. Thus in the performance tradition specific to anchoritic ceremony, the anchoress's status as both enclosed by her community and yet part of this enclosing community also allows her self-constitution through speech and silence.

It is important to recognize as well that the anchoritic context integrates the verbal and nonverbal through the specific vehicle of the female body, and so in this sense also anchoritism provides a lens through which to view the Marian play performing its object of enshrinement. Elizabeth Robertson's study of the *Ancrene Wisse* makes the point that women necessarily maintain a complicated relationship to reading and language: "the woman reader is one who must prepare her inner self as a nest for Christ while remaining continually aware of the desires of the outside world to violate that nest."[56] She argues further that writings for and about spiritual women asked them to make their bodies part of their devotional practice; even when the specific conduit through which they received instruction was verbal, their bodily world still had to become part of this experience.[57] The vision of the anchoress to which all these readings contribute suggests that, like a reliquary object, her layers of enclosure—her enshrinement—negotiate between language and image, between performed speech and silence. The figure of the anchoress thus provides a devotional context for understanding how the performance of the female Marian body on stage as enclosed and enclosing might also take on the identity of a devotional object of enshrinement.

The anchoritic context further emphasizes that the *Assumption* play functions not only as a performance of the Marian artifact, but also as a specifically performative constitution of that artifact. This devotional context showed us how ceremony named certain conditions into being. Correspondingly, the language of the play does not simply describe or subtly participate in the realization of the enshrining Marian object. Instead, at certain moments the play explicitly speaks this idealized object into being. This type of utterance is most clearly evident in Mary's own self-constitutive lines. Mary's self-referential speech forms part of a larger concern with self-examination in the N-Town cycle overall. As William Fitzhenry says, "the plays employ their self-reflexive characters and situations to stage the tension between the absolute and the concrete."[58] In negotiating the heavenly and earthly elements of her own dormition, certain aspects of Mary are reminiscent of the role of the modern theatre director. Her work as a director is based upon her function as a mediator. She receives messages from God about how her dormition should be staged and then communicates them to the characters around her. For example, after being given a "braunce of a palme" by the angel at line 134, she takes care later to say to John:

> He brouth me this palme from my sone thore,
>   Qwyche I beseke, as the aungyl me bade,
> That aforn my bere by you it be bore,
>   Saynge my dirige devouthly and sad.
>   (ll. 220–23)

As we saw earlier, Mary also gives specific instructions that she be surrounded by light and followers according to the instructions she has received. As is the case with a theatre director, what she speaks comes to pass because she speaks it. The *Golden Legend* points out this same aspect of Mary's reaction to the news of her Assumption, saying that "the Virgin showed [the apostles] the things that the angel had brought. She also gave orders that the lamps should not be extinguished until after her death."[59] As she prepares to die in the play, her speech interweaves a relaying of messages from heaven to her companions ("my son Jesu of his hye peté / Sent to me an aungyl, and thus he sayd..." [l. 291–92]) with her self-conscious desire to arrange herself in a tableau ("I beseke you than, tent me. / Now wyl I rest me in this bed that for me is rayed" [l. 297–98]). She asks that she be ceremonially arrayed in her bed as a visual prefiguring of entombment. The play establishes the performative potential of language by allowing Mary to speak herself into the specific being of the devotional object. This performative self-constitution forms part of the play's complex performance techniques for making the Marian artifact visible to the audience. Through mise-en-scène, the performance-based aspects of anchoritic tradition, and performative utterance, the N-Town *Assumption* brings an object of enshrinement into being on the stage.

Enshrining Poetry in the N-Town *Assumption*

As Pavis's remarks suggest, however, the play's text does not simply disappear into a kind of theatrical incarnation. Instead, text and spectacle exist in constant negotiation with each other. Mary's own performative speech makes up only one part of the play text's capacity for speaking her into being as enshrining object. Coexisting dialectically with this performative function is the play as poetry, its status as a written poetic text on the page. The idealized Marian reliquary, like many of the real and literary shrines we have seen so far, oscillates between a frame of inscription and a frame of performance. The vexed status of the N-Town cycle, and the questions it raises about whether and how it was actually performed, lends additional importance to the play's identity as inscribed text.[60] As a play text, the N-Town *Assumption* conflates interior and exterior not only through its visual and spectacular elements, but also through its poetic text. Focusing on the poetic components of the N-Town *Assumption* represents a somewhat unpopular approach, evidenced, for instance, by Rosemary Woolf's critique of the play as "stylistically at variance with the rest of the cycle: it is wooden, stilted, and lifelessly aureate in diction." Woolf perceives its poetic deficiencies as supporting the argument that "the impact of this play was clearly to the eye and to the musical ear: spectacle and music are essential to it."[61] But in fact, as this section of the chapter will argue, the play's language also contains the aesthetics of the inscribed shrine within its poetry as inscription on the page. As the process of the judge's representation in *Saint Erkenwald* occurred in two parts—through performance and through inscription—so the Marian artifact on stage is complete only when we acknowledge its elements of written inscription as well as its spectacular ones.

The *Assumption*'s use of rhyme in both its aural and visual capacities participates actively in the Marian reliquary's own dynamics of enshrinement. Various aspects of the N-Town cycle's language have come under critical scrutiny, from its macaronic use of Latin to its employment of verse patterns as "rhythmic signs."[62] The rhyming thirteener stanzas that (for the most part) make up this play have a circular and enclosing quality of their own; as we shall see, this poetic phenomenon appears more familiarly in *Pearl*, a poem whose structure and rhyme scheme are shaped by the culture of memorial artifacts on which it draws. But in the N-Town *Assumption* as well, the internal concatenation of this rhyme scheme in the long stanzas, with the last line's return to the b-rhyme of the opening couplet, mirrors the concentric aesthetic of Mary's representation in the play. Furthermore, in the previously cited section contrasting the cruel bishops with Mary praying in the temple, the language amplifies not only this contrast itself, but also its connections to the conventions of enshrining objects. The bishop's final lines rhyme "ded" with "hed" in his invective "the devyl smyte of here hed!" (ll. 92–93). Abrupt and largely monosyllabic, this final couplet emphasizes the violent fragmentation that the Jews want to deploy in order to compromise Mary's power. The following scene of Mary's prayer and the appearance of Wisdom and the angels, however, replaces these rhymes of fragmentation with rhymes that emphasize integrity. Latinate rhyming words such as "Vnité" (l. 100), "virginité" (l. 115), and "consorcyté" (l. 116) bind the section, and the speeches of the different characters, together. The arrangement of the play's rhyming words here makes the transition from figuring Mary's body as threatened with fragmentation to conceiving of it as reassuringly integral. Through this shift in register, the play's language elaborates upon the implications of Mary's positioning within the sacred structure of the temple. It is a place of enshrinement that defends against fragmentation. Performing Mary as artifact draws on the cultural traditions surrounding relics and reliquaries. The use of language in these scenes provides another way of invoking, through word arrangement and sound, the anxious dichotomy of fragmentation and wholeness universally associated with relic veneration itself.[63] This scene creates and examines its enshrining aesthetic as much through the arrangement of poetic language as through the enclosed and enclosing spectacle of the actor playing Mary.

Through its inscriptional features, the play's poetry contributes to the visual construction of the Marian artifact. Rhyme functions primarily at an aural level for spectators, but the attention it draws to itself also brings to light other poetic features of the language, some of which are more dynamically engaged with their visual status as inscription on the page. For example, at the moment of Mary's assumption, the placement and repetition of the word "body" create elaborate structures of enshrinement:

> *Dominus*: What worschepe and grace semyth you now here
> That I do to this body, Mary that hytht is?
>
> *Johannes*: Lord, as thou rese from deth and regnyst in thyn empere,
> So reyse thou this body to thy blysse that lyth is....
>
> *Mychael*: Ya, gloryous God, lo, the sowle here prest now
> To this blissid body likyth it you to fest now....
>
> *Hic vadit anima in corpus Marie.*
>
> *Dominus*: Go thane, blyssid soule, to that body ageyn.
>
> (ll. 500–509)

The dialogue's invocations of the word "body" here take the shape of the self-enclosing artifact structure. God's spoken references to Mary's body enclose the moment of the soul's reentry as a whole in the opening and closing lines of this passage. Within these twinned invocations, the phrases "body to thy blisse" and "blissid body" syntactically invert each other. Taken together, they echo through their chiastic form the self-enfolding effect we have discussed in material artifacts. The phrases also stage a separate, silent drama of inscriptionality, pointing out the process of marks interacting and making meaning through their spatialized placement and their relationality. The placements of the word *body* create an enfolding inscriptional pattern here in order to suggest the ways that the verbal sign places itself both within and without the physical body. The idealized Marian body, with its own self-enfolding infinitude, constitutes itself through this complex of inscribed signs. These gestures toward the formal and inscriptional status of the text— the physical shape of the words' arrangements—would be perceptible even in the auditory mode of performance. Perhaps more powerfully, however, they also call upon the audience to imagine the play as inscriptional object. The arrangement of words in this example creates a specific framing form that interacts with what we have seen as the existing conventions of inscriptional frames in devotional aesthetics. This inscriptional component of material culture suggests that even as the audience heard poetry, they also saw it inscribed in a coexisting system of visuality, and they incorporated this into their perception of the Marian artifact.

Performance theory's investigation of the relationship between signs and bodies on the stage can assist us in reading the role of inscription in the poetry of dramatic spectacle. As traditionally articulated through structuralist theories, the semiotics of performance necessarily maintains a conflicted relationship to medieval drama for a number of reasons. Most pressing is the fact that theories of performance as sign systems tend to build themselves around Aristotelian definitions of the aesthetics of drama, incorporating the classical ideals of unity and character development into the consideration of the ways in which all of what we see on a stage is a sign. As a result, the ideal of a kind of artistic illusion tends to prevail. It dictates, for instance, Viktor Shklovsky's pronouncement about defamiliarization, influential in theatre semiotics: "art is a way of experiencing the artfulness of an object; the object is not important."[64] And even in reformulating this structuralist model for analyzing drama, Keir Elam develops further the notion that everything on stage is a sign, and argues that an object's appearance on the stage "suppresses the practical function of phenomena in favour of a symbolic or signifying role."[65] For Elam, this dynamic occurs in a secular context, so that in considering the representational status of the actor's body, he argues that "the actor's body acquires its mimetic and representational powers by becoming something other than itself, more and less than individual."[66] Elam's vision of the actor's role creates a separation between the actor's body and what it represents. For example, he cites the problem of seeing scratches on an actor's leg, assuming that they are related to the world of the play, and then feeling disquieted upon realizing that they are not. In secular drama, the actor's body as physical reality has the potential to undermine the representation of the persona if that bodily reality is not transcended to form illusion. These ways of seeing the actor's body are generally incompatible with the far more complex status of the medieval body on stage, which often functioned as both sign and body. Bert O. States, however, proposes that there may be ways to accommodate a phenomenological perspective on performance studies within theatre semiotics, and in doing so he clarifies the relationship between sign and body in medieval drama. States acknowledges the semiotic nature of the reality that theatre creates, even though, as he also maintains, theatre "forestall[s] the retreat of the object into signification." Acts of performance and spectacle posit objects in "embodied form" as both "significative" and "self-given"; they are occasions for their viewers to be confronted by both an experience of the performance itself and the sets of signs that generate it.[67]

The language and spectacular elements of the N-Town cycle construct this relationship between sign and body as one of enshrinement, the conflation of enclosing and enclosed that we saw in the *vierge ouvrante*. And the nature of this relationship contributes to the possibility of the idealized reliquary on the stage. In medieval religious drama, the particular physicality of the performer became a relevant part of the process of representing the divine, not only as a sacred persona, but also as a sacred object. The Marian body on the stage is significant both for the representational process it actively examines and for its physical presence in the most concrete sense. In this dual nature lies its potential as a performed Marian artifact of devotion. Victor Scherb conceives of the sacred personage on stage as falling into W.J.T. Mitchell's category of the "sign that pretends not to be a sign, masquerading as (or, for the believer, actually achieving) natural immediacy and presence."[68] And yet, this sacred presence on stage depends upon the signs that constitute it. The formal arrangement of the language at the *Assumption*'s ending suggests that the concept of body exists both inside and outside the signs that represent it. In order to achieve its presence as a holy body, in other words, the Marian figure on the stage relies upon a culture of enshrining signs.

The cultural context of Marian artifacts suggests that inscription counted itself as an important enshrining sign. Relics, as we have seen, intensely engaged with their containers. For them, enshrining signs took the form of shape, decoration, iconography, and inscription. As we have seen so far in drama, the idea of the sign on the stage included the mediating representational elements—visual framing, light, and sound—that both constituted and inhered within the desired and idealized Marian body, the image of Mary as artifact.[69] But inscriptional characters also played a role in the devotional experience of the Marian artifact. The fact that copies of the narrative of the *Assumption* possessed talismanic force specifically as material written documents in late-medieval England suggests the role that inscriptionality might have played in the theatrical audience's perception of the idealized Marian artifact on stage.[70] And the *sacra cintola*, that most famous of late-medieval English Marian relics, was housed in the elaborate Chapel of Saint Edward at Westminster Abbey, where pilgrims also encountered rich inscriptional decoration. Until the sixteenth century, a framing inscription running along the cornice of the shrine told the story of the chapel's establishment in letters of dark blue glass set against a ground of gold mosaic. A fifteenth-century monk recorded this now-lost inscription, indicating its prominence in the venerating experience during the late Middle Ages.[71] Such inscriptional contexts for Marian artifacts suggest that part of the process of constituting the ideal Marian artifact on stage included not only the spectacular presentation of a self-enclosing body, but also an awareness of the play's inscriptionality as framing and framed by the body in performance.

Beyond the *Assumption* itself, other instances of the N-Town cycle's poetry signify through their spatiality on the page and also contribute a layer of inscriptional signs to frame their own Marian artifacts.[72] Turning back toward the N-Town cycle as a whole reveals a final example of poetic language functioning specifically as inscriptional enshrinement. At the conclusion of the *Presentation* play, an angel appears and makes an acrostic of Mary's name, associating identifying concepts with each of its letters:

> In ʒoure name, Maria, fyve letterys we han:
> M: mayde most mercyfull and meekest in mende.
> A: auerte[r] of þe anguysch þat Adam began.
> R: regina of regyon, reyneng withowtyn ende.
> I: innocent be influens of Jesses kende.
> A: aduocat most autentyk, ʒoure [anceter] Anna.
> Hefne and helle here kneys down bende
> Whan þis holy name of ʒow is seyd, Maria.
> (ll. 262–69)

In spelling out the name, the angel's utterance reaches toward enclosure and completion, with the enunciation of Mary's name preceding and following the articulation of its individual letters. The acrostic format—the emphasis on the letters as physical objects engaged in a visual pattern and signifying through their spatialized interaction—points toward their status as inscriptional. The recitation of the verse in performance, meanwhile, speaks the character into being. As Gibson points out, the incarnational aesthetic found one form of expression earlier in the Middle Ages through the idea of the "book visible."[73] But the poetics of enshrinement, somewhat differently, represents an earthly elaboration on the ideal of Incarnation. In the case of the N-Town cycle, the word does not become exactly the thing it denotes, as it might in a prelapsarian ideal of language. Instead, it is an object of both inscription and performance. The *Assumption* and other plays in the cycle enclose the body in iconographic and inscriptional signs, even as such signs engage in their own interiority, turning toward each other within the encompassing aura of the performance object. This dynamic as a whole produces the Marian artifact on the stage.

Finally, the act of spelling out the name exemplifies a form of temporality occurring throughout the play: the dialectical temporality of inscription and performance's mutual enshrinement. On the one hand, the character of Mary as a holy personage is performed through a serialized set of utterances. The creation of the character occurs within the temporality of verse narration. She is sequentially made through verbal declarations. On the other hand, the act of spelling her name, making her from letters, emphasizes the capacity of the letter as an object always already to encompass her. The form of this play's language thus imagines a Marian representation as existing in the temporality of the reliquary, a temporality of progression and anteriority. This moment in the cycle is one of many in which material and devotional cultures in late-medieval England maintain an aesthetic discourse with dramatic spectacle. This discourse describes the role that performance conventions played in the establishment of a poetics. At the same time, this passage from the play also suggests that even in the forms of poetry apparently most detached from their textual identities, inscription engages dialectically with performance.

Within the aesthetic context of other Marian plays and other related devotional traditions, the N-Town *Assumption* integrates poetic form and staging to create an enshrined and enshrining artifact. This artifact is idealized, and as seemingly "inpossible" (l. 146) as the miraculously reunited apostles themselves. Acts of enshrinement, as we have seen, are performances, the visual spectacle of the shrine or altarpiece ostentatiously indicating its sacred contents and dictating the choreography and protocol of the viewer's interaction with it. But it is ultimately just as useful, in trying to understand the nature of a divine figure on a stage, to read performance texts through the poetics of enshrinement. Focusing on a play has in this case demonstrated that poetic language not only draws upon performance conventions but also functions performatively in its own right. The play's performative function, its ability to speak sacred bodily artifacts into being, is intimately connected to its inscriptional identity as a set of signs to frame this body and be framed by it. The following chapter will continue to develop this understanding of poetic language as performative through its inscriptionality. By turning to a medieval dream vision, it will also treat explicitly the issues of visuality that readings of material spectacle always raise.

CHAPTER 4

ENSHRINING FORM: *PEARL* AS INSCRIPTIONAL OBJECT AND DEVOTIONAL EVENT

As an illustrated text, the alliterative dream vision *Pearl* gestures toward its status as an artifact of ink and vellum in a manner somewhat different from the texts we have examined until now.[1] Its inscribed characters on the page become part of the visual and material identity that the illustrated manuscript emphasizes. In this sense the manuscript's visual features draw attention to an inscriptionality that fixes, in Gabrielle Spiegel's terms, a material, historical, and social reality. This reality exists "both 'inside' and 'outside' the particular performance incorporated in the work."[2] As an inscriptional object, *Pearl* uses the poetics of enshrinement to investigate the very nature of analogies between verbal and visual forms of artistic expression. *Pearl* actively interrogates the process of forming analogies between verbal and visual modes in order to show the limitations of this exercise and to forge past it. Chapter 1 invoked Wendy Steiner's analysis of inter-art analogies to make the case that enshrinement functioned not only as a broad cultural aesthetic uniting visual and verbal artifacts, but also as a visual form of language for expressing verbal processes of representation. *Pearl* demonstrates this phenomenon in its own escape from the problems of analogy. In the dialectical enshrinement of inscription and performance, this chapter argues, the poem finds a way to move beyond being like an artifact. It instead frames inscription and performance within each other in order to recast its dream vision as devotional event. This event occurs through a specific kind of peripheral visuality that the poem suggests for both dreamer and reader.

The unique text of *Pearl* is part of a group of alliterative poems all thought to be by the same author, written in a Northwest Midlands dialect, and appearing in the late fourteenth- or early fifteenth-century British Library manuscript Cotton Nero A.x. The other poems are (editorially titled) *Patience, Purity (Cleanness),* and *Sir Gawain and the Green Knight.* Some have also considered *Saint Erkenwald* to be the work of this anonymous poet, but its authorship has been the subject of greater controversy.[3] *Pearl's* speaker mourns the loss of a young girl (possibly a daughter); he enters a green garden where, as he puts it, he lost his precious pearl.[4] Falling asleep, he dreams of an idealized landscape with a stream, on the other side of which he discerns a richly attired maiden whom he recognizes as his own beloved pearl. Although he is elated to see her, he does not understand her status as a privileged bride of Christ or the limits of his own literal-mindedness in thinking about her death, and so she proceeds to tutor him. Using scriptural allusion, she explains why, despite her early death, she still merits a place as one of the blessed virgins around Christ, citing the importance of God's grace as manifested in the parable of Matthew 20:1–16. She emphasizes as well that innocents are given a special place in Jesus' own teachings. She offers to show the dreamer a vision of the new Jerusalem, which is based on its depiction in the Book of Revelation and, like the maiden herself, recalls the physical sumptuousness of an artifact. Through the walls of the city the dreamer sees a procession of heavenly maidens and a vision of the Lamb of God. When he tries to cross the stream that still separates him from this holy manifestation, however, he awakens, and so in the end he must content himself with his earthly understanding of divine salvation.

Several contexts emerge as essential for understanding *Pearl's* negotiation between language and visuality. These include the poem's manuscript, its critical history, its reformist theological background, and the world of artifacts surrounding it. I shall briefly outline each of these contexts before turning to the poem. *Pearl's* occurrence in Cotton Nero A.x. provides an important context for the poem's interactions between visual and verbal expression. The illustrations suggest that visuality plays an important role in the dream vision's negotiations of different worlds and categories of being. Despite the commonplace characterization of these pictures as clumsy and crude, Paul F. Reichardt's observation that they necessitate a "literacy of interpreting visual scenes," and more specifically an account of the relationship between text and decorations, merits consideration.[5] One way to interpret these scenes involves identifying the nonverbal messages they send about the relationship between the maiden's and the dreamer's worlds. When the maiden is introduced in folio 42r., the paleness of her face and whiteness of her robe appear to set her emphatically apart from the saturated colors of the dreamer's clothing and surroundings (figure 4.1). Furthering her sense of separation from the

Figure 4.1 British Library MS Cotton Nero A.x., art.3, fol. 42r., ca. 1400. The British Library, London.

dreamer, the painting of the maiden in folio 42v. (figure 4.2) depicts her as part of an array of object-like images, including the tabernacle of the heavenly Jerusalem; in this scene the shape and color of her crown subtly reflect the turret and the top of the building enclosed within the crenellated wall. More than the wall itself (which as Jennifer Lee points out is a fairly conventional feature in depictions of medieval cities, both heavenly and earthly) the specific motifs of decoration in these paintings succeed in conveying a difference between the worlds that the dreamer and the maiden inhabit.[6] This picture speaks a surprisingly rich visual language of contrasts, juxtaposing the ordered lineup of the heavenly Jerusalem's components with the more naturalistically curving river that the dreamer follows in his own landscape.

At the same time, however, the visual language of these illustrations also hints at a potential connection between dreamer and maiden, and in this way it speaks to the poem's complex sense of the relationships among these different worlds. As Robert Blanch and Julian Wasserman have shown, hands are an important motif in all the illustrations of Cotton Nero A.x.[7] And it is through these hands, often exaggerated in shape and size, that we see the possibility of connection between the dreamer and the maiden despite the differences in the nature of their worlds. Jessica Brantley has made the point that there is optimistic potential in the maiden's reaching for the dreamer in folio 42v. (figure 4.2), a gesture toward their eventual reunion.[8] The illustrations experiment with a dynamic of distance and proximity, which we shall see as well in the poem's imagistic reference to the culture of reliquaries. In the case of both text and illustration, the gaze of the venerating subject experiences the simultaneous distance and accessibility of the exalted figure. The illustrations thus bear out visually the dream vision's verbal portrayal of the ambiguous relationships among its different environments and worlds.

The manuscript's juxtaposition of verbal and visual signs suggests that the sequential mechanics of reading make their way into the apprehension of visual art, while the instantaneous perception of the art object becomes a part of the experience of reading a text. As Brantley's study of the phenomenon of "performative reading" makes clear, texts that draw attention to their visuality (like W.J.T. Mitchell's concept of the "imagetext") prompt "a particular kind of performative reading, one that is nonlinear, reflective, even diffuse."[9] Michael Camille has discussed the related possibility of visual literacy, arguing, for instance, that by the thirteenth century, the "text/picture alignment" in manuscripts illuminates the extent to which visual signs demanded a literacy of their own.[10] In one sense, we might say that the visual images contained within these illustrations exist in an analogous relationship to the

Figure 4.2 British Library MS Cotton Nero A.x., art.3, fol. 42v., ca. 1400. The British Library, London.

text of the poem—they replicate a claim that the poem also makes about the complexity of intersection between divine and earthly worlds in the dream vision. But the presence of the illustrations does other important work as well. They remind viewers that *Pearl* is part of a visual artifact, that its words are inscribed characters whose visual form and existence might play an important role in the poem's ability to investigate its own comparisons to the realm of sacred artifacts. The illustrations provide their own kind of interpretive frame for the poem, one that we should keep in mind as emphasizing the poem's own visual identity on the page, its capacities as material inscription. As a frame, the illustrations sustain the possibility that *Pearl*'s material form, its inscription on the page, participates in the formation of the dream as a visually apprehended event. To exercise visual literacy in the consideration of both the illustrations and the poem involves acknowledging this possibility.

If the artifact of Cotton Nero A.x. provides one kind of crucial context for *Pearl*, the poem's extensive critical history provides another; like the manuscript illustrations, this history engages the poem in questions concerning visuality and the accessibility of the divine. One important critical perspective on the narrative of *Pearl* has concerned the extent to which the poem and the dreamer succeed in achieving an understanding of the divine. In considering the poem's own statements about its achievement of divine understanding, Nicholas Watson has observed that *Pearl* points to a discrepancy between the poem's events and its resolution. He understands this discrepancy as espousing a worldly theology for the active (courtly) rather than the contemplative Christian.[11] Sarah Stanbury reads the poem's meditative and devotional project though its interest in "descriptive art," a focus on specific perceptual acts as generating a "visual hermeneutic."[12] Other readings use the *sermo humilis* or the doctrine of participation in exploring *Pearl*'s capacity to approach an incarnational ideal.[13] Lynn Staley Johnson focuses on *Pearl*'s particular identity as poetry; she looks to the mode of allegory to characterize the dreamer's progression toward understanding through language and figuration.[14] This aspect of *Pearl* criticism brings to the forefront the theme of incarnational language in understanding the poem's interaction with the material world. One critical mode of thinking about *Pearl*'s form in relation to incarnational language is exemplified in Sandra Prior's work, which sees in *Pearl* an ultimate failure and "falling off" of circular form that allows the poem to confirm that "the fairest *formeȝ* are not humanity's but God's."[15]

Reformist thought contemporaneous with the poem contributed to this idea that human forms of expression could not successfully mediate the divine ideal. The reformist theological context of late-fourteenth-century

England dictates that these progressions toward the divine inherent in the poem must inevitably fail, and this context should also be taken into account when considering *Pearl*. Late-fourteenth- and early-fifteenth-century Lollard ideology, for instance, potentially intersects with the project of *Pearl* in two ways. In the first place, it questioned the idea of language as a mediating force in articulating and encompassing the divine and miraculous. *Pearl* becomes relevant to this discussion, Elizabeth Schirmer argues, because its author's goal is to reject the notion that unmediated access to the divine is possible, and instead to use poetic expression as a form of mediation comparable to more exclusively clerical methods.[16] In the second place, as Stanbury argues, Lollard discourse reflected conflicted cultural attitudes toward images that drew attention to their own material splendor and value.[17] The sermon of William Taylor (1406) contains a passage displaying a striking convergence of these concerns, first using the imagery of building to emphasize the potential of an individual worshipper to gain access to spirituality, and then extending the building metaphor to express disapproval of the material excesses of traditional Catholic worship:

> But whanne ony man spekiþ of þis mater sum men anoon caren for susteynynge of greet bildyngis of tree and stoon, and reckne not of þe susteynynge of þe hooly temple of God þat is man, þe which, glorified in body and soule, shal be euerlastynge tabernacle of God, for þe which to be repareiled Crist fro þe myddis of his herte shedde out his precious blood endelesly, lasse reckinge of sich costlew bilding. Herfore whanne þe apostlis of a maner worldly curiouste shewiden Crist þe bildynge of þe temple, he seide, "Not a stoon shal abide upon anoþir but þat it be distryed."
>
> But ȝit meene I not oþerwise but þat cristen men shulden haue an honest hous, not ful costlew, neþer abiect, for to come togidere þere to preye God.[18]

This is not simply an articulation of the old problem of *latria* and *dulia*; instead it points out the place of representational practice itself at the heart of a conflict over devotional images. In this early-fifteenth-century instance, the Wycliffite preacher discounts the human impulse toward craft and mediation by emphasizing the human body's own potential as a "tabernacle" for the divine presence of God. He then uses this point to shift toward emphasizing the importance of simplicity and moderation in actual houses of worship, rejecting the deceptively mediating arts of traditional Catholic material and devotional culture.

Despite these cautions, the culture of elaborate devotional objects was still thriving in the world of the *Pearl*-poet, and offered other models for representing sanctity. Providing a few examples before turning to *Pearl* will establish a final important context for it: the aesthetic background on which the poem draws to test the boundaries between verbal and visual culture. Various readings of *Pearl* have identified in passing both the apparent influence of shrines, reliquaries, and artifacts on the poem's individual images, and the potential for drawing analogies between a kind of overall aesthetic ascribed to the poem and its artifact context. Felicity Riddy reflects the assessment of many readers of the poem when she calls *Pearl* "the poem about jewels which is itself a jewel" for its ornate encircling structure and lapidary imagery.[19] Devotional objects from this period indicate the similarity between the poem's images of pearls and whiteness and the materials and techniques of contemporary art. The late-medieval vogue in northern Europe for white enameling *en ronde bosse*, a technique in which a three-dimensional metalwork object has enamel applied to its roughened surface, has been suggested as an aesthetic practice that is reflected in the dreamer's description of the maiden. The fifteenth-century "Goldenes Rössel" (Little Gold Horse), notes Riddy, contains not only a number of pearls and other jewels, but also a white-enameled and golden-haired image of the Virgin, as well as a horse figure enameled in white *en ronde bosse*, all recalling elements of *Pearl*'s aesthetics.[20] Inventories of Richard II's own jewelry and plate mention a jeweled reliquary cross, as well as other objects from his collection that displayed the *ronde bosse* enameling style. This style was visible most familiarly on the white hart badges of the Wilton diptych.[21] In addition, an eighteenth-century painting exists of a reliquary produced around 1400 and decorated *en ronde bosse* (figure 4.3). Its visual features—the intricate metalwork and use of white—resonate with the dreamer's image of the lost jewel. Marian Campbell describes a possible influx of precious objects from other parts of Europe during Richard II's reign, in particular the jewels that accompanied Anne of Bohemia. Based on surviving examples from the region, including a reliquary pendant (figure 4.4), these seem to reflect particularly elaborate craftsmanship.[22] They also provide a potentially relevant backdrop for *Pearl*'s aesthetic.

Through the categories of sculpture and architecture as well, *Pearl* reflects certain existing aesthetic practices of its period. For instance, English sculpture in the fourteenth century reflected a taste for "subtly contrasting tonal relationships, achieved perfectly by high grade white alabaster."[23] The spectacle of the maiden, dominated by shades of white ranging from pearl to ivory (l. 178), corresponds suggestively to these traces of visual evidence of the period's aesthetic. "Blysnande whyt," "glysnande golde" (ll. 163, 165), the maiden in her garment of "myryeste margarys" (l. 199) seems to draw her physical aspect from the artifact culture in which she was envisioned. She is a complex exercise in what has been termed "notional ekphrasis," a verbal description of an imagined

Figure 4.3   "Maria mit Heiligen und Stifter," eighteenth century. Painting of a reliquary. Bayerisches Nationalmuseum Inv. Nr. MA 2608.

Source: © Bayerisches Nationalmuseum München.

artifact.[24] Finally, and most comprehensively, Ann R. Meyer has suggested that *Pearl* responds to the late-medieval English proliferation of chantry chapel architecture. For Meyer, the *Pearl*-poet becomes "a master builder, a literary architect."[25] In this reading, *Pearl*'s "epistemological process" builds itself around the poem's use of ornament, its awareness

Figure 4.4 Reliquary clasp with eagle, mid-fourteenth century. Germany (Bohemia?). Silver, enamel, precious stones. Inv. Cl. 3292. Musée national du Moyen Âge–Thermes de Cluny.

Source: Photo by Gérard Blot. Réunion des Musées Nationaux/Art Resource, New York.

of the transformative potential of architectural decoration, to show "the mechanism of philosophical allegory."[26] Meyer's perception of the epistemological process at work in the poem plays an important role in my own reading; my argument here, however, focuses not on the allegorical process itself, but instead upon a more metadiscursive inquiry in which the poem engages. Through this inquiry it critically examines the very processes of analogy—the features that make it possible to think of the poem as literary architecture or artifact—toward which it tends.

The Art of Analogy

This section of the chapter will spend some time developing the analogy between *Pearl*'s images and the realm of enshrining artifacts. The presence of reliquary busts in late-medieval England provides us with a useful point of access into the poem itself, in what they offer to our understanding of the maiden as a figure both accessible and inaccessible. As late as the sixteenth century, silver gilt head reliquaries of Saint Ursula were found in English cathedrals. And in the late Middle Ages, a number of head shrines existed in major cathedrals throughout England, often in the shape of busts.[27] Looking briefly at the example of a bust reliquary of Saint Ursula (figure 4.5), one notices its remarkable ability

Figure 4.5 Bust of Saint Ursula, ca. 1300–1325. Inv. No.1955.77. Historisches Museum, Basel.

Source: Photo by HMB M. Babey. Historisches Museum, Basel.

to display a gaze at once intimate and remote, both personal and symbolic. This effect results in part from the twin gestures that such reliquaries make, toward both heaven (through their rich materials) and earth (through their compelling gazes at their earthly worshippers). In a unique way, this object creates a sympathetic relationship with the viewer even as it gestures toward heavenly perfection. The bodily matter reliquaries contain is a memento of saintly martyrdom. As Brian Stock has demonstrated, one function that the reliquary served—especially to its more learned viewers—was as a memorial to the saint.[28] But the relic and reliquary also mark earthly loss and death as an immediate source of distress to the medieval viewer. Peter Brown sees in the origins of relic veneration in Western Europe an attempt to comprehend loss and mourning. Brown describes the "slow adjustment to the great sadness of mortality" as transpiring through an investment in a belief in the afterlife. The late-antique graves of regular people were interspersed with those of martyrs, creating "an imaginative dialectic which led late-antique men to render their beliefs in the afterlife palpable and directly operative among the living by concentrating these on the privileged figure of the dead saint."[29] The death of the exalted martyr played a role in understanding more immediate instances of death. This poignancy is still visible in the representation of this virgin martyr, whose eyes and subtly expressive features draw the viewer into a dynamic of reciprocity and involvement.[30] But at the same time, the sacred nature of the relics within lends a divine aspect to the stylized perfection of the reliquary's hair, clothing, and facial features. Similarly, the Saint Foy statue creates a memorial through her intensely articulated features, personal and poignant, while she is simultaneously implicated in a system of figuration that evokes the idea of the heavenly Jerusalem through the earthly materials that enclose the saint's remains (figure 4.6).[31] In enshrining these sacred remains, reliquary likenesses embody a universalizing symbol of heaven that intersects powerfully with the intimate and affective dynamic they create with their viewers.

The language and formal features of *Pearl* replicate these aspects of the encounter with a beautiful reliquary bust or majesty. When he first sees the maiden, the dreamer is "astount" [stupefied, astonished] by the strangeness of the vision.[32] As he continues to look, though, his steady gaze makes him feel that he knows her "more and more." The repetition of this phrase as a verse refrain conveys both the progressive and recursive aspects of this encounter. It is through this very scrutinizing gaze, or "frayste"—simultaneously intimate and alienated—that he feels her glory approach him, and he experiences her as both present and holy: "Suche gladande glory con to me glace / As lyttel byfore

Figure 4.6 Reliquary of Sainte Foy, ninth century, with Gothic additions. Gilded silver, copper, enamel, rock crystal and precious stones, cameos, wooden core. Treasury, Abbey Ste. Foy, Conques, France.

Source: Photo by Erich Lessing/Art Resource, New York.

þerto watȝ wonte" (ll. 171–72) [Such rejoicing glory did glide to me/ As it was rarely wont to do before]. The dreamer draws attention to an internal conflict that arises within him as a result of what he sees as the maiden's simultaneous proximity and distance. His nostalgic long- ing to be reunited with her helps her to retain a human identity; as Patricia Kean points out, she "can be approached with human feelings of tenderness."[33] The dreamer wants to call to her, but seeing her in "so strange a place" (l. 175), with a face as discouragingly flawless as "playn yuore" (l. 178), creates an insurmountable distance between them. The maiden levels the gaze of the reliquary bust—the devotional object's gaze of both particular sympathy and the aloofness of the symbolic—at the mournful dreamer. Thus what occurred visually in the poem's illus- tration, as we saw earlier, occurs here through the narration of a visual experience that finds a parallel in the material culture of the enshrining object.

Reliquaries designed to show their contents (figure 4.7) provide another dynamic analogous to *Pearl's* imagery and structural tech- niques. European devotional artifacts in the thirteenth and fourteenth centuries displayed relics at the same time that they enclosed them, making the fact of the body's mortality evident through their particular shape and iconographic programs. Caroline Walker Bynum describes a reliquary monstrance as "sheath[ing] the body of the saint or of Christ in the crystalline permanence of heaven while at the same time reveal- ing that it was of the stuff of earth."[34] Relics and reliquaries, she argues, gestured in complex ways toward the reintegrating potential of res- urrection. The eschatological aspect of reliquaries contributes to their complicated relationship to temporality. On the one hand, as artifacts of a medieval death culture, reliquaries that make their contents visible seal off their bodily fragments to memorialize them. On the other hand, they perpetually invoke the possibility of the body's reintegra- tion as another version of its physical self through these enshrining mechanisms as well.

This dual temporality also functions in other ways: such reliquaries show the narrative of earthly time through their bodily vestiges while they also transcend this time through their eternalizing materials and decorative structures. Bynum discusses an earlier tradition, found in Peter the Venerable's work, of understanding the relationships among the body, personhood, and eternity through images of seeds and flora as well as through the reliquary: "Peter can speak of bones germinating because he is sure those bones *are* the resurrection body. Any flesh that grows upon them will be similar to the flesh they wore here below. A 'something' that continues undestroyed in the reliquary will 'green' and

Figure 4.7 Reliquary in the form of a tower, 1380–90. Gilded silver and rock crystal; h. 28 cm. Cathedral and Museum, Salzburg, Austria.

Source: Photo by Erich Lessing/Art Resource, New York.

'germinate'...at the end of time; even now it throbs with a potentiality that can spill over into miracles."[35] The material inside the reliquary is understood as possessing an earthly, organic, temporal quality. At the same time, in the case of the object pictured here, decorative elements also enshrine in stasis the vestige within. This object represents through its visual language and shape an ascendancy toward a divine ideal, even as its form constantly draws the eye back toward the enclosed relic itself. It signals through its features a timeless ideal of divine understanding at the same time that it makes central the temporally progressive fragment of the saint's earthly body. In this way it mediates, like the saint, between heaven and earth. Reliquaries such as this one invoke their own duality of temporal progression and timelessness and transform their contents by enclosing them.

The first part of the poem, in which the maiden appears to the dreamer and then interacts with him, develops the analogy between poetic form and the conventions of sacred enshrinement. Through imagery, word placement, and stanzaic structure, the pearl reference introducing the maiden models the late-medieval reliquary's juxtaposition of earthly and heavenly material. During its opening lines and its entire first stanza group, for example, *Pearl*'s basic conceit and verse structure link death with gold, pearls, and an aesthetic of artifice through the poem's stanzaic symmetry:

> Perle, plesaunte to prynces paye
> To clanly clos in golde so clere,
> Oute of oryent, I hardyly saye,
> Ne proued I neuer her precios pere.
> So rounde, so reken in vche araye,
> So smal, so smoþ her sydeȝ were,
> Quere-so-euer I jugged gemmeȝ gaye,
> I sette hyr sengeley in synglere....
>
> For soþe þer fleten to me fele,
> To þenke hir color so clad in clot,
> O moul, þou marreȝ a myry iuele,
> My priuy perle wythouten spotte.
> (ll. 1–8; 21–24)

> [Pearl, pleasing for a prince's pleasure
> to enclose flawlessly in bright gold,
> in all the orient, I can boldly say,
> I never found her precious peer,
> So round, so noble in each setting,

so small, so smooth were her sides,
Wherever I judged gems to be bright/beautiful
I set her alone in uniqueness....

For truly many (songs) floated to me,
To consider her color so wrapped in clods of earth,
O, earth, you mar a merry jewel,
My secret spotless pearl.]

In these opening stanzas, references to the "oryent" pearl, the bright
enclosing gold, and the uniqueness of the jewel's beauty and symmetry
alongside the image of the body in the grave mimic in particular the
late-medieval reliquary's vivid juxtaposition of death's power to disinte-
grate with the defiant eternity of these glittering materials. As with the
reliquary, the time of the earth and the stasis of eternity exist alongside
each other.

But as we have seen before, reliquaries do not simply juxtapose;
they in fact blur the boundaries between container and contained.
The *Pearl*-poet also makes explicit through the formal technique of
linked verses the process that transforms the maiden's body, decorated
with and surrounded by pearls, into a pearl herself, subverting the distinction between contained body and containing artifact through the
medium of poetic form. Because Section IV's stanzas are joined by the
words "perlez" and "py3te" [decorated], many of these stanzas end with
descriptions of the ways in which pearls decorate the maiden. These
include "A precios pyece in perlez py3t" (l. 192) and "Wyth precios
perlez al vmbepy3te" (l. 204). The section's fourth stanza focuses on
the pearl that sits "Inmyddez hyr breste" (l. 222). When this stanza ends
with a reference to "Þat precios perle þer hit wat3 py3t" (l. 228), the
emphasis upon the single pearl begins to draw our perception of the
image of the pearl away from mere adornment and toward an object
that represents the maiden herself, even as the pearl in this stanza section remains an image concretely connected to the maiden's dress and
decoration. The next stanza section, however, uses the pearl as a figure
for the maiden's reintegrated body. Section V opens with an apostrophic
address that combines the pearls decorating the maiden with her own
identity as a pearl (in contrast to the epithet "swete" which the dreamer
applies to her in line 240): " 'O perle,' quod I, 'in perlez py3te' " (l. 241).
The repetition that characterizes *Pearl*'s formal strategy charts the process by which the poem identifies the maiden herself with the material
that decorates and contains her. In this manner, the device of repetition reinterprets her as an aesthetic object whose center is merged with
the decoration that contains it. The account of the pearl maiden here

becomes an ekphrastic description—a representation of her as an art object—that also draws, through its form, upon signifying techniques analogous to those of the objects referred to.

The poem's structure and imagery thus mimic the reliquary's effect of merging the containing with the contained; this comparison between text and object can help us to understand the nature of the maiden's bodily integrity. In the visual realm of the reliquary, enshrinement becomes a way of organizing and conveying meaning, so that the evidence of mortality engages in a dialogue with the preserving and static sculpture that surrounds it. Kevin Marti and Ian Bishop have pointed out a dilemma inherent in the *Pearl*-poet's need to describe the maiden in an integral and comprehensible form before the actual Resurrection has taken place. This dilemma requires the poet to "draw from characteristics that theologians believed resurrected bodies would possess at the end of time."[36] Understanding her reintegration as a reflection instead of the culture of reliquaries, which used enshrinement to make integral artifacts from the inescapably fragmenting matter of death, suggests an immediate means for achieving her beautifully integral presence.

Like the reliquary, the progression and arrangement of the poem's subsequent imagery also enclose earthly fallibility within celestial permanence.[37] Section V, for instance, contains images of death's decay inside images of artifice in order to stage a transformation from one into the other. The maiden refers to the pearl's enclosure inside the "cofer" of the garden (ll. 259–60), to a "forser" (l. 263), and to a "kyste" (l. 271), which are also words that signify caskets or coffers.[38] Marie Borroff points out that there are a number of levels of enclosure in the poem, from the pearl cleanly enclosed in gold to the garden itself, the root meaning of which is "enclosed place," the Edenic bower.[39] The pearl maiden elaborates in particular on the image of the enclosing coffer in this section with her reference to the rose, a central symbol of metamorphosis in the poem.[40] The first several lines of one stanza in particular give the rose an important position:

> Bot jueler gente, if thou schal lose
> Þy ioy for a gemme þat þe watȝ lef,
> Me þynk þe put in a mad purpose,
> And busyeȝ þe about a rayson bref;
> For þat þou lesteȝ watȝ bot a rose
> Þat flowred and fayled as kynde hyt gef.
> Now þurȝ kynde of þe kyste þat hyt con close
> To a perle of prys hit is put in pref.
>
> (ll. 265–72)

[But gentle jeweler, if you must lose
your joy for a jewel that was dear to you,
it seems to me that you are set on a mad intention,
and concern yourself with a fleeting cause;
for that which you lost was but a rose
that flowered and failed as nature decreed.
Now through the nature of the coffer that has enclosed it,
it has become a pearl of great price.]

The rose represents the reality of bodily decay, as in, for instance, the legend of Saint Stephen Protomartyr, in which the image of the rose acts as a symbol of the sacred dead body, with a dream image of a basket of red roses betokening Stephen's coffin and sacred remains.[41] The stanza above has sometimes been read as an allusion to microcosmic structure in *Pearl*, whereby the poem participates in the medieval belief in Christ's body as the center of a concentrically structured universe.[42] The centrally placed moment of jewels and roses in *Pearl* elaborates on the concentric model of the metaphysical universe by considering how layers of containment inform each other and even transform what they contain. The form of the poem bears this idea out in the sentence's arrangement of images. It begins with the reference to the seemingly permanent jewel, followed by a central reference to the rose, and then moves outward again to the realm of jeweled objects with its references to the coffer and chest. The concentric structure contains the organic within the artificial.

Pearl's alliterative form as laid out on the page demonstrates how its layers of enclosure bring about the transformation between earthly matter and celestial stasis. In lines 270–71, the alliterating "f" conveys the earthly transience of flowering and failing, and the word "kynde" appears to designate this natural characteristic. In the following line, meanwhile, the "k" in "kynde" becomes the basis for the alliteration, and corresponds to "kyste" and "close," words specifically designating the artifice of enshrinement as the means of transforming the dead body. Thus, through the pattern of alliteration, "kynde" becomes the fulcrum between these two different states for the body. The poem is not simply making the point that "kynde"'s meanings allow it to function in this dual manner; it is also suggesting that the form of the poem itself creates such a fulcrum and enables the shift. "Kynde" operates not only as a concept but also as an inscriptional object here, defined by its spatial relationships to what surrounds it. Thus the analogical relationship to material culture occurs in both the poem's imagery and its formal patterns.

Pearl's concatenating structure at other specific moments also contributes to an interaction between circular completeness and earthly fallibility. Its form sets up in this way as well the analogy to the conventions of the reliquary.[43] Patricia Kean suggests that the dichotomy between preservation and decay exists at a generalized, thematic level in the poem: the focus on the "grave in a garden of delights is…the central motif around which the twin themes of earthly and heavenly treasure and of mortality and regeneration are organized."[44] But more specifically than this, the poem achieves this interweaving of "twin themes" through its arrangement of verse form and its use of refrain. For example, lines 22–23 bring the presence of "clot" and "moul" into the dreamer's mental image of his pearl: earth mars and corrupts his treasure, leaving the dreamer with a picture of disintegration into darkness.[45] Meanwhile, the refrain-line "precios" or "pryuy perle wythouten spotte" in this first stanza group repeatedly impels a movement in this part of the poem from its images of earthly decay back to the invocation of the spotless pearl in each stanza's final line.[46] In the third stanza, images of seeds and spices, drawing the reader's attention again into the earth, are supplanted in the final line with the repeated reference to the symmetrical and transcendent jewel. "Þat spot of spyceȝ mot nedeȝ sprede, / Þer such riches to rot is runne" (ll. 25–26) [That spot must needs be overspread with spices / Where such riches are run to rot] gives way again to the precious pearl without spot (l. 36).

While the opening section's interweaving of mortality and an aestheticized vision of cultivation has been read as a comment on the "natural cycle of life," *Pearl*'s stanzaic structure also suggests that these natural cycles ultimately resolve themselves in the kind of preserving artifice that underlay the reliquary's promise of bodily resurrection.[47] In this way, *Pearl* develops further its analogy between poetic structure and the properties of the devotional artifact. When the narrator states in the poem's third stanza that "Flor and fryte may not be fede / Þer hit doun drof in moldez dunne, / For vch gresse mot grow of graynez dede" (ll. 28–30) [Flower and fruit (tree) may not be faded / Where (the pearl) has been driven down into the dun earth / For each plant must grow from dead seeds], he appears to allude to an image of natural renewal.[48] This stanza returns, however, as do the others in this opening group, to the image of an aesthetic object: "So semly a sede moȝt fayly not, / Þat spryngande spycez vp ne sponne / Of þat precios perle wythouten spotte" (ll. 34–36) [So seemly a seed could not fail / nor springing (flourishing) spices to shoot up / from that precious pearl without spot].[49] Rather than presenting a simple cycle of growth, death, and rebirth, the arrangement of the poem's lines renders inextricable the organic process it represents and the integrating artifice of jeweled embellishment.

Recalling the venerated relics at a saint's shrine, mediating between earth and heaven, *Pearl* acknowledges the necessity of physical remains in the process of approaching the holy. As the pearl maiden herself points out, in order to cross over into the realm of the heavenly Jerusalem, "Þy corse in clot mot calder keue" (ll. 320) [your corpse must sink colder into the earth]. She also describes her body this way when she explains to the dreamer that the heavenly Jerusalem is the place to which her soul has fled "Fro þat oure flesch be layd to rote" (ll. 958) [from the place where our flesh has been laid to rot]. This last declaration appears in a stanza set whose refrain-line repeats the phrase "wythouten mote" [without spot], again using the poem's structure to create a connection between unearthly perfection and mortal fallibility and transience, an integration of body and enshrining artifact.

Such impulses to perceive a sympathetic current running between visual and textual modes of devotional expression in *Pearl* ultimately extend from an established methodology of comparison among various art forms relevant to *Pearl*. One category for this comparison involves late-medieval representations of the Apocalypse and the heavenly Jerusalem. Muriel Whitaker, for example, has argued that *Pearl*'s own visions of both the celestial city and the pearl maiden herself find clear sources in fourteenth-century Apocalypse illuminations, and that this shared aesthetic fulfills important representational goals having to do with the project of truth-telling.[50] Stanbury's work on visuality and the *Pearl*-poet has continued this line of investigation, suggesting that "the ocular programs of illustrated Apocalypse manuscripts," joined with contemporary pilgrimage texts, dictate the narrative strategies of *Pearl* as well as its distinctive use of space.[51] In the realm of art historical analysis, the examination of metalwork and manuscript imaginings of the afterworld provides another means of perceiving how the spatial language of one mode of representation might be connected to other means of expression, and how the reliquary in particular provides a governing aesthetic for forms outside its own. Harvey Stahl, for instance, makes a useful case for the influence of the reliquary's visual representation of jeweled cities upon illuminated frontispieces from a fourteenth-century French book of hours in Cambrai; this analysis takes the additional step of seeing the reliquary itself, more conceptually, as "a medium for developing new visual strategies of disclosure, presence, and authority." Stahl explains that because the illuminations he examines use "the imagery of reliquaries and utilize their characteristic strategies of presence and revelation, they raise issues of bodily continuity and perception at a time when both were central to debates about the soul's knowledge of God before the general resurrection."[52] This scenario of shared goals among varied methods of representation ultimately motivates my own and other critical perspectives on the *Pearl*-poet's allusions to visual and material languages in his own work, and on the attendant construction of analogies.

Inscription and the Transcendence of Analogy

This field of comparative inquiry exists, however, within a broader tradition of critical self-awareness about boundaries between visual and verbal expression. V.A. Kolve has asserted, for instance, that trying to imagine poetry as able to "imitate the effects proper to painting," or vice versa, is in the end a "fanciful" exercise.[53] Jeffrey Hamburger, approaching the issue from an art historical perspective, explains his position on the ways that one might read visual as opposed to verbal signs:

> The texts and images of female monasticism suggest, and at times insist on, the nondiscursive character of visual experience. By nondiscursive I do not mean ahistorical and free from the encodings of culture or context, akin to the physiological processes of perception. I merely wish to underscore what the sources themselves suggest: that visual images served functions distinct from those of texts and that they elicited a type and range of response unlike, if not unrelated to, those elicited by words, whether written or spoken.[54]

For Hamburger, this distinction becomes important to maintain because it casts into relief devotional imagery's capacity for teaching us about the psychology and culture of visual encounters. But it is also in some ways exemplary of a broader epistemological position on the specific ways that words and images signify. Thus while analogies are possible and even suggestive in thinking about medieval arts, caveats also exist about certain fundamental distinctions between visual and verbal ways of signifying.

Even the analogies that we have just examined raise related questions. How, for instance, does a reader negotiate between imagery and form as two possible locations for constructing analogies to the visual world? What role does visuality play in the experience of perceiving analogy between verbal and visual expression? What kinds of material forms, and what kinds of spectacles, can poetic form itself construct? As *Pearl*'s narrative continues, moving into a depiction of a performance, the poem is able to take up these questions. In doing so, *Pearl* ultimately transcends analogy itself by becoming inscriptional object and devotional event.[55]

As *Pearl* progresses, it presents us with a scene that explicitly pushes against the limitations of comparative acts. This scene involves the interaction between the dreamer and the maiden. The section in which the encounter takes place is organized around a rhetorical strategy of comparison. This occurs first through the comparative force of its refrain phrase, "more and more," and second with a series of internal statements of comparison, such as "Þe fyrre...Þe more" (ll. 127–28); and "if hit watz fayr þer I con fare, / Wel loueloker watz þe fyrre londe" (ll. 148–49) [If it was fair where I was passing, / Much lovelier was the farther land]. These lines create a general aesthetics of the comparative for this section, reflecting some of the comparative impulses underlying analogy. But at the same time, this moment in the poem actually shows comparison's limitations as an interpretive strategy. The dreamer's articulation does not ultimately allow him to move outside his present position; he is frozen where he is and can engage with the lovelier land only in terms of its comparison to where he stands. The act of comparison does not create for him a change in consciousness, context, or material situation. If the strategy of explicit comparison itself does not hold transcendent power, then the poem's implied comparisons between visual and verbal forms might also have certain limitations. The force of this moment liberates the poem from its project of simply analogizing visual and verbal expression.

Instead, *Pearl*'s inscriptional identity contributes to the constitution of a devotional event, the dreamed vision as exterior to the narrative utterance of the dream itself. As we saw, the manuscript features of this poem in particular emphasize the importance of encountering it visually, and the context of its illustrations emphasizes the visual work that its material inscription on the page might do as well. In order for us to understand *Pearl*'s progression toward the event through inscription, we must first consider briefly the function of inscriptionality in late-medieval religious art. Medieval iconographic evidence suggests that written words take on a dual capacity in religious art, at once linguistic signs and at the same time physical objects entered into a network of nonverbal signification in the image. For example, Roger Ellis, in examining the different ways that words appear in late-medieval and Renaissance religious art, distinguishes between words as printed on an image without incorporating themselves into the visual mimesis at stake, and words that become part of the image's own surfaces, that participate in the material qualities the picture is trying to convey. Ellis argues that

Figure 4.8   Simone Martini, Annunciation with Saints Ansano and Margaret, 1333. Four medallions: Jeremiah, Ezekiel, Isaiah, and Daniel. Tempera on wood; 184 x 210 cm. Inv. 451, 452, 453. Uffizi, Florence, Italy.

Source: Photo by Erich Lessing/Art Resource, New York.

the first use of words in particular "inhabits an alternative reality to that of the other signs in the painting.... [T]he word points us both away from and towards the heart of the physical universe."[56] He provides the example of the Simone Martini *Annunciation* to illustrate this phenomenon (figure 4.8 and detail).

Both the image itself and Ellis's commentary upon it demonstrate the dialectic of inscription and performance. In this moment of hailing, Gabriel famously speaks the fullness of Mary into being. The positioning of the inscription between the two figures implicates it in this performative act. As Ellis points out, however, it simultaneously exists on a separate plane, or in the silent and self-referential realm of the inscribed character, part of a system of signs that weaves itself into, and yet is distinct from, the other categories of signs in the painting. The central inscription interacts with the framing inscriptions throughout the piece, including the name labels at the bottom and the banners within the medallions at the top. The inscription of Gabriel's utterance concatenates with these framing inscriptions, but its materiality also differs from theirs. Thus while the inscription visually interacts with the inscriptional frames for the piece, it also finds itself, as a separate materiality, enclosed within the visual depiction of a performative encounter.

The *Annunciation* illuminates some of the mechanics behind *Pearl*'s own uses of inscription and visuality in its depiction of the heavenly Jerusalem. As Stanbury has pointed out, *Pearl*'s adaptation of Revelation is actually somewhat unusual. By her account, "In most Middle English references to the New Jerusalem, the city is only invoked by name; when the city is described, it is modeled after Ezekiel's vision, rather than John's, and details chiefly the city's walls as seen by the approaching pilgrim." *Pearl*, on the other hand, is markedly visual and concrete in its recapitulation of its scriptural source.[57] As part of this visual concreteness, the passage explicitly refers to written inscription as part of a system for embellishing devotional objects. This section of the poem points toward the inscriptional traditions incorporated into actual devotional artifacts in the reference to the "scrypture" (l. 1039) [inscription] on each of the sets of three door plates enclosing the heavenly city:

As John hym wrytez ȝet more I syȝe;
Vch pane of that place had thre ȝates,
So twelue in poursent I con asspye,
The portalez pyked of rych platez,
And vch ȝate of a margyry,
A parfit perle that neuer fatez.
Vchon in scrypture a name con plye
Of Israel barnez, folewande her datez.
          (ll. 1033–1040)

[As John wrote, yet more I saw;
each wall of that place had three gates
so I saw twelve in the enclosing wall,

the gateways adorned with rich metal plate,
and each gate (adorned) with a pearl,
a precious pearl that never fades.
Each one contained an inscribed name
of the sons of Israel, corresponding to their dates.]

The heavenly Jerusalem's square and symmetrical shape, "As longe as brode as hyȝe ful fayre" (l. 1024); its "streteȝ of golde as glasse al bare" (l. 1025); its walls of jasper; and its chrysolite adornments all contribute to the vision of the city as an object of enshrinement. Figure 4.9, a reliquary from the Sainte-Chapelle, indicates the passage's potential relationship to an available culture of inscribed reliquary artifacts in its imagining of the heavenly Jerusalem. The object's architectural features, triple gates, and inscribed names all reflect features of the dreamer's vision. A correspondence between object and literary description clearly suggests itself here. But perhaps more important than this correspondence is the way that religious visual culture explicates the poem's use of inscriptionality. The *Annunciation*'s suggestion that its inscribed component exists as both interior and exterior to the angel's central performative has useful implications for *Pearl*. In the poem as well, inscription both occupies interior formal spaces and exists as an exterior and constitutive frame. *Pearl* conceives of inscription as intersecting layers. It is part of the image of the gates contained within the line, expressed through the word "scrypture" near the center of the stanza. But it is also the inscribed characters of the verse itself. As an entity encountered visually, *Pearl* uses inscription to move past its descriptive correspondences to the world of artifacts. It exists as a self-enfolding object through the particular visual materiality of its inscribed characters, in a dynamic that we see as well as read.

The role of visuality becomes especially important in this part of the poem, and in its ultimate identity not only as inscriptional object, but also as devotional event. *Pearl* locates in the Jerusalem vision a fundamental epistemological question about the relationship between writing and seeing. The form of the poem's syntax intertwines these two concepts with each other: "As derely deuyseȝ þis ilk toun / In Apocalyppeȝ þe apostel John" (ll. 995–96); "As John deuysed ȝet saȝ I þare" (l. 1021); "As John hym writeȝ ȝet more I syȝe" (l.1033). Writing, devising, and seeing emerge as the terms that proliferate between the dreamer and his invocation of the apostle in this section. The words linking the parts of Section XVII together through their repetition are "Apocalypse," "apostle," and "John," incorporating a reference to the scriptural source for the imagery in this passage into the enclosing *concatenatio* structure itself; in this way as well, an act of writing articulates itself through artistic expression that requires an

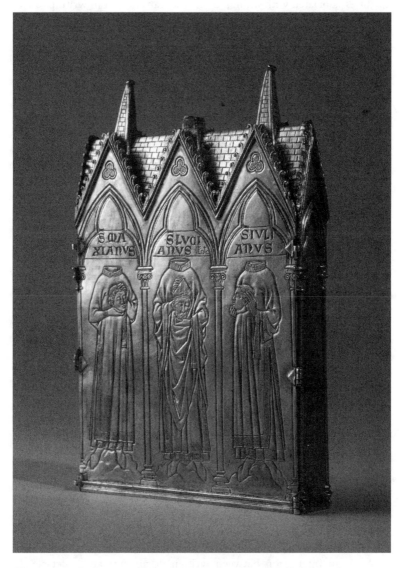

Figure 4.9 Reliquary of Saints Maxien, Lucien, and Julien from the treasury of Sainte-Chapelle, ca. 1261–62. Cl. 10746. Musée du Moyen Âge–Thermes de Cluny, Paris, France.

Source: Photo by F. Raux. Réunion des Musées Nationaux/Art Resource, New York.

act of seeing. Some critics have emphasized the "physical" and "carnal" qualities associated with seeing, so that the transition from writing to seeing would have to map itself onto an underlying awareness of the material aspects of both writing and sight.[58] Barbara Newman asks the important question "What did it mean to say 'I saw'?" in the Middle Ages. Part of her answer involves the work that the visualization of a scriptural text might perform. According to Newman, "through visualization the scriptural text could be deeply internalized, and this inner landscape prepared the ground for new visions and vision texts."[59] Thus textuality and visuality intersect to create a space of profound interiority. But at the same time, this interiority holds the potential to exteriorize itself. As Newman continues, Pseudo-Bonaventure enjoins the reader to become not only a spectator but also a "participant," so that what he visualizes moves from something internal to something external to him: "For the Christian practitioner...visualizing *becomes* seeing."[60] When *Pearl* interweaves the terms of writing and seeing, it emphasizes the written word's potential to contain a spiritual vision that then moves into a space beyond its articulation. Encountering *Pearl* visually thus means more than perceiving how a poem can be like an artifact. Instead, its inscriptionality folds in upon itself to produce a kind of vision that unfolds outward from itself.

Processional Performance and the Dream as Devotional Event

Pearl also refers to John's scriptural vision as a dream, and the overall dream frame allows the poem to take a further step away from analogy and toward the devotional event.[61] Like *Saint Erkenwald* and the N-Town *Assumption*, *Pearl*'s dream incorporates various forms of reference to performance culture. The last chapter in particular suggested that poetic language and performance conventions are mutually illuminating. The references to such conventions in *Pearl* thus exist as an underlying visual and material language for describing the poem's processes of representation. And ultimately, *Pearl*'s representation of its central performance— the heavenly procession—provides a structure for understanding the dreamer's relationship to his dream as devotional event.

The tradition of processions in late-medieval Europe formed itself through an interaction between written documents and spectacle. In her study of the documentary practices of medieval Paris and London, Brigitte Bedos-Resak claims that civic authorities used the strategy of "embellishing the routines and techniques of their documentary writing through ceremony."[62] Written documentary culture thus had a relationship to ceremonial performance. In discussing specifically late-medieval cultural practice, Wendy Scase demonstrates a related point about the "poetics of spectacle" (Gordon Kipling's term) informing fifteenth-century entry processions. For Scase, the concrete and visual elements of spectacle contain the potential—obvious to the politically powerful deployers of such spectacle—to become "textualized," "working within a complex system of interplay between the idioms of visual spectacle, liturgical ritual, and historical narrative" in order to establish their meaning.[63] Kipling himself argues that in the case of Richard II's reconciliation with London in 1392, the urban pageant sought to "identify London as a type of the New Jerusalem," so that its goal was to "transform this verbal metaphor into visual imagery" through St. John's apocalyptic account, also featured in *Pearl*.[64] To the extent to which written signs served the purpose of regulating authority or communicating in other ways within the landscape of the city, they acted interdependently with visual, aural, and other signifiers associated with the arts of procession and spectacle. Thus procession specifically as a representational occasion (not only as a devotional or political one) provides a relevant context for *Pearl*'s own investigation of visuality and textuality.

The *Pearl*-poet himself might have had access to certain specific processional performances. Speculation exists concerning the connections between *Pearl*'s processional scene and royal grieving and memorializing upon the death of Anne of Bohemia in 1394. Anne's death was marked by a funeral procession that took place—as it does in *Pearl*—in August, on the octave of Saint Anne's day.[65] This reading of John Bowers's posits a definite trajectory between pageant and poem. Focusing for the most part on the possibilities underlying the social and political world of the poem, Bowers makes the case that the *Pearl*-poet's familiarity with the Ricardian court (through the oft-acknowledged Cheshire connection) creates potential resonance between the elegiac content of *Pearl* and the other expressions of grief surrounding Anne of Bohemia's death. Bowers has used the occasions of the death of Anne and Richard's subsequent marriage to the young Isabelle of France to reconstruct a life for the *Pearl*-poet as connected to the Ricardian court. He cites the evidence of *Pearl*'s obsession with both mourning and sexual chastity. Bowers contends that despite our inability to know for certain how personal was the loss that *Pearl* describes, "the author worked diligently to encode the representation of loss in a field of religious and regalian symbolism that would have allowed interpretation toward wider public ends. Everything in his mode of composition bespeaks the performance of a courtly poet." Both the maiden herself and, as Bowers points out, the procession of the Lamb in the celestial city potentially reflect a genre of carefully orchestrated Ricardian spectacle.[66] As Staley argues, however, this association between

Anne of Bohemia and the maiden does not account for the latter's specific designation as a child.[67] It might be useful, then, to expand upon Bowers's work by moving away from the exercise of linking specific processional occasions or cultural productions to specific literary depictions, instead asking how this cultural context elucidates the poem's representational strategies.

One answer to this question lies in *Pearl*'s use of performance traditions to engage the dialectics of inscription and performance. Specifically, in the sections preparing for and detailing the procession, *Pearl* uses the imagery of light, and the procession's forms of illumination, as a means to enshrine inscription and performance within each other. Light is an important element in these sections:

> Þur3 wo3e and won my lokyng 3ede,
> For sotyle cler no3t lette no ly3t.
> Þe hy3e trone þer mo3t 3e hede
> Wyth alle þe apparaylmente vmbepy3te,
> As John þe appostel in terme3 ty3te.
> (ll. 1049–53)

> [Through wall and dwelling place my gaze passed,
> for all being transparent and clear, nothing hindered any light.
> There you might see the high throne
> embellished with all adornment,
> as John the Apostle set forth plainly (in words).][68]

At one particular point in the Jerusalem description, light allows visual spectacle to enclose the poem's inscriptionality. The Lamb, who will ultimately be at the at the center of the procession, is introduced in Section XVIII through images of light: "Þe self God wat3 her lombe-ly3t, / Þe Lombe her lantyrne, wythouten drede" (ll. 1046–47) [God himself was their lamp light, / the Lamb their lantern, doubtless]. The Lamb functions as a performance object. Like the Christ images and statuary sometimes used in medieval processions, it is a silent artifact engaged in the movement and sound of ceremony.[69] As a performance object, the Lamb is both at the center of the ceremony and, through the light it casts, a force that surrounds it. The link-phrasing for this section fairly consistently involves a negation of the light of the sun and moon: "Hem nedde nawþer sunne ne mone" (l. 1044) [there was no need of sun nor moon for them]; "bry3ter þen boþe þe sunne and mone" (l. 1056) [brighter than both the sun and moon]; "The mone may þerof acroche no my3te" (l. 1069) [the moon could not acquire any strength from there]. The Lamb therefore outdoes the network of earthly light references that this inscriptional pattern weaves. His divine light encompasses the scene. We saw earlier that in this section, inscriptionality turns in on itself, through the interaction between the reference to inscribed characters and the inscriptional materiality of the poem itself. Introducing the element of performance here, we find as well that inscriptionality—in the form of the patterned link-phrases—momentarily disappears into the light of the divine spectacle. The repetition of negating constructions in these link phrases emphasizes the momentary eclipsing of this element. Thus in this section, performance and spectacle, as embodied in the Lamb as performance object, become the encompassing and defining mode of expression.

The next section of the poem, however, suggests that this is not a stable dynamic; here light instead serves as an instrument for establishing an inscriptional frame. Two consecutive stanzas in this section begin and end with the word "delyt" (ll. 1117, 1128, 1129, and 1140), a pattern not common for *Pearl*'s link-words overall. The word "delyt"'s possible pun on "light" suggests that in this section, unlike the previous one, the inscriptional reference to light enshrines the performance. The concatenation here creates a frame of verbal signs around the spectacle of the procession. Through its form on the page, the poem reasserts the capacity of inscription to enshrine, enable, and even constitute the performance. More than the appearance of the single word itself, its repetition this section emphasizes this constitutive capacity of written inscription. In a sense, the word's repetition stands in for the iterability of all written words, their generation of meaning through self-reference and relationality. This repetition of the single word, over the time and space of the section, signals the inscriptional character as always already there. It is a constitutive, anterior, and exterior force, shaping the spectacle itself.

In using light to identify its poetics of enshrinement, *Pearl* suggests that the dialectic of inscription and performance occurs not only in visual terms, but also through the poem's complicated relationship to vision. Light's implication in this dialectic obliges us to ask about the extent to which the poetics of enshrinement is a visible poetics. This poetics, as we have seen, derives from a visual language, but *Pearl* raises additional questions about whether, and how, the poetics of enshrinement relies upon visualization. There are two ways to approach this question, and both lead us toward *Pearl*'s break with analogy through its identification as a devotional event. One approach involves characterizing light's role in visual processes related to texts and textuality. The other is to suggest that, in the dream framework, the poetics of enshrinement uses light to oscillate between interior and exterior forms of vision.

In certain areas of medieval thought, light not only illuminated texts but also participated in their potential materiality. Hugh of Saint Victor elaborates on *lumen* as emanating from the reader to illuminate the manuscript page. As Ivan Illich puts it, Bonaventure's later commentary on Hugh imagines that "the text has…begun to float above the page," so that the use of light in constituting the book as object shifts into an act of constituting the text as object.[70] In Herbert Kessler's analysis, medieval artistic expression "recapitulates the very materialization of divine light."[71] Thus, through the channels of both textuality and divinity, light possesses a kind of ambiguous materiality of its own. It is both an object and a means toward understanding.[72] Hugh's comment on fire elaborates upon this model. In *De unione corporis et spiritus*, he distinguishes fire from the other elements because of the unique nature of its materiality and refers to it as "sapientia vitalis."[73] Fire in his terms becomes both an object and a process of understanding. But as Shoshana Felman shows, within this very equivocation between object and process lies the definition of performativity itself.[74] Allusion to light in a medieval text can therefore carry performative force, initiating a process of understanding while also existing as an independent object. Through its ambiguous materiality, light foregrounds the extent to which a text has its own constitutive claims to materiality. In using light to enshrine inscription and performance within each other, *Pearl* suggests that the text not only inscribes a processional performance object, but also performs an inscriptional object. The poem is both narrative process and light-filled inscriptional object, and it achieves this identity not through analogy but rather within the particular materiality that light bestows upon the text.

Pearl also takes a step beyond analogy, and toward the devotional event, by using the poetics of enshrinement to move between interior and exterior forms of vision. In its inscription on the page, the vision exists through, but is also anterior to, the process of its performative constitution through the dreamer's narrative utterance. The specific terms in which the dreamer describes his experience of the vision suggest its identity as devotional event, something that exists outside his own performative capacities. *Pearl*'s language suggests the possibility of a liminal space that is object and process, not only in the content of the dream, but also in the dreamer's interaction with his vision. The procession contained within the city functions as an object, but at the same time it performatively constitutes itself through the dreamer's utterance. In the moment of introducing the procession, the dreamer uses the famous simile of the "maynful mone" to describe the way in which the procession takes him by surprise, coming suddenly into being:

> Ry3t as the maynful mone con rys
> Er thenne the day-glem dryue al doun,

So sodanly on a wonder wyse
I watz war of a prosessyoun.
                    (ll. 1093–96)

[Just as the mighty moon rises
before the gleam of day sinks down,
so, suddenly, in a wondrous manner,
I was aware of a procession.]

This moment exceeds the bounds of the dreamer's narration into something genuinely unexpected. Throughout the rest of the description of the
heavenly Jerusalem, the dreamer's acts of narration speak into being the
space of the inscriptional artifact—visual and verbal, a pattern of worlds
and words. At the point when he witnesses the procession, however, his
language allows for the possibility that something exists outside it as well.
The procession is an event that comes into being without a perceptible
narrative process through language; instead it occurs in the space between
the generalized "maynful mone" and the dreamer's specific awareness of
what he sees. *Pearl*'s narrative situates itself both within and without the
dreamer. Its relationship to visuality is elusive, existing over his shoulder,
like a shadowy daylight moon.

The dream functions as an appropriate space for such an effect to
occur. Dreams, as chapter 1 suggested, provide a mechanism for articulating the relationships among different worlds that a text might narrate.
Kathryn Lynch elaborates further on this idea, pointing out that "dreams
and visions naturally raise questions of ontology, of how the flesh and
spirit can interpenetrate"; they are "liminal" in nature.[75] As Brantley
has proposed, the Carthusian miscellany known as British Library MS
Additional 37049 engaged its readers, through its own intersections of
various literary genres as well as images, in a process that "made the
individual's quiet encounter with a static book itself a species of sacred
performance." This point forms part of her argument about performative
reading, to which I have previously referred.[76] We might perceive the
transition from scriptural reading to the vision of the procession across the
river in the dream as staging the generation of such an interior spectacle.
Pearl, however, also demonstrates how its vision constitutes itself not only
through the reader's imaginative interaction with it, but also within the
functioning of the poem's language and narrative techniques, its deploy-
ment of dream, form, and light. The status of the dreamer's vision is suggestively indeterminate as far as the categories of interior and exterior are
concerned. While the dream always remains in the private realm of the
narrator's imagination, it has a logistical valence that distinguishes it from
the type of interiorized apprehension involved in absorbing words on a

Figure 4.10 All Souls College MS 6, fol. 4r. (Codrington Library), ca. 1250–60.

Source: The Warden and Fellows of All Souls College, Oxford.

page. An illumination in Oxford, All Souls College MS 6 (ca. 1250–60) visualizes a similar distinction, with the content of a book manifesting itself as a vision external to the reader's figure; the vision exists as exterior to the nun, hovering over her shoulder, and yet at the same time has been produced by her experience praying before a book, and is linked imagistically to the book as object and instrument (figure 4.10).[77] The poem's dreamer and reader stand within a dynamic of enshrinement in relation to their own experience of the ontologically complex dream. The procession begins as an act of performative self-constitution, but it also becomes an event, borrowing the ambiguous substantiality of light to move into a devotional space between the seen and unseen.

In a study of the "poetics of the mind's eye," Christopher Collins describes Shakespeare's "O, for a muse of fire" prologue (*Henry V*) as an example of poetry that is asking for permission to use the mind's eye.[78] This formulation can help us to define what *Pearl* does as well. Rather than simply asking the reader to visualize something, *Pearl* uses the poetics of enshrinement to participate in that process. It generates interior and exterior vision not only through images and content, but also through its inscriptional form on the page and the particular materiality of the light upon which it calls. Perhaps what Barbara Newman terms "scripted visions" in the late Middle Ages were also, as in the case of *Pearl*, inscriptional visions.[79] Their form as well as their content contributes to their interaction with the visual world. In certain ways the poetics of enshrinement is a poetics of the hidden and the revealed; we have seen instances in which the form of the reliquary frames, conceals, and reveals its contents at once, and this becomes a way of understanding poetic representation as well. For the articulation of a vision located, like the daylit moon, outside the corner of one's eye and at the same time occupying a place of centrality in the imaginative life, a poetics of enshrinement seems an appropriate vehicle. Having explored this poetics' ability to unfold its own visualities as a way of moving beyond an analogical aesthetics, we shall now turn inward, toward other cognitive acts. If the poetics of enshrinement in *Pearl* illuminates a path beyond analogy, and toward the complex visuality of the devotional event, then in *The Pardoner's Tale* this poetics reveals the performative process of poetic figuration itself.

CHAPTER 5

RELIQUARIES OF THE MIND: FIGURATION, ENSHRINEMENT, AND PERFORMANCE IN *THE PARDONER'S TALE*

The Pardoner's own accoutrements seem to provide an obvious key to identifying the dialectical enshrinement of inscription and performance in *The Pardoner's Tale*. Presenting himself to the pilgrims as habitually carrying a combination of relics and inscribed, sealed documents, the Pardoner describes how he initiates his performances by showing off both. At the end of his exemplum, he reminds his listeners of the power of the inscribed document in his promise that "Youre names I entre heer in my rolle anon."[1] We might say, therefore, that the presence of an inscriptional form frames the occasion at one level, while at another the performance itself, dynamic, ambiguous, and varied in its representational modes, forms an enclosing context for the documents, whose meaning exists relative to the Pardoner's deceiving spectacle. This exchange between container and contained occurs in the fulcrum of the reliquary objects themselves, and all the complex meaning this tale gives them.[2]

Exercising some suspicion about this easy application of the model, however, will ultimately yield a more useful way of reading *The Pardoner's Tale*. It will also reveal additional dimensions of the poetics of enshrinement itself. For in the context of my overall claim, the Pardoner's documents represent a more problematic reference to inscription than might appear to be the case. The artifacts of enshrinement imagined in *Saint Erkenwald*, the *Assumption* play, and *Pearl* all reflect the reliquary's own use of inscriptional signs. Inscriptions appeared, for instance, on the judge's lettered tomb, the "scrypture" engraved on the gates of the artifact-like heavenly Jerusalem, and the imagined Marian reliquary as a theatrical object made of verbal and visual signs. In *The Pardoner's Tale*, on the other hand, the inscriptions and relics exist in such emphatic parallel to each other that they do not seem to intersect with each other. Each comes in its own bag, and the Pardoner displays them in succession: "That shewe I first..." (VI. 338); "Thanne shewe I forth...." (VI. 347). The reliquaries themselves lack inscriptions. Neither the glass tubes the Pardoner carries nor the Host's vividly imagined reliquary of the "hogges toord" in which to enshrine the Pardoner's testicles incorporates inscriptions. While inscriptionality is visible in the text overall, it seems to be erased from the culture of relic objects it invokes. *The Pardoner's Tale* thus prompts us to ask how the poetics of enshrinement might function with its inscriptional element seemingly occluded. It answers this question by transforming what we have seen as the representational model of the reliquary into a model of cognition. The text posits a reliquary of the mind—a reliquary that requires neither inscriptional labels nor belief in its authenticity, both of which are notably missing from this tale's devotional objects.

The reliquary of the mind, as revealed through the imagery of *The Pardoner's Tale*, serves as a space in which to create metaphor, and in doing so reveals metaphor's performative and enshrining character. As a space for the imaginative work of figuration, the reliquary of the mind elaborates on the relationship between objects in the world and processes of thought. Both Marx and readings of Marx suggest that physical objects can be "the bearers of our most important thoughts." In Christopher Cannon's explanation of the Hegelian universe of mind, "form is the materialization of thought."[3] When, in *Specters of Marx*, Derrida reads Marx on the table as commodity, he provides another conceptual context for the reliquary of the mind. Derrida describes the work of the table's mind as the production of "a whole lineage of fantastic or prodigious creatures, whims, chimera, non-ligneous character parts." The table is not simply mindful here, nor simply an animated creature. In its ambiguous identity ("animated-inanimated," "dead-living"), it contains processes of figuration, the manufacture of imagined figures.[4] Through *The Pardoner's Tale*, the enshrining reliquary materializes a process by which different layers and levels of performance enshrine each other in the mental construction of metaphor. Ultimately, I will suggest that a different kind of inscriptional frame also exists for this text, but this chapter will mostly take advantage of inscription's apparent suppression to focus on performance, performativity, and the mind's metaphoric processes.

Other readings of *The Pardoner's Tale* link the truth claims of relics and shrines more closely to its semiosis; this study takes a somewhat different approach by focusing on the tale's mechanics of figuration. As Eugene Vance demonstrates, the pilgrims' project in this tale and in the

Canterbury Tales as a whole shifts between questions of truth and semiosis. The Pardoner, he argues, wishes to make of himself a shrine in order to deflect the pilgrims from the true shrine that they all seek. At the end of the tale,

> the Host's castrating invective deflates the Pardoner's urge to enshrine his own disclosure, to be sure; yet the Host's refusal to kneel and adore the Pardoner's smelly and excrement-stained breeches may very well have summoned to the pilgrims' memory one of the sublimer relics they would soon kneel to adore at Canterbury.[5]

Vance reads this opposition between the Pardoner's words and the Host's as demonstrating the significative role of framing in the *Canterbury Tales* and in medieval poetic language. He argues that we can consider "some of the dramatic links between the Pardoner's discourse and the pilgrimage to Becket's tomb as a framework of the *Canterbury Tales* as a whole," reflecting the idea that "medieval semiotic theory tends to see proper signification as a *framing* of meanings that extends beyond the *sign* to the *utterance*, next to the *discourse*, and finally to the *edifice* of discourses that are the living expression of the social order [emphases in original]."[6] In this view of medieval semiotics, framing moves outward, from sign to lived and social utterance. I would elaborate further on this model by considering the complete culture of reliquaries, which, as we have seen, complicates the designations of framing and framed. In Vance's perspective as well as mine, formal features, particularly enclosure, provide a bridge between signification and the material world. The present study builds on this formulation by suggesting that the reliquary shrine as a conceptual term reveals the performativity of metaphor.

Discarding the Reliquary

The tale's first set of references to reliquaries is its most literal and its most debased. But the abandonment of any hope of truth in these first relics is a necessary step in the tale's overall process of explaining figuration through enshrinement, because it allows the reader to move from physical reliquaries to reliquaries of the mind. The Pardoner's relics reveal the material realities of death and ask the viewer to envision a process of symbolic and literal transformation through their enclosure within glass and "latoun" (VI. 350). As we have seen, this juxtaposition of body and decorative or symbolic materials gestures toward a heavenly ideal of integrity and eternity. But at the same time that the Pardoner's relics recall this existing cultural belief, they explicitly introduce the necessity of acknowledging their own possible falsity through the Pardoner's disavowal.[7] "Relikes been they, as weene they echoon" (VI. 349), he declares, and he also refers to his proffering of the relics as a "gaude" (VI. 389), undermining both their legitimacy and their efficacy. Lee Patterson reads the Pardoner's abuses of relics as signaling the tale's doubt in the relic's capacity to gesture toward the resurrection of the body, and to "eras[e] the line between material and spiritual."[8] *The Pardoner's Tale* aggressively limits their meaning and potential as objects, and it provides us with an important reminder that the practice of enclosing relics did not protect them as physical objects from the possibility of emptiness and falsity.

The contemporary reformist context that questioned the relic's meaning and value also makes the point that as signifying objects, physical relics and reliquaries in the world were problematic in their ability to control and determine their own signification. As Anne Hudson points out, one prevalent branch of Lollard thought held that "false is the imagination of those who think that pilgrimage must mean the visiting of images and the bones of saints."[9] Wyclif himself was known to "commen[t] tartly on images of Christ and the saints with golden locks and garments encrusted with gold, silver, and jewels."[10] Reformists argued with increasing force that God dwelt in men's souls "bettere þan all ymagis made of man in erþe, and better þan alle bodies of seyntis, be þe bones of hem neuer so gloriously shreyned in gold."[11] The *Twelve Conclusions of the Lollards* makes its point about devotional objects and artifacts vividly clear: "if þe rode tre, naylis, and þe spere and þe coroune of God schulde ben so holiche worchipid, þanne were Iudas lippis, qwoso mythte hem gete, a wondir gret relyk."[12] In addition, rich and costly artifacts not only emphasized the tenuousness of the devotional object's hold on what it might signify to viewers, but also represented a misuse of funds. "[M]en erren foul in þis crucifixe making, for þei peynten it wiþ greet cost, and hangen myche siluer and gold and precious cloþis and stones þeronne and aboute it, and suffren pore men...to be by hem nakyd, hungry, thrusty." The most "ryaly tabernaclid" of the "dede stones and roten stokkis" shamefully inspire the largest monetary tributes.[13] As Carolyn Dinshaw has argued, this hesitation in assigning unequivocal meaning to the relics finds a parallel again in the Pardoner, who maintains a necessary indeterminacy in his own identity.[14] Lollard critique also emphasizes that relics, as integrations of object and sign, can in fact be empty of devotional content, and instead signify only greed and vanity.

The tale's relics and reliquaries introduce many of the conventions we have seen throughout this study as associated with physical relics, and yet at the same time their avowed falsity liberates us from having to adhere to the realm of the concrete relic, encouraging us to look beyond it.

Reliquaries function in the tale as conceptual objects, powerful not for their authenticity but exclusively for their interpretive potential.

In order to delineate the various aspects of this interpretive potential, we might return briefly to certain elements of the cultural context relics invoke, even within larger questions about the legitimacy of this devotional tradition. As indicated earlier, one of the forms of reliquaries in use during the fourteenth century was the reliquary monstrance, incorporating a crystal component—sometimes columnar—that allowed the relic to be seen within the reliquary. Some of these objects contained either relics or the host, so that their shape referred to both relic veneration and the ceremony of the Eucharist.[15] This form of reliquary began to develop in the thirteenth century and continued to be interpreted into the fourteenth and fifteenth.[16] We have discussed already Caroline Walker Bynum's important points about these reliquaries' potential for at once making visible earthly matter and at the same time suggesting its eventual transformation into something newly integral and ideal in the ultimate vision of resurrection and the heavenly Jerusalem. Michael Camille also points out, in an argument about optical theory in the late Middle Ages, that conceptions of the sacred were affected by the "earthly luminosity" and "the transforming power of transparency" that such objects suggested for their viewers.[17] Camille reveals that these objects dramatized a process of transformation in their use of visual symbol and metaphor. He uses as an example a fourteenth-century reliquary monstrance. Like the reliquary monstrance referred to earlier (figure Intr.5), it contains several architectural components, which provide a means for the reliquary to allude to an idealized heavenly Jerusalem. The artifact's central transparency elucidates an act of transformation occurring between the organic matter of the body and the reintegrating ideal of the heavenly Jerusalem. This reliquary monstrance embodies the idea that death is understood in certain areas of late-medieval material culture through an acknowledgment of transformative process, of translations made concrete and visual through light and transparency.[18] The fifteenth-century angel reliquary at the Louvre fulfills a similar function (figure 5.1). Its arresting juxtaposition of stylized, integral body and visible fragment asks us to imagine a process of transformation within the context of its static and iconic affect. These objects remind us of the conceptual work that medieval reliquaries did for their viewers.

This cultural backdrop suggests that visual transformation and the juxtaposition of organic matter with iconic, static integrity comprise the remaining conceptual residue once *The Pardoner's Tale* has invoked and then discarded its actual relics as meaningful objects. The tale's subsequent references to enshrinement continue to turn away from relics and

Figure 5.1 Angel with reliquary, also called "Angel of Brittany," fifteenth century. Gilt silver. Inv.: MR 550–551. Louvre, Paris, France.

Source: Photo by M. Beck-Coppola. Réunion des Musées Nationaux/Art Resource, New York.

reliquaries that mimetically represent such objects in the world. Instead, *The Pardoner's Tale* becomes increasingly invested, as it progresses, in the imagined object of enshrinement, the reliquary of the mind. The conceptual terms ordinarily attached to physical reliquaries—visuality, transformation, degeneration, stasis—float through the rest of the tale. Within the space of an imagined artifact of enshrinement, they articulate a performative process of figuration.

A Figure of *Figura*

In order to reveal its own imagined spaces of enshrinement, *The Pardoner's Tale* first posits a figure of *figura* surrounded by images of death and enclosure. This is the old man "al forwrapped save [his] face" (VI. 718). The exemplum describes the old man through images of enclosure, from the cloak in which he shrouds himself, to the mysterious chest and the chamber he mentions, to the wistfully desired "heyre clowt to wrappe" (VI. 736) his body, as well as the image of the ground on which he persistently knocks in order to ask to be taken into the earth and entombed. The old man gathers around himself not simply the imagery of death but more specifically the imagery of death's containment—graves, caskets, and winding sheets. He embodies through his self-accounting the juxtaposition inherent in medieval artifacts of death between the slow process of death within this world and the stasis that devotional artifice creates for it. And like the images of "cofer" and "kyste" in *Pearl*, the old man's description proposes enclosing structures as instrumental to acts of transformation.

Through this use of the imagery of enclosure, deeply rooted in artifact culture, the old man becomes a figure of figuration itself. His depiction employs the reliquary shrine's visual language of layered enclosure to portray the transformative space of metaphor. The old man has motivated a large number of interpretations, along with an equally large number of warnings against the danger of limiting his potential meaning to one type of analysis. I suggest here that the Pardoner's old man, in his dramatization of an attempt at enclosed transformation, models figuration as possessing the structure of devotional objects. As Ann W. Astell demonstrates, *translatio* and transformation play an important role in *The Pardoner's Tale*'s instances of signification and figuration, whether these involve the "identity of the rioters and the Old Man as *translationes* of each other" or the old man himself as "a sign that has strayed away from its proper grounding."[19] The medieval mechanism for theorizing these acts of transformative figuration takes the form of the reliquary as a culturally prevalent signifying object.

At the center of the old man's depiction is his face, and the text's attention to it suggests the old man's ability to stand in for figuration through a long history of association between face and *figura*. When he says of himself, "ful pale and welked is my face" (VI. 738), he enters himself into a network of face images in the tale. The old man's line, for instance, recalls the Pardoner's opening condemnation of the drunken man: "disfigured is thy face" (VI. 551). One of the rioters points out as well that that the old man is "al forwrapped save thy face" (VI. 714).[20] As Paul Ricoeur states, discussions of metaphor need to take into account the trope's basis in the idea of the figure as face, something visual: "By providing a kind of figurability to the message, the tropes make discourse appear."[21] Erich Auerbach ends *"Figura"* by describing the "the dominant view in the European Middle Ages: the idea that the earthly life is thoroughly real, with the reality of the flesh into which the Logos entered, but that with all its reality it is only *umbra* and *figura* of the authentic, future, ultimate truth, the real reality that will unveil and preserve the *figura*."[22] He claims here a historical basis for acknowledging the importance of *figura*'s concrete aspect, the idea of earthly reality itself as *figura*. Protruding from the veiling and enclosing objects all around him, the old man's face similarly suggests a complex relationship between figuration and the realm of the concrete and visible. Through its history as a concrete term, *figura* aligns itself with the old man's face, cast into relief by its enshrouding.

The old man's process of shifting between the concrete and the symbolic also makes him a figure of figuration.[23] As is probably evident to most readers of *"Figura,"* Auerbach's methods of choosing support for the particular trajectory of the term's development are not always clear. Nevertheless, his assessment of *figura* as a term capable of shifting between the senses of "form" or "model" and "copy" identifies the term's dual nature and transformative properties. In this context, Auerbach refers to Ovidian uses of *figura* as those that bring out most effectively the word's investment in "changing form." Auerbach's description of figural reading as a practice that both acknowledges the concrete and earthly and encompasses the *umbra*, the conceptual figuration, of some other truth emphasizes again this aspect of the dual nature of *figura*.[24] The duality of *figura* as both concrete and symbolic finds expression in other examinations of poetic language as well. For example, as Maggie Kilgour states, Ovid's conception of metaphor enables itself in the concrete and literalized terms of physical metamorphosis.[25] Transformative process thus stands as a necessary component in understanding acts of metaphor. These dualities of concrete and conceptual, and their role in metaphor, find application in the Pardoner's old man. John M. Steadman argues that Chaucer's portrayal of the old man indicates an interest in the tension between the "general idea rather than the individual example, the universal rather than the particular." Steadman points out that Chaucer's "attempt to delineate the general through the particular brings him close to the frontiers of allegory, but he does not actually cross."[26] Instead he navigates—albeit unwillingly—between the concrete and symbolic.

We see this navigation in the old man's struggle to transform himself in death, and this struggle reveals the nature of figuration as a process. A theological reading might define the old man's position—caught in both change and stasis—as Augustine's "second death." This is the idea of eternal punishment as eternally dying, or an "immortal death."[27] But his struggles with transformation have other conceptual resonances as well. Through his own self-description and his invocation of death, the old man hovers, like a character at the moment of Ovidian metamorphosis as metaphor, between an identity as an individual and as a conceptualization. But more specifically, the old man's words and actions emphasize that the transformation from any one state to another, whether understood as a shift from life to death or from death to a spiritual rebirth, is painful, difficult, and weighted with resistance. Detailing the process of his attempts at some kind of transformation, the old man claims:

> ...For I ne kan not fynde
> A man, though that I walked into Ynde,
> Neither in citee ne in no village,
> That wolde chaunge his youth for myn age;
> And therfore moot I han my age stille,
> As longe tyme as it is Goddes wille.
> (VI. 721–26)

The quest for change is laborious; it involves a pilgrimage of its own in order to find a suitable means of self-translation. On the one hand, as he points out, death itself will not take his body, forcing him into a painful state that does not allow him to change and die. On the other hand, he laments "Lo, how I vanysshe, flesh, and blood and skyn!" just before asking when his bones will finally find their resting place, depicting himself as undergoing an excruciating and perpetual transformation, one that renders his face "pale and welked" (VI. 738). He is frustrated in his suspension in time, ruefully explaining that it is "As longe tyme as it is Goddes wille" (VI. 726). At the same time, he is tortured by the unending transformation of his body. Through his paradoxical engagement with temporality, the old man shows how painful and difficult the transformative intersection can be. He makes the slow process explicit, and displays the toll it takes through his physical body.

The compromised body in *The Pardoner's Tale* must always also refer to the very process of verbal representation. Rita Copeland demonstrates that *The Pardoner's Tale* reflects a longstanding perspective on rhetorical expression through the imperiled body. Rhetoric, she argues, is conceived of, and expresses itself, as a fragmented and "transgressive" body, and it draws attention to its own transgression and fragmentation in order to stage its own correction (discipline) and necessary control.[28] Copeland has also argued that rhetoric becomes involved in the political dissension surrounding Lollardy through questions about the nature of literal meaning. Again, she invokes the trope of discipline and taming, explaining that rhetoric was able to remain involved in scriptural discourse by being "tam[ed]" and "confin[ed]...within the fixed boundaries of literal, grammatical exposition." The "institutional history" of rhetoric she creates in her account of the Pardoner usefully clarifies the connection between the concreteness of the body and the strategies that words employ in order to persuade or represent. By positing rhetoric as participating in its own correction, Copeland moves beyond a discussion of static principles to a discussion of active process and technique. She contends that the Pardoner "achieves his curative effects...not through his tale, but through his very presence as an embodiment—literally a bodying forth—of the danger of rhetoric." In doing so Copeland emphasizes the extent to which the symbolic, fragmented body is understood in the tale as a process of representation and of formulating meaning through its status as an object.[29] The old man locates himself at a transformative intersection between translation and the enclosure of artifice, and he is caught there, dramatizing and delimiting representational process.

Having established his engagement with transformation, we can now examine how the old man's enclosure functions as a mechanism for the transformative action of figurative language in particular. The language describing the old man emphasizes his potential for transformation by shrouding him in various kinds of (literal and figurative) obscurity. In recounting to the rioters his attempts to die, the old man repeats his habitual plaint to the earth:

> Allas, whan shul my bones been at reste?
> Mooder, with yow wolde I chaunge my cheste
> That in my chambre longe tyme hath be,
> Ye, for an heyre clowt to wrappe me!
> (VI. 733–36)

The closest source for this lament is the "Regret de Maximian."[30] This poem details sorrow at the disintegration of the body but does not incorporate the specific images of enclosure that Chaucer names here. The first elegy of Maximian contributes the scene of the aged man knocking on the ground, but similarly fails to display chests, chambers, or the other enclosures that Chaucer builds into his passage.[31] The device of alliteration here associates "chaunge," "cheste," and "chambre," connecting on the one hand a cluster of enclosing structures with, on the other hand, a reference to transformation.[32] *Chaunge* in this passage is most accurately understood as "exchange," although it included transformation among its meanings by the late fourteenth century.[33] The exchange of layered frameworks of enclosure (chest in chamber for haircloth and grave) in these lines creates a structure around the old man that incorporates the themes not only of enclosure but also of translation from one place—or one state—to another. He demonstrates R.A. Shoaf's point that metaphor, to Chaucer, offered "liberation from the fear of definition and category and nomination" through its implication in structures of exchange.[34] If the old man resists metaphoric attachment to any one particular vehicle—death, despair, greed—he can instead contain figurative representation within his body; in the chain of alliterative terms surrounding him he becomes the *translatio* inherent in metaphor.[35]

In using the form of enshrining artifacts to detail the process of figuration, the Pardoner's old man helps us to address some persistent theoretical questions about metaphoric language and how it functions. In his essay on metaphorical process, Paul Ricoeur argues that metaphor is a predicative construction, one constituted by the interaction between its two parts. The challenge in explicating the function of metaphor, Ricoeur says, is how to visualize that process, or see what is in the space between the two terms.[36] Ricoeur introduces the terms "feeling" and "imagination" to try to construct this oscillating and transformative space, but he expresses some hesitation about the psychologizing move required here. The Pardoner's old man refines Ricoeur's invocation of imagination by suggesting that in the medieval poetics of enshrinement, the act of imagination that enables metaphor takes an enshrining form. Enshrinement, as a practice in material culture and a visual system of signification, provides Ricoeur's transition point from "literal incongruence to metaphorical congruence between two semantic fields." This is the point he finds difficult to envision without recourse to the psychologizing terminologies of feeling and imagination; they become a way of explaining a "shift in the logical distance, from the far to the near."[37] In Ricoeur's terms, metaphorical congruence seems to imply that the two semantic fields become present to each other. As an object of enshrinement, the old man's body provides just such a space for these transformative processes. The accoutrements hung around his body, as well as his utterances, juxtapose death with its enclosing artifices in the culture of reliquaries. His relationship to his own death, articulated through references to his entombment, fluctuates between the near and the far, the illogical and the congruent. The old man continues his statement about his far-flung wandering, cited above, by saying:

> And on the grounde, which is my moodres gate,
> I knokke with my staf, bothe erly and late
> And seye, "Leeve moder, leet me in!"
>
> (VI. 729–31)

In these lines we see the old man's body again as containing both spatial and temporal paradox in its desire to be entombed. The ground as mother is both intimate and unattainable, and he finds himself always in the process of transforming but never fully transformed, specifically through his relationship to entombment and enclosure. His ambiguous occupation of space also acts out the reliquary shrine's traditional negotiation, what Peter Brown calls "the carefully maintained tension between distance and proximity."[38] In these ways the old man's status as surrounded by death's enclosures provides an alternative engine for the process of metaphor to Ricoeur's feeling and imagination. What enables the particular dynamics required for metaphoric expression is the structure of enshrinement, which bestows a shape upon the imaginative act.

Figuration and Event

The enclosing devices of the old man lead toward an enshrining dynamic for metaphor. If the old man figures figuration through his images of enclosure, then we might ask how *The Pardoner's Tale* uses this model throughout in the functioning of its figurative language. When we see the tale's metaphoric language in the terms of devotional objects, we also see the ways that metaphoric utterances frame and are framed by what they name into being. One example of figurative language elsewhere in the exemplum occurs during the youngest rioter's musings as he procures his fellows' mock-eucharistic meal:

> This youngeste, which that wente to the toun,
> Ful ofte in herte he rolleth up and doun
> The beaute of thise floryns newe and brighte.
> "O Lord!" quod he, "if so were that I myghte
> Have all this tresor to myself allone,
> There is no man that lyveth under the trone
> Of God that sholde lyve so murye as I!"

And atte laste the feend, oure enemy,
Putte in his thought that he sholde poyson beye,
With which he myghte sleen his felawes tweye.
(VI. 837–46)

In this passage, the use of "rolleth up and doun" as a metaphor conveys an act of thought at the same time that it associates itself more concretely with the physical properties of the florins themselves. The conditional constructions of desire in this passage are also paired with the conjuring of the florins in the rioter's mind. "Up and doun" appears as a ubiquitous motif in the *Canterbury Tales*, and many of its usages designate acts of imagination, figurative expression, and interpretation. For instance, in the *Knight's Tale*, walls are painted "up and doun" with images of hunting and "shamefast chastitee" (I. 2054–55). Egeus, meanwhile, "knew this worldes transmutacioun, / As he hadde seyn it chaunge bothe up and doun" (I. 2839–40), indicating that the phrase is used to describe transformation as well. More famously, the Wife of Bath sets up her argument with the statement, "Men may devyne and glosen, up and doun" (III. 26), associating the phrase with both rhetorical embellishment and interpretive practice. The rioter's own imaginative act participates in the transformative figuration of "up and doun" by creating a shift between literal and figurative registers. While the verb *rollen* can evoke the physical nature of the florins themselves as "gold ycoyned rounde" (VI. 770), its pairing with the phrase "up and doun" preserves the description's reference to a more abstracted act of the imaginative life, the temptation that the situation presents to wonder at potential and possibility. These physical and figurative meanings of *rollen* are both attested in the fourteenth century.[39]

The lessons that the old man teaches can explicate the metaphoric functioning of "rolleth" as imaginative process in this passage. The old man's embodiment of figuration revealed that the incongruous terms of figurative expression come together in a space of enshrinement. His strange and paradoxical body also confronted us with a meeting of the experiential and the aesthetic, death and the traditions of artifice surrounding it. In this passage's use of the term "rolleth," we see the constant oscillation between the reference to the physical object and the impulse toward ideation. "Rolleth" is always in a transformative process, but never fully transforming. It provides a set of images for an act of thought, and yet it never fully moves away from the concreteness of the round florins being pictured. "Rolleth" shows how a metaphor can always be on its way to death, like the old man (and like the rioter himself in this instance), but never quite arrive at death.[40]

When the rioter thinks about the coins, he also, according to medieval perspectives, employs the mechanisms of sight and visuality. The
episode at the end of the tale has been aptly described as a "brief glorying
over gold" placed in the context of a larger representational structure
that ultimately subsumes metaphor to the literal.[41] Within the youngest
rioter's brief act of supposition, however, exists an illuminating depiction of metaphor as a cognitive process that also has a visual identity.
The medieval mind, as both object and process, was in general highly
attuned to the mechanics of visuality and the formation of visual images.
This was the case not only in the particular context of devotional vision,
as the last chapter discussed, but also more generally around conceptions
of cognition and perception. Aquinas privileged sight in the hierarchy
of the senses, arguing that it required no change or mediation between
the eye and the spectacle.[42] And despite Augustinian cautions about the
fallibility of corporeal vision, the more absolute truth that "seeing and
knowing are inextricably linked in Western culture," as Suzanne Akbari
puts it, tends to obtain in medieval discussions of cognition and acts of
the mind.[43] Akbari has discussed the epistemological force of vision, the
similarities between its mediatory principles and those of language, and
the fact that medieval perceptions of brain function were closely linked
to sight and optics.[44] This relationship between seeing and knowing also
meant that medieval thinkers conceived of the mind's own structures in
terms of vision. The workings of the mind were themselves understood
through patterns of visual imagery, the architectural spaces of chambers
and *cellulae*.[45] This tradition suggests that the mind's very processes articulated themselves, and made themselves comprehensible, through tropes
of visuality and the imagery of the visual.

In the context of the mind's visually understood work, the rioter's
imaginative act demonstrates metaphoric process as a reliquary of the
mind. In the passage from *The Pardoner's Tale* cited above, the rioter's
mind specifically becomes an enclosing space. It holds a visual image of
the coins and also the process of "rolling" them—a figure for thinking
about them—within itself ("in herte"). The mind's status as an object of
enclosure receives further elaboration at the moment when we learn that
the devil has put a murderous thought into it. In the enclosure of the
rioter's consciousness (a kind of combination of "herte" and "thought"),
we thus see juxtaposed the golden florins, with their metaphoric connection to death, and the poison, a more literal and concrete rendering
of death's process.[46] Within the mind's reliquary, figurative expression
generates itself first by the constant shifting and transformation of *rollen* as
metaphoric usage. But *rollen*'s figural identity forms itself as well through
the enclosed juxtaposition of coins and poison. The introduction of literal

death through the thought of poison allows the coins' metaphoric connection to death to begin to construct itself within the enclosing space of the rioter's mind. In his own consciousness, desire connects the two, so that the coins signify the specific death of his fellows. But in the broader context of the tale, the enclosing space of the rioter's mind becomes a mechanism for making the coins a more general metaphor: they transform into a universal death through their enshrined juxtaposition with an instrument of death.

In this occurrence, the mental formation of metaphor leaves the realm of mere enclosure, and begins to participate in the dialectic of enshrinement. Through the transformation it engenders, the rioter's mind is both container and contained. The desiring utterance that exists within it transforms into an event, and each frames the other. Thomas Greene has suggested that the origins of all poetry locate themselves around the expression of a wish as a performative act. Poetry's ancestry includes spells in which the expression of desire brings an appropriation of some kind into being, and the poetic legacy of the invocation continues to call realities into being for the speaker.[47] Thus we might understand the rioter's statement of desire—"if so were that I myghte / Have all this tresor to myself alone..."—to function as a performative act set within the reliquary of the mind as a space of figuration. In conjunction with the figurative reference to death, the rioter's mental utterance performatively constitutes a situation in which murder and death are inevitable. This scene, however, goes further than simply allowing the rioter to speak something into being. The rioter's speech is part of an act of transformative figuration, and through this transformative context, the murder ultimately transfers itself out of the speech and into the unforseeability and exteriority of the event. Ultimately it takes all three rioters by surprise. As we have seen in other texts as well, performative language in medieval expression does not only constitute a reality that is then bounded by that language. Through the act of figuration, performative language also produces a condition separate from that language, genuinely unlooked-for. Whereas this dismantling of interiority and exteriority happened elsewhere through devotional practice, here it becomes, through the reliquary of the mind, a way of performing death itself.

Figuration and the Performative

These points provide a context for the tale's final imagined reliquary, which also becomes a performative space. The phrase "reliquary of the mind" does not necessarily imply only a mind as reliquary, as in the instance above. It can also potentially refer to a reliquary created in the mind, which is exactly what famously happens at the end of *The Pardoner's Tale*. In its closing section, the tale not only explicitly imagines a reliquary but also shows how the mental construction of this reliquary makes metaphor possible. Cursing the Pardoner, the Host calls forth an especially unsavory devotional object from his own mind. The Host's rhetorical gesture silences the Pardoner by imagining the Pardoner's "coillons," the bodily emblem of his indeterminacy, placed within a humiliatingly earthly enclosure:

> "Lat be," quod he, "it shal nat be, so theech!
> Thou woldest make me kisse thyn olde breech,
> And swere it were a relyk of a seint,
> Though it were with thy fundement depeint!
> But, by the croys which that Seint Eleyne fond,
> I wolde I hadde thy coillons in myn hond
> In stide of relikes or of seintuarie.
> Lat kutte hem of, I wol thee helpe hem carie;
> They shul be shryned in an hogges toord!"
>   (VI. 947–55)

In one sense it seems that a substitution takes place in this passage between "relikes"/"seintuarie" and "coillons." But in fact, the word "shryned" is the locus of figuration in this passage, allowing the hog's turd to be reimagined as a reliquary shrine. As was the case with "rolleth," the metaphoric impulse in this utterance lies in a verb, in, as Ricoeur describes it, the predicative and the process-oriented. Although the Host's words here silence the Pardoner for the remainder of the tale, they also introduce a final reference to the realm of relic veneration, one that reinforces the connection between cultural practice and figurative expression. But in addition, the Host's speech sets up a metaphoric expression that depends upon enshrinement not only in its content but also in its formal and imagistic means of conveyance. The reliquary, as we have seen, is an object in which such suspensions become possible. The host's imagined reliquary is both the metaphor itself and the structure that makes metaphor possible.

There are a number of ways in which the Host's reliquary displays a dialectics of spatial enshrinement in its own construction and the functioning of the language that represents it.[48] *Seintuarie* exists as an important term in this regard. The word generally refers to a shrine, but in this sentence it could also designate an actual relic. Benson refers the reader to Chrétien de Troyes's *Cligés*, lines 1194–1996; this text also capitalizes upon this term's potential dual meaning. In certain *Cligés* manuscripts, as I have discussed elsewhere, the Old French version of this word appears in a description of the holy shrine Jehan has built for a saint, but in which he plans to place the falsely dead Fenice. In this case the word emphasizes Fenice's holiness in the face of her apparent worldly debasement by adultery, in addition to the interaction she creates between containing edifice and contained holy object.[49] In designating both the contained relic and the reliquary as container, the word itself embodies a dichotomy characteristic of enshrinement: the oscillation between what is enclosed and what encloses. In an argument whose purpose is to locate the Pardoner's pants, and their fate, within a *fabliau* tradition, Richard Firth Green describes a Norman tale that similarly conflates relic and reliquary, observing that "the pants are precious not in themselves but for what they contain."[50] Thus the text invokes several inversions of container and contained around the Host's wishful utterance.[51]

Through the materials he chooses with which to construct it, the Host's specific image elaborates on the mechanism of transformation. The *seintuarie* to which the Host refers in his speech actively investigates the process of transformation between the actual bodily fragment in the cult of relics and its reinterpretation and reintegration, its transition between evanescence and permanence. It does so in part through its scatological associations. One explanation for the specific nature of the object the Host conjures is the capacity of the scatological to represent liminality, and specifically, in the context of the *Canterbury Tales*, the space between life and death. The *Prioress's Tale*, for instance, dramatizes this association with the depiction of the clergeon's body cast into the privy. As Richard Rambuss points out, drawing upon Mary Douglas's argument, "defilement...is typically framed as a matter of the marginal, as what has passed from the inside to the outside." This trope of marginality applies itself in the case of this tale to the boy's status as "suspended between this world and the next."[52] The excremental nature of the Host's shrine similarly alludes to this concept of liminality, creating a place of transition. The physical matter of the reliquary in this case reminds us of the inevitability of transformation even as it fulfills its enshrining function. Thus the physical features of this enshrining object embody the transformative and transitional act required in figurative expression. In creating his metaphor the Host is also creating the possibility of metaphor.

The materials of the Host's artifact also point toward the sacred artifact's temporality through its unique composition. The "coillons" it enshrines are indeterminate in status, and their invocation draws attention to the possibility of their absence, their removal from time. Simultaneously, the "hogges toord," as the material of enshrinement, exemplifies decay as the most earthly reminder of temporal passage. The process of metaphorization, the transition from hog's turd to shrine, draws attention to the shrine's manipulation of temporality. Actual shrines engage in forms of both stasis and progressive temporality in their acts of sacred enshrinement, juxtaposing degenerating materials with static ones. In the Host's imagined construction, the material of the enshrining artifact—usually one of permanence—here embodies a narrative of degradation and decay. The vividness of the Host's statement lies in the way that it powerfully combines the eternizing associations of the shrine with the transitory nature of bodily matter in the physical nature of the artifact itself. The Host's shrine takes to an extreme form the unusual temporality of the reliquary. Its freedom from the ontological limitations of actual reliquaries allows the imagined shrine to caricature the reliquary's transformative act through its particular enshrining material.[53]

This caricatured temporality of the reliquary helps us to make sense of the temporality of the Host's metaphor. The Host begins with a conditional statement of desire: "I wolde I hadde thy coillons in myn hond." He then, however, shifts the mood and tense of his declaration by introducing an imperative construction, an expression of volition combined with futurity: "Lat kutte hem of, I wol thee helpe hem carie." We saw that the old man as *figura* brought together time moving and time stagnating. The grammar of the Host's lines leading up to the final creation of the metaphor ("They shul be shryned in an hoggs toord!") demonstrates the necessity of this kind of complex temporality in the process of forming metaphor. The Host's yoking together of terms requires first that he imagine a kind of alternative present in which the testicles were in his hands. This puts him outside his habitual place in temporal progression. But in order to complete the metaphor, he reenters a progressive temporality and imagines his unique shrine by placing it in the future.[54] De Manian criticism has established one tradition for thinking about the relationship between time and figuration, largely through the essay "The Rhetoric of Temporality." In this work, de Man opposes symbol and allegory by referring to them, respectively, as spatial and temporal. Allegory "corresponds to the unveiling of an authentically temporal destiny," while symbol creates a problematic perception of simultaneity and coincidence.[55] This schematization allows us to see the relevance of temporality to figuration. But it also seems that the model of figuration articulated in *The Pardoner's Tale* offers a somewhat modified vision of the relationship between time and figurative expression. In the Host's speech, the process of figuration operates both in time and out of time. The reliquary provides a space in which this manipulation of temporality is not only possible, but also necessary. Thus, in terms of time as well, the construction of the metaphorical reliquary in his mind also becomes the site that accommodates this construction.

By juxtaposing his imagined reliquary with a reference to the True Cross, and specifically the narrative of its *inventio* by Saint Helena, the Host seems at first to return the tale to a discussion of truth and falsity. In one sense, the Host places what might be thought of as a "real" reliquary, the image of the True Cross as found by Saint Helena, alongside one that is clearly false. Melvin Storm proposes that this comparison allows Chaucer to emphasize the falsity of the Pardoner's own relics and the way in which they have almost distracted the group from their purpose, which privileges authenticity.[56] In this sense, the comparison speaks to the questions about truth claims often taken up in the criticism of this tale.

But this juxtaposition also allows the reader to move beyond the relic's legitimacy and toward the performative nature of the Host's metaphoric language. Both relics are performatively uttered. The Host's invocation of the True Cross appears in the form of an oath—"by the cross"—and its syntactical and logical integration with Host's imagined reliquary suggests that both take on the performative force that oaths imply. Throughout the tale, anxiety exists about the performative power of oaths. The Pardoner criticizes the swearing of the rioters by saying, "Oure blissed Lordes body they totere—/Hem thoughte that Jewes rente hym noghte ynough." (VI. 474–75). "Hir othes been so grete and so dampnable" (VI. 472), the Pardoner implies, because they are performative, and have the power to bring something into being between their own rhetorical energy and their connection to the Passion of Christ. The Host's final comment surrounds both true and false relics with the performative force of oath. The true cross asserts a legitimate materiality through the invention narrative implied in Saint Helena's invocation. The nature of the false relic's materiality, then, needs to be accounted for as well in its placement within the same context of the performative utterance. Its legitimacy and materiality inhere within the speech act itself. Like the rioter's mind, the Host's reliquary becomes a space of performativity. The verbal representation of the object is interwoven with some of the formal conventions of performative speech. As a result, a reliquary that seems to be situated in the mind becomes instead a reliquary of which the mind's processes are constructed.

Sermon Structure and the Reliquary of the Mind

When the Host names his imagined reliquary, he speaks into being a structure, a visual and material language with which to frame and understand the tale as a whole. This final section will use the visual terms of the poetics of enshrinement to suggest some ways of connecting different elements of the tale, and of considering its structure through the temporality and spatiality of the reliquary. The performative use of metaphor, seen in the exemplum's language and the Host's shrine image and oath, exists within the frame of the performed sermon. But the nature of this framing sermon is in turn inflected by the poetics of enshrinement located within it.

In other instances, the poetics of enshrinement has involved the dialectical enclosure of inscription and performance. But *The Pardoner's Tale*, as I suggested earlier, tends to separate inscriptional objects from performance objects. One reason that it does so might involve its need to emphasize the tale's formation by layering modes construed as speech and spectacle: the performance of preaching to the pilgrims and to the other audiences the Pardoner describes. As the conclusion to this study will eventually argue, inscriptionality is merely hidden in, rather than absent from, *The Pardoner's Tale*, and suggests itself in another form. But for the present, I contend that the tale models a version of the poetics of enshrinement in which various levels of performativity—often articulated through metaphor—enshrine each other. The blank reliquaries of *The Pardoner's Tale* emphasize not necessarily a poetics of orality over writing, but a structure of performance and the performative that enshrines itself, or that folds in upon itself.

The Pardoner's Tale is a performance first and foremost in its designation as a sermon. A long history of criticism exists concerning the extent to which the Pardoner's performance obeys the dictates of late-medieval preaching. H. Leith Spencer's survey of English sermon material asserts that while on the one hand there are "features of the Pardoner's *Prologue* which adequately indicate his author's familiarity with contemporary vernacular preaching styles," on the other hand it is important to "sto[p] readers attempting to force the text to seem to obey the rules of an *ars praedicandi*." The relationship between *The Pardoner's Tale* and the conventions of late-medieval preaching is one of experimentation and allusion rather than direct applicability.[57] For Alan J. Fletcher, "Even if the Pardoner preached 'som honest thyng' well, suspicion could have attached to his *form* [emphasis in original] of preaching" because of its "demotic" associations.[58] Thus form becomes a political issue here rather than a means of aesthetic categorization. And in some ways, Spencer's analysis of the sermon tradition suggests that to think about sermons at all means to think not about the establishment of form, but rather about the possibility of at once recognizing and undermining formal constraints. As a medium necessarily responsive to audience reaction, the structure and length of any given sermon were dictated to some degree by that audience. The "appearance of order" rather than an ideal of symmetry became the goal.[59] The stucture of the tale reflects these issues.

One clear element of Chaucer's use of the sermon and exemplum form in his tale, however, is its reliance upon patterns of enclosure, as well as the complication of such patterns. The presentation of the sermon and exemplum structurally involves a few layers of enclosure. At the center is the exemplum itself, which in somewhat conventional fashion is surrounded by the sermon commentary and the return to the Pardoner's inveighing against the catalogue of sins (VI. 895–99), which launched his oratory. Outside this layer are the Pardoner's interactions with the other pilgrims. These layers, however, intersect in different ways. For example, within the scaffolding of the Pardoner's discourse on sin, the story of the three rioters finds itself transformed and affected by that which encloses it. Fletcher assesses the Pardoner's remarks as paralleling a particular type of sermon in John Mirk's *Festial*, in which the category of "modern" form is somewhat loosely understood and in which the exemplum "acquires inflated importance."[60] This parallel suggests that, relative to sermons in the modern style, the Pardoner's sermon uses its opening and closing oratory—whether or not one considers this a "theme" in the traditional sense—to make the central exemplum into a more significant object. Its dictates move outside and define the layers that enclose it.

In a similar fashion, the opening and closing invocations of the relics determine the meaning of the sermon and performance to the other pilgrims. These references also participate in the dynamics of enshrinement. As Glenn Burger characterizes the frame around the tale, "Harry Bailly's simplistic attempt to re-form the pilgrimage body by excising the Pardoner replicates the desire of relic worshippers to fetishize a part rather than a whole and thus falsely appropriate the meaning of the relic as their own." But relics themselves are both material and transforming, "highlighting sameness and difference." Their qualities affect their ability to convey the holy and define our relationship to it. They thus define the relationship of the pilgrimage to the tale. Even if, as Burger contends, the kiss at the end of the tale provides the clearest emblem of the moral complexity that the Pardoner reflects in the rest of the pilgrims, it is the relics that allow his actions to suspend themselves between truth and falsity. The ambiguous way in which the Pardoner presents them in his performance underlies both the pilgrims' and the reader's uncertainties about him.[61]

Reading the tale's structure through the mechanism of enshrinement means that the tale as a whole becomes legible specifically by means of a poetics, rather than only through its cultural and generic associations. Another way to think about the structure of the whole tale as a series of concentric enclosures informing and reaching back out to each other is through Lee Patterson's argument about penitential process in this tale.

The framework upon which Patterson's argument about *The Pardoner's Tale* focuses is that of confession and penance, and the Pardoner's speech and actions work out his relationship to, and place within or without, this system. The choices the Pardoner makes in telling his tale and offering his relics to the pilgrims form a process of devotional practice even as they critique this practice; as Patterson puts it, "the Pardoner's confession contains within it an anti-confession. It is a penitential act that challenges the legitimacy of the very penance it seeks to perform."[62] Reexamining this assessment through the structure of enshrinement, we see a moment of performance folding in upon itself. The critique frames the performance of the penitential act but is at the same time an integral part of its construction and embedded within it. This effect resonates with the rioter's performative metaphor. In both cases, the speaker utters something at once constitutive and unexpectedly self-canceling. Seeing this parallel allows us to include the structure and mechanics of the sermon within the tale's poetics of enshrinement.

This association between the sermon structure and the tale's forms for poetic figuration obtains as well when we consider that *The Pardoner's Tale* is already a copy of a previously imagined performance. It involves the Pardoner replicating an originary ideal of another performance: the actual sermon preached before his followers. Performance inheres within the aesthetic of *The Pardoner's Tale*, from the Pardoner's self-descriptions as a performer to his declamation to the pilgrims.[63] But performance here also carries the performative sense of speaking something into being, making the utterance into an occurrence or object through its structure. Britton Harwood applies traditional Austinian categories of the performative to this discussion, seeing in the tale essentially a shift between performative and constative utterances.[64] It is equally possible to understand the Pardoner's performance as once again folding in upon itself, borrowing the visual language of enfolding objects like the Stavelot triptych to illuminate the text's structure. The frame and exemplum create a narrative moment, unique to the pilgrims' situation, in which the Pardoner's speech holds the capacity to constitute the spectacle he was only attempting to represent mimetically. It then becomes difficult to determine which category of utterance frames and which is being framed: do the Pardoner's direct addresses to his audience essentially comprise an actual sermon, or are they conventions of the sermon as verbally created spectacle, carrying a separate performance identity? The Pardoner's declaration to his audience that he is going to mimic one of his own sermons seems to enclose his subsequent narration. And yet that narration becomes a performance occasion in its own right, encompassing the experience to such an extent that the Pardoner himself loses sight of the frame he established. We saw a related dynamic at work in *Saint Erkenwald*'s speech within a speech, a moment when what appeared to be the representation of performative speech ended up functioning performatively. In *The Pardoner's Tale* structural enshrinement functions to describe the indistinction between a description of a scene of utterance and an actual scene of utterance potentially taking over. The fact that this formal dynamic originates in the tale's construction of metaphor suggests again that the sermon structure itself in *The Pardoner's Tale* is not simply a gesture toward historical conventions or a thematic exercise in the problem of signification. It is rather a participatory element in the tale's poetics of enshrinement.

Viewed as a kind of self-enshrining performance, the Pardoner's sermon becomes a copy of something whose original identity is entirely indeterminate. In this way, the tale finally reenters the dynamics of inscriptionality that it has seemed for the most part to occlude. The Pardoner's performance embodies the complex iterability of inscription itself. In the tale's negotiation between absent and present performance, and the difficulties inherent in this distinction, lies the *différance* of the written character. This chapter's reading of *The Pardoner's Tale* has for the most part capitalized upon the text's submersion of inscriptional thematics in order to explore another possibility for the poetics of enshrinement— one that privileges performance itself, and the ways that performative acts might frame each other. *The Pardoner's Tale* shifts the materials of the dialectic into a different cognitive realm, in which metaphor itself takes place through spatial form. But as we see here, the difference and deferral of inscriptionality are ultimately not absent from this tale's formal identity. The conclusion to this study will investigate this point further by means of a reminder that lyric—a form of poetry deeply connected to inscriptionality in the Middle Ages—played a vital role in medieval sermon tradition. Lyric reinstates this study's awareness of the inscriptional work of poetry even as it illuminates poetry's performative dimensions.

CONCLUSION

A LYRIC POETICS OF ENSHRINEMENT

As a dialectical interaction between inscription and performance, the poetics of enshrinement traces cultural trajectories in the late Middle Ages among visual art, conceptual discourses on representation, and narrative poetic form. But this method of understanding poetic representation also applies itself to a category of verse that dominates poetic culture after the Middle Ages: the lyric. This study will end by investigating the possibility of a specifically lyric poetics of enshrinement for the late Middle Ages. As with other forms of poetry we have examined, medieval lyric similarly negotiates between the modes of inscription and performance. The enshrining dialectic of inscription and performance provides a way of characterizing the nature of lyric voice. And as I shall ultimately argue, this characterization of voice and the lyric self not only has relevance in medieval literary traditions but also contributes usefully to the study of certain postmedieval lyric traditions.

Both during the Middle Ages and in critical studies of this period, lyric's status as a genre has appeared both vexed and degraded; however, some of these very complexities lead to intriguing possibilities for understanding the nature of the medieval lyric speaker. Glending Olson concedes that English court lyrics are thought to be "at best graceful and charming and at worst (the condition that usually obtains) repetitive and vapid."[1] Gregory Roper suggests that English lyrics' dialectal vernacularity, combined with their folk associations, made them "less a part of the high literary culture" as well.[2] Lyric's particular means of occupying the spectrum between sacred and secular is also complex. Some of the most famous devotional lyrics, such as "I sing of a maiden," display secular and popular elements in their formal features.[3] The tradition of courtly and secular lyrics, meanwhile, often finds ways to ally itself with devotional convention, as in the case of Froissart's love lyrics carefully kept inside reliquaries.[4] But through some of these ambivalences and ambiguities, the medieval lyric provides interesting opportunities for a conclusion to this study. Its complexity as a genre allows it to forestall simple constructions of the lyric speaker. It raises questions about agency and collectivity in poetic voice, to which later experimental traditions return. Some of these later traditions can help us to understand more deeply the medieval poetics of enshrinement, but in addition, the medieval poetics of enshrinement provides some ways of defining and shaping the lyric self in other traditions that struggle with this concept.

Like inscription, lyric is an occluded element in the Pardoner's performance. Although his sermon stays within the realm of narrative, medieval lyrics often appeared as part of sermon manuscripts. As Siegfried Wenzel speculates, they took their specific forms and functions from their usefulness to the preacher's work.[5] Lyric's link to sermon tradition offers one way for this poetry's language to function performatively. As *The Pardoner's Tale* suggested, the performative force of the sermon speaks its components into being; Claire Waters has pointed out the performative and embodying power of the vivid example in preaching tradition.[6] The lyrics embedded in sermons participate in this performative work. While Wenzel's account of preaching texts as a "generative center for the production of English lyrics" might in some instances seem to exaggerate the case, his point about the role of rhymed sermon divisions as part of the evolution of English lyric is extremely suggestive.[7] Through its formation within the sermon, lyric also contributes to the performance of the sermon. Wenzel's findings imply that rhymed embellishment, "devices that we would consider 'poetic,'" made important contributions to the performed occasion of the sermon, and lent to the sermon's performative work of bringing new consciousness into being.[8] Within the context of the sermon, the lyric verse's "ulterior intention is to affect the will and to move; and this relates them closely to the rhymed advertisement jingles and political slogans of our day."[9] Alan J. Fletcher sees a complex generic and stylistic relationship between the poetic texts embedded in sermons and their prose contexts, distinguishing between lyrics that evolve as part of the transitional structures of a sermon, and those that do not.[10] In these latter cases as well, lyric functions as part of the performance of the sermon and defines its purpose through the conditions of faith that the sermon produces. If late-medieval English culture saw an opportunity to experiment with the lyric form in particular, then this desire to experiment existed in part within the performative, constitutive contexts of actual sermons and their literary reconstructions.

While the sermon as performed occasion provides one avenue for seeing lyric language's performative potential, other, more subtle ways also exist in the institutions of readership and reception. For instance,

Jessica Brantley's identification of the mode of performative reading obtains with particular relevance for the lyric poems she examines.
Looking at lyrics in the context of the images and layouts that accompany
and define them, she reads such poems as asking for "a kind of 'looking' in the mind." Focusing on the visual qualities of meditative lyric,
Brantley argues that "the reader...enacts...meditative lyrics, as they take
up performative modes of both authorial and readerly kinds."[11] Thus even
in situations that appear private, internal, and silent, the lyric displays performative force. Through the interaction of text and image in which certain lyrics engage, Brantley argues, "the meditational dynamic is blurred
and changed, transformed finally into a performative one."[12] Beyond lyrics located in a manuscript tradition that encourages this kind of visual-
ized, performance-based perspective, we also find poems, as Christiania
Whitehead argues, that "belong in settings of public celebration."[13] These
are lyrics that formally identify themselves as carols, and therefore suggest
an aesthetic attachment to sung performance even if their primary identity
appears to be private and meditative. Whitehead reinforces her point by
alluding to the number of nativity lyrics that make explicit references to
acts of singing within their imagery and narrative. In addition, she uses the
Passion lyric "I sike al when I singe" to demonstrate a charged interaction
between singing and seeing.[14] In this way as well, lyric poetry builds itself
upon the aesthetics and conventions of spectacle and performed occasion.

While it draws on these conventions, however, the medieval lyric also
foregrounds its inscriptional aspects. In different ways, medieval lyrics
draw attention to the materiality of their inscribed characters. Emily
Steiner has suggested that in the perspective of medieval poets, lyric
was a "material genre."[15] Lyrics such as the fifteenth-century love poem
"Go! little bill..." use self-reference as a written document, as well as
the imagery of "imprinted" (l. 19) and "iwrit" (l. 24) beauty, to draw
attention to their own status as inscriptional objects.[16] The fourteenth-
century meditational lyric "Jesu, that hast me dere iboght" engages in
a similar strategy by repeating the command to Christ to "Write upon
my hert boke" (l. 29); "write in my hert depe" (l. 41); and "yit write in
my hert" (l. 49).[17] Furthermore, the manuscript-based purpose of lyrics relates explicitly, in a somewhat different way, to their identity as
marks on the page. As Julia Boffey has argued, "Lyrics were...frequently
used as fillers in manuscripts, copied to occupy what would otherwise
have been blank space at the end of a gathering or a whole work." Some
were part of the copyist's plan, while others appear more randomly motivated.[18] In either case, however, the lyric again functions spatially as a
set of inscriptional marks; its potential to help the copyist manipulate
the way that physical space is used on the page again defines its identity

through its inscribed status. As Boffey and Wenzel both discuss, the verse forms of lyrics sometimes engaged in dynamic visual interactions with their surrounding prose contexts.[19] Because of their generic features, such as compactness and elaborate verse structure, lyrics were a form of poetic expression especially suited to asserting the materiality of physically and visually inscribed characters.[20]

The lyric offers its own ways of integrating the two traditions of inscription and performance. In discussing lyrics in sermons, Wenzel refers to the "Elopement of Princess" exemplum tradition, which featured a series of inscribed gift-objects; when rendered on paper, these inscriptions took the form of short verses, in both Latin and English. Wenzel illustrates that lines from one of the inscriptions also appear elsewhere in a manuscript containing the exemplum, as part of a verse illustrating the characteristics of Christ. The verse appears once again in the moralization for the elopement exemplum.[21] We might at first, thus, characterize the relationship of inscription and performance as a kind of simple embedding: within the vocal performance of the sermon is inlaid a reference to verses that exist in material form, attached to the symbolic objects that the sermon enumerates. But the fact that these verses, whose original identity marks them as physical inscription, then interweave themselves into other sermon-based contexts as well suggests the possibility of a more multilayered model for describing the interaction of inscription and performance through lyric verse.

I would argue that the lyric articulates this interaction through the poetics of enshrinement. In order to make this case, I shall focus on a late-medieval lyric appearing in the fifteenth-century Cambridge Magdalene College MS Pepys 1236, folio 128r. (figure Cn.1):

> In 8 is alle my love) _
> And 9 be isette before;) IHC
> So 8 be iclosed above,)
> Thane 3 is good therefore.)[22]

This short poem operates as both visual puzzle and serialized speech act. The manuscript catalogue calls this piece of writing a "number puzzle in verse" and a "single quatrain." On the spine of the manuscript appears a later label indicating that it contains "monkish rhymes."[23] The lyric fills out the space left on a manuscript page otherwise taken up by a musical passage. This is a monophonic sacred chant that might have functioned as a recessional upon the conclusion of the Sarum rite, which occupies much of the rest of the manuscript.[24] Thus the manuscript page stages a suggestive convergence of many issues relevant to this discussion: the

Figure Cn.1 Cambridge Magdalene College MS Pepys 1236, fol. 128r., ca. 1460–65.

Source: The Pepys Library, Magdalene College, Cambridge.

visible and spatial function of the inscribed verse; the performance-based connotations of the musical setting; and finally, the intriguing shadow of the individual voice (in the monophonic chant) hovering over the short poem, an issue to which I shall presently return.

More specifically, however, "In 8..."'s form on the page engages in intersecting and juxtaposed layers of enclosure. Like the reliquaries we have examined throughout, the poem's proliferation of enclosing structures also raises questions about the meaning of interiority relative to exteriority, and the role of juxtaposition in creating frameworks of enclosure. The H of the monogram is spatially enclosed within the I and C, while at the same time the poem makes reference to the mark by which the H is "iclosed" (1. 3). The poem's form investigates the act of enclosing a central vestige of Christ. In the transverse crossing the H, the manuscript also contains and unifies the monogram and subtly suggests the shape of the cross.[25] Furthermore, interweaving braces connect the lines of the quatrain and are also crossed by the transverse running through the H. This structure creates a graphic link between the monogram and the poem, one that seems visually to combine enclosing and juxtaposing impulses. The network of lines juxtaposes the iconic monogram with the narrative verse, but at the same time it also raises two alternative possibilities for a structure of containment—that either the IHC encompasses its explanatory narrative, or the series of verses shapes and contains the monogram.[26] As medieval reliquary shrines suggest, narrative or aesthetic representations coexisted with visible fragments and vestiges of the holy dead, so that each one might be seen to contain and contextualize the other. Here, the short lyric can express through the visual languages of reliquaries a conceptual model of dialectical enclosure in its form.

The means by which the poem's text represents the Christ figure involves a frame of performance. We might say that the poem's performative dimension enables, produces, and frames the monogram. The sequential enunciation of the lines builds the monogram as both language and physical object. In each line's enactment of a step to create the monogram, the poem as utterance brings it into being. Its language does not just narrate, but in fact performs the Christ monogram through temporalized process. Looking at the two components side by side on the page, then, we might see the serially performed verses as exterior and anterior to the iconic monogram.

We might equally say, of course, that the inscriptional aspect of this poem underlies the performative gesture in the first place. This lyric's interesting use of numbers to correspond to letters highlights the letters' capacities to function as marks on a page; they become part of a code that functions visually, a relationship of spatial correspondence between letters and numbers as signifying marks. But this very correspondence also points toward the internal differences of the inscriptional marks. By introducing the system of numbers, the poem emphasizes the relational quality of its inscriptional characters, the extent to which they define themselves through their interactions with other characters. And in their pairing with numbers, another category of signs, the letters become indeterminate within their own natures. The interaction between letters and numbers emphasizes both the relational play of difference in each system, and each system's potential arbitrariness as inscriptional marks. The letters in this context are both productive and fragmented from themselves, like Hillis Miller's dehiscent seedpods.[27] "In 8..."'s central conceit thus emphasizes the features of the characters as inscriptional marks, so that the implications of inscriptionality become an essential element in the construction of the monogram.

The IHC monogram itself goes even further by carrying within itself a particular inscriptional anteriority, functioning as a constitutive frame. IHC embodies the material residue of the performative process embedded in the verse. But it is also a *vestigium* of Christ—in name and body—whose origin locates itself outside the poem's constitutive utterance. It is a mark existing as anterior and exterior to the verse's temporal performance of it. IHC is an inscriptional locus that contains difference and deferral within itself, because it seems both to precede and follow, to exist both inside and outside the narrative declaration with which the braces and lines on the manuscript page bind it. But in addition, the IHC monogram suggests that even if linguistic trace is always already effaced, in Derrida's vision, material traces in other cultural forms can be essential ingredients in understanding language's inscriptional self-reference and codes of *différance*. In Miller's reading of Derrida, inscriptional marks can "turn into forces" through only the most mysterious, indefinable, and problematic channels.[28] "In 8..."'s combination of coded verse and monogram elucidates the process by which inscriptional marks take on constitutive force. The lyric suggests an encounter between absence (Christ emptied out of the monogram, which is only a vestige of what was once bodily there) and presence (the devotional occasion performed through the sequential recitation of verse, which makes Christ present in the monogram). The culture of devotion and the uses of the material vestige elucidate the means by which the inscriptional monogram functions as at once absent and present. The monogram as a set of inscriptional marks is always already engaged with the complexities of representing Christ. Its constitutive force derives from the fact that it establishes a representational process anterior to the poem's act of narration. The monogram brings into being not Christ, but the nature of representational process surrounding Christ, an interaction between verbal and material form. As a set of strategies for representing Christ, this brief quatrain crystallizes the poetics of enshrinement for the lyric.

If the poetics of enshrinement functions as a way to understand lyric as a poetic mode, then it becomes possible to ask how such a poetics might inform a discussion of this mode beyond the historical moment of the Middle Ages. Because the poetics of enshrinement bases itself upon the interaction between verbal and visual representation, one potential answer to this question lies in later lyric engagement with visual art. In determining what kinds of later lyric traditions resonate most powerfully with the poetics of enshrinement in this way, however, we must acknowledge that certain forms of modern and postmodern poetry emerge as more relevant than the early modern lyric tradition immediately following the fifteenth century. In assessing the viability of analogies between poetic language and visual images, early modern and modernist critical discourse has acknowledged certain anxieties about dismantling or preserving the very categories of text and image. W.J.T. Mitchell uses the phrase "ekphrastic fear" to describe the moment "when we sense that the difference between verbal and visual representation might collapse and the figurative, imaginary desire of ekphrasis might be realized literally and actually."[29] In discourses preceding Mitchell, this fear is apparent. Examinations of the "sister arts," painting and poetry, have in particular traditionally reflected hesitations about the limits inherent in drawing analogies between the two forms; the limits, that is to say, of the Horatian *ut pictura poesis* formulation.[30] These hesitations have located themselves, for instance, in Leonardo da Vinci's distinction between the successive temporality of linguistic signs and the liberating and natural instantaneousness of the visual image; and, most famously, in Lessing's *Laokoön*, which addressed what its author saw as a growing sense of confusion about the characterization of the arts by distinguishing between poetry as a temporal art and painting as a spatial one.[31]

Twentieth-century poetics and criticism, on the other hand, have experimented in different ways with this relationship. In his examination of ekphrastic poetry, for instance, Murray Krieger draws upon the work of E.H. Gombrich to question the distinction between natural and conventional signs and to posit the narrative and temporal capacities of visual images.[32] Criticism from the 1980s draws upon the Hegelian possibility of transcending language's temporality to achieve aesthetic stasis. It complicates from another angle the earlier distinctions between the representational strategies of painting and poetry.[33] In addition, Krieger and Mitchell have turned toward ekphrasis as a way of understanding what they see as all poetic language's movement toward its own spatiality.

Michael Davidson takes this line of thinking in another direction, and away from traditional conceptions of ekphrasis. He argues that rather than conceiving of inter-art relationships in terms of ekphrasis, we might see them instead as an interaction of verbal and visual language. Specifically, the "painterly poems" of the New York School represent a tradition of postmodernity (independent of more drawn-out narrative poetic forms) that challenges the notion of simply "recover[ing]" a painting through linguistic narrative in order to emphasize the complexity of the materiality constituted in poetry. This particular postmodern tradition, represented in certain poems of O'Hara's and Ashbery's, works out instead "the instability of the object, its extension in a larger world of signs."[34] These poems capitalize on intersections between verbal and visual forms of signification, not simply by attempting to replicate content, but rather by focusing on formal features—fragmented imagery, framing, "semiotic and stylistic factors within the canvas"—in order to illuminate the relationship between painting and poetry.[35] As a poetics that argues for the potential of visual languages to elucidate verbal strategies of representation, the medieval dialectics of enshrinement might therefore hold potential for illuminating some of the buttresses and cantilevers supporting postmodern poetry's connections to the world of visual art.

I would like to make a slightly more encompassing case here, however, and suggest that through its interactions between inscriptionality and the material arts of performance, the poetics of enshrinement constructs lyric voice itself in both medieval and postmedieval contexts. As aspects of lyric that have always occupied critical attention, voice and self have suspended a bridge (albeit a sometimes fragile one) between earlier and later lyric. The poetics of enshrinement provides a means of describing the lyric self both in the Middle Ages and beyond. Even in the short devotional quatrain just discussed, the first person asserts itself in the first line, foregrounding the role of "my love" as a frame of its own for the monogram's constitution. In addition, the lyric's placement underneath a script for performance emphasizing the individual speaker raises questions about the nature of the speaker's voice in the poem as well. Returning to this study's opening invocation of the *Book of the Duchess*'s inset lyric will develop further the claim that the lyric self emerges through the mutual framing of inscription and performance at work in the poetics of enshrinement.

As a specifically medieval phenomenon, the lyric "I" maintains a productively indeterminate relationship to the concept of personhood. Leo Spitzer's foundational essay on medieval lyric suggests that the poetic "I" was universal in this tradition: "literature dealt not with the individual but with mankind."[36] For didactic purposes, the "I" was autobiographical only to the extent to which everyone participated in the human weakness it represented. The medieval poetic "I" was personal, yet not individual.[37] Revisitings of this argument refine the process by which the poem constructs a lyric self, but they continue to maintain that the articulation of this self has a complex relationship to the idea of the person. Judson Allen, for instance, sees the medieval poetic "I" as articulated through the "serial experience" of the medieval lyric text. In this process-oriented view of the poem's construction of a lyric self, Allen argues, "pronouns...exist as ideal or universal to each member of the audience's own particularity and invite him to perfect or universalize himself by occupying that language as his own."[38] Thus Allen refines Spitzer's earlier claim by specifying the formal means by which the process of universalization takes place. Gregory Roper and David L. Jeffrey interpret the "I" as carrying specifically penitential force. Roper directly challenges his predecessors' arguments with his own claim that the lyric self "is trying not just to allow us to *occupy* its 'I,' but to *reshape* us, ourselves, our 'I's, through its experience."[39] Jeffrey's reading of the lyric's place in Franciscan spirituality similarly reinforces lyric's contribution to a "psychological movement toward penance."[40] Thus for many of these critics, the lyric "I" continuously approaches and retracts from its own potential personhood.

Exploring this "I" further will entail a return to the knight's inset lyric in the *Book of the Duchess*, which provided an initiating demonstration of the poetics of enshrinement. This text illustrates that the complexity of the medieval lyric "I" exists through lyric's engagement with the dialectics of inscription and performance. As Louise Fradenburg and others have shown, voice stands out as an important issue in the *Book of the Duchess* as a whole.[41] While we looked before at the lyric's narrative frame, I shall focus now on the enshrined poem's own language, some of the verses associated with the knight himself:

> I have of sorwe so gret won
> That joye gete I never non,
> Now that I see my lady bright,
> Which I have loved with al my might,
> Is fro me ded and ys agoon.

> Allas, deth, what ayleth the,
> That thou noldest have taken me,
> Whan thou toke my lady swete,
> That was so fair, so fresh, so fre,
> So good that men may wel se
> Of al goodnesse she had no mete!
>
> (ll. 475–86)[42]

As I argued in chapter 1, the lyric utterance's setting within the poem delineates a double triptych form involving the knight's performing body and his poem as material inscription. In this dialectical enshrinement of inscription and performance, the voice of the lyric speaker emerges as having a specifically formal connection to his body. The "I" of the knight's inset lyric articulates its unique relationship to the self through the body's implication in enshrining forms. The references to the knight's body surrounding and containing his utterance reach toward an ideal of the present speaker in this scenario. And yet, the knight is in several ways fragmented from this section's allusions to voice. His song is songless—a complaint expressed without a note—and by line 503 he seems unable to speak. Poststructuralist doctrine maintains that the self-identical utterance cannot really exist, that the written sign always exists in a state of having been broken from its context and source.[43] The poetics of enshrinement shows us how this dynamic functions in the case of the knight. The narrative's ambiguous uses of performance and inscription resist an easy association between the knight as embodied figure and his poem's lyric voice. The double triptych form enshrining this verse shifts the knight between frames of embodiment and silent inscription, so that his relationship to voice in his lyric utterance is always indeterminate. With its ties to both silent inscription and voiced performance, the "maner song" imagines the memorial voice as constituted by the "functional structure" of the inscriptional mark, while at the same time existing as performance.[44]

The form of the knight's lyric also pushes the voice outside its self-construction and into the unforeseen event. As Arthur Bahr points out, the knight's language is for the most part deeply conventional, and Bahr sees its "psychological interest" as "supported by rhetorical structure."[45] These rhetorical techniques involve self-enfolding chiastic patterns.[46] Like Bahr, Robert A. Watson reads the vision as occupying an identifiable form, that of the Platonic dialogue.[47] In both these readings, the poem creates a sense of agency, and generates a speaking persona, through the occupation of a form. In the specific instance of the knight's inset lyric, the particular formal device of the pronoun shift similarly dictates its strategies of representation. The first stanza focuses on the "I" in the present tense, while the second addresses the "you" of death and moves into the past. In the larger context of the dream vision, the lyric appears in one sense to use its stanzaic and pronoun structure to create a series of temporalized layers: within the present of the dreamer's experience lies the present of the knight's self-accounting—"Now that I see..." (l. 477). And within this present is buried a recollection of the past, the moment of death itself that is fragmented from the speaker through his turn in address to "you." His desire to have been taken instead of the lady represents another form of fragmentation from the self as well here. Like the physical inscriptions within the dreamer's utterance of his vision early in the poem, the inset lyric exists in the form of poetic inscription within the layers of the dreamer's and knight's bodily performances. But in this poem that is also a memorial artifact, the poetics of enshrinement complicates the above formulation even as it constructs the lyric subject. The shift into the past tense emphasizes the anteriority of the second stanza. This second stanza, thus, is not simply an inset scrap of verse. It is a death-driven event, formed as a lyric stanza, which frames the knight's entire performance even as it exists at the center of the dream's many layers.

In their negotiation between past and present, and between I and you, the two lyric stanzas accordingly render indeterminate the location of the knight's own presence in the poem. As the dramatic texts from N-Town and the devotional contexts of *Saint Erkenwald* suggested, the artistic manufacture of intersections between poetic language and performing bodies necessarily complicates the location of presence. Furthermore, in the larger multilayered vision of the dream, the knight is himself constructed of inscription, a "whit wal or table" (l. 780) engraved with laudatory signs. The lyric "I" in this poem therefore contains itself alternately within bodily acts and written inscription. This poetic "I" suggests that the medieval lyric "I" situates itself through its inscriptional and performative aspects, each of which provides a potential frame and encompassing context for the other. The lyric subject's own identity as inscriptional and performative oscillates between inscription and performance as framing each other. In this way, a poetics derived from material culture gives form to the specific elusiveness of the medieval lyric "I."

The historical and critical trajectory emerging subsequent to this late-medieval sense of lyric voice, however, seems in certain respects to abandon this indeterminacy. Lois Ebin's characterization of an earnestly self-designating aureate style in poets making the transition into the early modern period differs significantly from the more ironic and distanced sense of poetic voice associated specifically with the lyric tradition in the Middle Ages. The poetic voice seems to change in spirit as it moves from an unlocatable and multidimensional sense of the lyric subject to a less equivocating declaration of the worthy work of the poet.[48] This is not to imply that the poetic self of Chaucer's inheritors lacks complexity, but rather that this self bears a definite relationship—albeit a sophisticated one—to what Robert J. Meyer-Lee calls a "historically specific *person*" as "a normative formal feature." As Meyer-Lee has argued, this fifteenth-century transitional group preoccupies itself with "constructing a first-person poetic speaker" as part of "a practice of English laureate self-representation."[49] This kind of speaker possesses a being and consciousness that differ from the lyric tradition we have been discussing.

Instead of following the trajectory from the Middle Ages into the beginnings of the early modern period, therefore, I shall embrace a different strategy and consider again an instance in lyric tradition whose features, while more distant in time from the Middle Ages, may in fact speak to and explicate the aims of medieval lyric more fully and deeply. The tradition of contemporary lyric poetics has demanded a revisiting of the nature of lyric voice, particularly in the context of language poetry and other experimental traditions. We have in a sense cycled back to a situation in which the humanist subjectivity of the lyric "I" is once again as subtly complex as it was in the Middle Ages. Marjorie Perloff has argued that language poetics have developed with a view toward "the dismissal of 'voice' as the foundational principle of lyric poetry." She situates this impulse within the larger context of poststructuralist criticism.[50] Michael Greer sees in language poetry a "collective, multiply voiced poetic project" and "an impulse to disperse and displace the speaking subject as it is conventionally known."[51] Oren Izenberg offers a critique of this invocation of collectivity, pointing out that in attempting to define itself in terms of oppositional communities, language poetry chooses one culture or community over another only to subject itself to new forms of convention. This tradition problematically results in a "fantasy of no situation."[52] Other poets and critics approach in different ways the resulting problem of negotiating between the self and community in poetry, as in Lyn Hejinian's point that "the 'personal' is already a plural condition.... One can look for it and already one is not oneself."[53] Perloff suggests that the unequivocal separation of the humanist subject and the poetic "I" might bear re-examination, and her discussion of the poet Ron Silliman expands upon his own sense that "the relation between agency and identity must be understood as interactive, fluid, negotiable."[54] This view of the relation between agency and identity provides an apt description of the knight as lyric speaker, both embodying and detached from his own utterances. The lyric "I" in that poem recalls in certain ways the interactive and fluid qualities Silliman and others ascribe to the postmodern lyric subject.

But it is equally the case that some of the terms by which these experimental poetic traditions articulate their objectives might receive useful elaboration from a model like the poetics of enshrinement. The title of Bob Perelman's collection *Writing/Talks* indicates the importance of the interaction between the inward-turning of inscription and the world-contacting activity of performance.[55] And as Greer suggests, one of the central conflicts in the criticism of experimental poetry occurs around the attempt to reconcile the poststructuralist impulse to trace language's inward turn and the Marxist and materialist need to look outward to cultural and economic context.[56] The poetics of enshrinement is an interpretive mode that draws upon dialectical framing to understand the relationship between these two components of representational process.

This poetics might therefore suggest some reading strategies for poetic traditions that share with those of the Middle Ages a desire to sustain productive indeterminacies around voice. Michael Palmer's "Sun" has been described as an instance of experimental poetry that reflects a traditional "lyric sensibility."[57] This poem's interweaving of the phrases "Write this" and "Say this" into its stanzas throughout gestures toward a dialectics of inscription and performance. But one stanza in particular demonstrates how the poetics of enshrinement might locate and explain the nature of its lyric voice:

> Say this. There is a sentence in my mouth, there is a chariot in my
> mouth. There is a ladder. There is a lamp whose light fills empty space
> and a space which swallows light[58]

The initial command to "Say this" lends performative force to the stanza, and the subsequent images of words within the mouth bear out the idea that the spoken performance encloses written inscription as object. The second part of the stanza, however, abandons paratactic structure for a hypotaxis that allows a chiasmus between "light" and "space." Like the chiastic structure in the Mary play's poetry, the alternation between light and space here creates a self-enfolding dynamic in visual, inscriptional terms. While the lamp, light, and space appear at first to create a simple series of enclosures, the formal reversal of terms allows us to imagine a more complex interaction among these layers: an enshrinement. In addition, the resonance between the containing images "mouth" in the first part of the stanza and "swallows" in the second generates a larger frame for these two parts. The lamp, the mouth, the chariot, and the lighted space all suggest a space of enshrinement, a reliquary of the mind in which the work of poetry and imagination occur, a way of seeing and constituting poetic process through the visual language of objects.

The lyric voice does not construct itself here simply through a single, coherent historical subjectivity; rather, it does so more fully through the mutual containment of inscription and performance as representational modes in the culture. The conflation of container and contained that characterizes the medieval poetics of enshrinement is of course deeply linked to this poetics' devotional source: the possibility of divine presence is one of the main instruments by which the enclosed becomes enclosing. And yet, the model of a poetics drawn from visual, material, and artistic practice, as well as one that uses its visual and material terms to sustain the indeterminacy of poetic voice, holds potential in the experience of reading this later tradition. The terminologies of inscription and performance, and the mutual enshrinement between them, become a means of understanding poetry's relationship to other cultural forms.

This concluding argument might seem in many ways to join a fairly established chorus of claims that the medieval contains certain forms of postmodernity, that it anticipates much of what follows it.[59] Such arguments play an important role in articulating the discipline's meaning in wider intellectual culture; however, these assertions do not parallel mine. It is crucial to recognize the historical, political, and cultural specificities that help to construct each of these literary cultures. And a legitimate rejoinder to my argument exists in the point that the frequently oppositional politics of these experimental poetic traditions differ vastly from the medieval material that this study has explored. What the medieval poetics of enshrinement offers—to both medieval studies and to postmedieval literary inquiries—is a poetics embedded in the materialities of cultural practice, rather than overlaid descriptively upon the poetry. Medieval studies has for some time now been turning to new formalist inquiry as a way to complicate productively its relationship to historicism.[60] The poetics of enshrinement offers a historicized perspective on form deeply engaged with, but not limited to, literary and textual realms. When criticism characterizes experimental poetry's "insistence on poetics as the *enactment* (rather than the description) of a certain discursive strategy," it seems to be searching for such a model of approaching representational practices in poetry.[61] The poetics of enshrinement seeks out these practices beyond comparisons between visual and verbal expression. Within inscription and performance as cultural practices, it locates a shaping language for poetic processes. In doing so, the poetics of enshrinement renegotiates the relationship between poetry and culture.

NOTES

Introduction

1. By the time of the Sainte-Chapelle's construction France had developed for itself a national identity as the destined receptacle of the relics of the True Cross. See L. Levillain, "Essai sur les origines du Lendit," *Révue Historique* 157 (1927): 254 [241–76]. See also Daniel H. Weiss, "Architectural Symbolism and the Decoration of the Sainte-Chapelle," *The Art Bulletin* 77 (1995): 308 [308–20]. Weiss discusses the building's purpose as housing the most important Passion relics. On English kings modeling building projects on the Sainte-Chapelle, see Ann R. Meyer, *Medieval Allegory and the Building of the New Jerusalem* (Woodbridge, UK: D.S. Brewer, 2003), p. 112.

2. Nicola Coldstream, "The Kingdom of Heaven: Its Architectural Setting," in *The Age of Chivalry: Art in Plantagenet England, 1200–1400*, ed. Jonathan Alexander and Paul Binski (London: Royal Academy of Arts, 1987), p. 93 [92–97].

3. Meyer discusses exchanges of form and feature among a variety of metalwork and stone memorial enclosures in *Medieval Allegory*, pp. 134, 156–61.

4. The negotiations between these two models, and their attendant theoretical constructs, will receive detailed examination throughout this study; however, one well-known point of reference for initiating thought about the conflict between inscriptionality and performance occurs in Walter Ong's work. He acknowledges, for instance, his opposition to Derridean constructs of inscriptional self-reference and contrasts the "participatory" quality of oral utterance—its engagement with the world—with the "sequester[ing]" nature of the "mark on a surface." Ong's somewhat essentialist view of spoken language and mother tongues can be problematic; however, his articulation of an epistemological conflict between voiced and silent expression encapsulates a basic problem. See Ong, *Interfaces of the Word: Studies in the Evolution of Consciousness and Culture* (Ithaca, NY: Cornell University Press, 1977), pp. 10–22.

5. Jay David Bolter and Richard Grusin, *Remediation: Understanding New Media* (Cambridge, MA: MIT Press, 1999), p. 21.

6. Henk van Os, *The Way to Heaven: Relic Veneration in the Middle Ages* (Amsterdam: de Prom, 2001), p. 122.

7. Herbert L. Kessler, "Turning a Blind Eye: Medieval Art and the Dynamics of Contemplation," in *The Mind's Eye: Art and Theological Argument in the Middle Ages*, ed. Jeffrey F. Hamburger and Anne-Marie Bouché (Princeton: Princeton University Press, 2006), p. 413 [413–39].

8. van Os, *The Way to Heaven*, p. 122.

9. J. Hillis Miller, *Speech Acts in Literature* (Stanford: Stanford University Press, 2001), p. 67. This is one of Miller's many characterizations of Derrida's perspective on words and inscription.

10. van Os, *The Way to Heaven*, p. 40.

11. Jeffrey F. Hamburger, "The Medieval Work of Art: Wherein the 'Work'? Wherein the 'Art'?" in *The Mind's Eye*, p. 376 [374–412].

12. Jacques Derrida, *Limited Inc*, trans. Samuel Weber and Jeffrey Mehlman (Evanston, IL: Northwestern University Press, 1988), pp. 152–53.

13. See, for instance, Gail McMurray Gibson, *The Theater of Devotion: East Anglian Drama and Society in the Late Middle Ages* (Chicago: University of Chicago Press, 1989), p. 13, on Rhabanus Maurus's *carmina figurata*. See also Sarah Beckwith, *Signifying God: Social Relation and Symbolic Act in the York Corpus Christi Plays* (Chicago: University of Chicago Press, 2001), p. 88. Jessica Brantley points out that medieval poetic texts found many ways to ask their readers to "attend to" the physicality and materiality of the text besides the shaped poem of the *carmen figuratum* tradition. Brantley, *Reading in the Wilderness* (Chicago: University of Chicago Press, 2007), p. 122.

14. On the performativity of language (in the Derridean sense) as a concept that occupies temporalized structures, see Catherine M. Soussloff's point that "it is precisely because the communication is iterable that it must be able to refer to the past." Soussloff, "Like a Performance: Performativity and the Historicized Body, from Bellori to Mapplethorpe," in *Acting on the Past: Historical Performance across the Disciplines*, ed. Mark Franko and Annette Richards (Hanover, NH: Wesleyan University Press, 2000), p. 75 [69–98].

15. Jacques Derrida, *Memoires: For Paul de Man*, trans. Cecile Lindsay, Jonathan Culler, and Eduardo Cadava (New York: Columbia University Press, 1986), p. 58.

16. Derrida, *Memoires*, p. 85.

17. Derrida, *Memoires*, p. 38: "But what defies the simple and 'objective' logic of sets, what disrupts the simple inclusion of a part within the whole," is "the non-totalizable trace...interiorized *in* mourning *as* that which can no longer be interiorized, as impossible Erinnerung, in and beyond mournful memory—constituting it, traversing it, exceeding it."

18. See Caroline Walker Bynum, *The Resurrection of the Body in Western Christianity, 200–1336* (New York: Columbia University Press, 1995), pp. 211–12, 327, on the reliquary's conflation of container and contained. This idea will receive further elaboration in chap. 4.

19. Cynthia Hahn, "The Voices of the Saints: Speaking Reliquaries," *Gesta* 36.1 (1997): 20, 27–28 [20–31].

20. Julia Reinhard Lupton, *Afterlives of the Saints: Hagiography, Typology, and Renaissance Literature* (Stanford: Stanford University Press, 1996), pp. 64–65.

21. This conception of sacred enclosure as engendering permeable boundaries and conflations of inside and outside has incarnational aspects. The Augustinian understanding of the sacrament (*Confessions* 7.10), examined by Hugh of Saint Victor, involves the idea that "the Body of Christ is eaten in the sacrament in order that we might be incorporated into Him." See Ann W. Astell, *Eating Beauty: The Eucharist and the Spiritual Arts of the Middle Ages* (Ithaca, NY: Cornell University Press, 2006), p. 38.

22. Sarah Stanbury uses a Bachelardian "dialectics of inside and outside" to read the enclosed spaces of the Middle English *Patience*; in her argument, Jonah himself orders the relationship between interior and exterior through the motif of vision. Stanbury's reading of *Patience*, and of the *Pearl*-poet in general, elucidates the role of visuality in understanding relations among structures of enclosure in medieval texts. Stanbury, *Seeing the* Gawain-*Poet: Description and the Act of Perception* (Philadelphia: University of Pennsylvania Press, 1991), p. 72.

23. This study refers throughout to various critical discourses, most frequently deconstruction, performance theory, and theories of performativity in language. I have tried to create a coherent framework from these references, rather than using them opportunistically and without consideration for the intellectual and cultural history that they themselves represent and participate in. I suggest that the specific move that poststructuralist theories of language and representation make toward ideas about performativity in language provide an important template for understanding the representational strategies of medieval poetic language. On medieval language philosophy's resonance with the Heideggerian conception of relationality in language, see, for instance, R.A. Shoaf's comment that the Middle Ages had the capacity to see "a text or a word [as] a node in a skein of relations constantly changing its contours as it, the text or word, assimilates to other texts or words," in Shoaf, "Medieval Studies after Heidegger after Derrida," in *Sign, Sentence, Discourse: Language in Medieval Thought and Literature*, ed. Julian N. Wasserman and Lois Roney (Syracuse, NY: Syracuse University Press, 1989), pp. 12–13 [9–30].

24. Theresa Coletti, *Naming the Rose: Eco, Medieval Signs, and Modern Theory* (Ithaca, NY: Cornell University Press, 1988), p. 75.

25. Jacques Derrida, "Composing 'Circumfession,'" in *Augustine and Postmodernism: Confessions and Circumfession*, ed. John D. Caputo and Michael J. Scanlon (Bloomington: Indiana University Press, 2005), pp. 20–21 [19–27]: "I assumed for a long time, despite a number of reservations I had about Austin's theory of constative and performative speech acts, that the performative speech act was a way of producing an event.

I now think that the performative is in fact a subtle way of neutralizing the event."

26. Katherine O'Brien O'Keeffe, *Visible Song: Transitional Literacy in Old English Verse* (New York: Cambridge University Press, 1990), pp. 4, 153. Her analysis of systems of "pointing" suggests a self-referential system that bases itself on the mechanics of difference and relationality we have begun to discuss here (pp. 150–52).

27. Emily Steiner, *Documentary Culture and the Making of Medieval English Literature* (New York: Cambridge University Press, 2003), pp. 9–10. Glending Olson's essay "Toward a Poetics of the Late Medieval Court Lyric" similarly turns to other cultural elements to find a language in which to articulate a lyric theory not entirely explicit in the medieval period itself. In *Vernacular Poetics in the Middle Ages*, ed. Lois Ebin (Kalamazoo, MI: Medieval Institute Publications, 1984), p. 228 [227–48].

1   The Poetics of Enshrinement

1. Wendy Steiner, *The Colors of Rhetoric: Problems in the Relation between Modern Literature and Painting* (Chicago: University of Chicago Press, 1982), pp. xi, 16.

2. As n. 21 of the introduction indicates, Hugh of Saint Victor explicates *Confessions* 7.10 through this device.

3. A number of critics in the fields of both literary studies and performance theory have articulated the inevitability of performance's connection to performativity. Keir Elam has asserted that "speech act theory itself is founded on a dramatic model of language use." Elam, "Much Ado About Doing Things with Words (and Other Means): Some Problems in the Pragmatics of Theatre and Drama," in *Performing Texts*, ed. Michael Issacharoff and Robin F. Jones (Philadelphia: University of Pennsylvania Press, 1988), p. 42 [39–57]. See also, for instance, Andew Parker and Eve Kosofsky Sedgwick, "Introduction," in *Performativity and Performance*, ed. Parker and Sedgwick (New York: Routledge, 1995), p. 2 [1–18]. They discuss two potential ends of the spectrum of performance—"the *extroversion* of the actor" and "the *introversion* of the signifier," but also refer to Paul de Man's invocation of "the torsion, the mutual perversion…of reference and performativity" (pp. 2–3). Steven Connor also provides a helpful account of how the word "perform" itself contains implications of both "acting" (doing something, or bringing something into being) and at the same time of "enacting" (impersonating or imitating). Performing implies at once a spontaneous event and a "doubling." See Connor, "Postmodern Performance," in *Analysing Performance: A Critical Reader*, ed. Patrick Campbell (New York: Manchester University Press, 1996), pp. 107–8 [107–24].

4. Antonina Harbus, "Text as Revelation: Constantine's Dream in *Elene*," *Neophilologus* 78.4 (1994): 647 [645–53].

5. *The Epitome of S. Eucherius About Certain Holy Places*, trans. Aubrey Steward (London: Palestine Pilgrims' Text Society, 1971), pp. 13–14.

6. Julia Bolton Holloway, "*The Dream of the Rood* and Liturgical Drama," *Comparative Drama* 18.1 (1984): 35 n. 6 [19–37].

7. Jeffrey F. Hamburger, *The Visual and the Visionary: Art and Female Spirituality in Late-Medieval Germany* (New York: Zone Books, 1998), p. 19.

8. Dunbar H. Ogden, *The Staging of Drama in the Medieval Church* (London: Associated University Presses, 2002), p. 51.

9. Lisa Victoria Ciresi, "A Liturgical Study of the Shrine of the Three Kings at Cologne," in *Objects, Images, and the Word: Art in the Service of the Liturgy*, ed. Colum Hourihane (Princeton: Princeton University Press, 2003), pp. 208, 202 [202–30].

10. Peter Draper, "Architecture and Liturgy," in *Age of Chivalry*, p. 86 [83–91]. See also Paul Binski, "Liturgy and Local Knowledge: English Perspectives on Trondheim Cathedral," in *The Medieval Cathedral of Trondheim: Architectural and Ritual Constructions in their European Context*, ed. Margrete Syrstad Andås, Øystein Ekroll, Andreas Haug, and Nils Holger Petersen (Turnhout, Belgium: Brepols, 2007), pp. 21–46. Binksi uses English cathedrals, such as Canterbury, Lincoln, and Ely, to examine the methods by which we perceive connections between physical spaces and the ceremonies within them, and the importance of local and specific traditions in such readings.

11. Eleanor Townsend, "Pilgrimage," in *Gothic Art for England 1400–1547*, ed. Richard Marks and Paul Williamson, assisted by Eleanor Townsend (London: V&A Publications, 2003), p. 425 [424–35].

12. Ciresi, "Liturgical Study," in *Objects, Images, and the Word*, p. 212.

13. Ogden, *Staging of Drama*, p. 63.

14. Ogden, *Staging of Drama*, pp. 17, 71.

15. John D. Caputo, "Shedding Tears Beyond Being: Derrida's Confession of Prayer," in *Augustine and Postmodernism*, p. 100 [95–114].

16. Caputo, "Shedding Tears," in *Augustine and Postmodernism*, p. 102.

17. Derrida, "Composing 'Circumfession,'" in *Augustine and Postmodernism*, pp. 20–21. As Derrida argues in "Signature Event Context," the condition of the performative utterance as dictated by context and *différance* is ultimately a condition of all language. Jacques Derrida, "Signature Event Context," in *Margins of Philosophy*, trans. Alan Bass (Chicago: University of Chicago Press, 1982), p. 325 [307–330].

18. Kelly McKay Holbert, "Mosan Reliquary Triptychs and the Cult of the True Cross in the Twelfth Century" (Ph.D. diss., Yale University, 1995), pp. 260–66. It should be acknowledged that this somewhat elaborate reading of the triptych's iconography is vulnerable to the criticism that it relies on what might have been an unrealistic opportunity for detailed examination. At the same time, it seems to me that the convention of enfolding enshrinement, on which this reading depends, would be something apparent to a worshipper familiar with such objects even without microscopic scrutiny.

19. Holbert, "Mosan Reliquary Triptychs," p. 227.

20. Sarah Stanbury, *The Visual Object of Desire in Late Medieval England* (Philadelphia: University of Pennsylvania Press, 2008), pp. 4–5.

21. Donald L. Ehresmann, "Some Observations on the Role of Liturgy in the Early Winged Altarpiece," *Art Bulletin* 64.3 (1982): 359–69.

22. Draper, "Architecture and Liturgy," in *Age of Chivalry*, p. 87.

23. On the scarcity of late-medieval English metalwork as a result of its destruction, see, for instance, Marian Campbell, "Metalwork in England, c. 1200–1400," in *Age of Chivalry*, pp. 162–67; and Kathleen Kamerick, *Popular Piety and Art in the Late Middle Ages: Image Worship and Idolatry in England 1350–1500* (New York: Palgrave Macmillan, 2002), p. 4.

24. Stanbury, *The Visual Object*, pp. 5, 13–14. Stanbury's point that medieval authors had as their cultural context not only a rich culture of images and artifacts but also conflicting social and religious ideas concerning these objects provides an important context for my own readings.

25. Benjamin Nilson, *Cathedral Shrines of Medieval England* (Rochester, NY: Boydell, 1998), p. 37.

26. A fifteenth-century depiction of such a juxtaposition occurs in Lydgate's *Troy Book*, with the shrine of Hector incorporating both his body and an image:

> Ther were degres, men by to ascende...
> Parformed up al of cristal stoon,
> Attenyng up fro the table bas
> Where the standing and the resting was
> Of this riche crafty tabernacle,
> Having a-boue, up-on eche pynacle,
> A riche ruby; and reised high on heighte
> Stood an ymage, huge & large of weighte,
> Of massyf gold, havynge the liknes
> Of worthi Hector...

> (John Lydgate, *Troy Book*, ed. Henry Bergen
> [London: Kegan Paul, 1906–20], III, ll. 5639–50.)

Hector's body in the *Troy Book* is bloodless, having been drained thoroughly by embalmers. Its placement alongside a golden memorial likeness of him complicates some of the categories of temporality we assign to artifacts—the body in its embalmed state both gestures toward temporal fallibility and at the same time attempts to participate in the same dynamic of stasis as the golden image.

27. On earlier depictions of reliquaries, which "make explicit the artifice intervening between picture and God," see Herbert L. Kessler, *Spiritual Seeing: Picturing God's Invisibility in Medieval Art* (Philadelphia: University of Pennsylvania Press, 2000), p. 128.

28. On late-medieval English image shrines, see, e.g., Katherine J. Lewis, "Pilgrimage and the Cult of St. Katherine," in *Pilgrimage Explored*,

ed. J. Stopford (Rochester, NY: York Medieval Press, 1999), pp. 145–60; and Nilson, *Cathedral Shrines*, p. 57, on empty tombs at major shrine sites in England. See also Eamon Duffy, "The Dynamics of Pilgrimage in Late Medieval England," in *Pilgrimage: The English Experience from Becket to Bunyan*, ed. Colin Morris and Peter Roberts (New York: Cambridge University Press, 2002), pp. 164–77.

29. Lewis, "Pilgrimage and the Cult of St. Katherine," in *Pilgrimage Explored*, p. 159.

30. Duffy, "Dynamics of Pilgrimage," in *Pilgrimage*, pp. 171–72.

31. Gibson, *Theater of Devotion*, pp. 140–42.

32. See John Dillenberger, *Images and Relics: Theological Perceptions and Visual Images in Sixteenth-Century Europe* (New York: Oxford University Press, 1999), p. 7, on the Western practice of viewing images as though they were relics.

33. Eric Jager, *The Book of the Heart* (Chicago: University of Chicago Press, 2000), pp. xvi–xvii.

34. Steiner, *Documentary Culture*, p. 3; see also her discussion of the archive on p. 94.

35. Amy G. Remensnyder, "Legendary Treasure at Conques: Reliquaries and Imaginative Memory," *Speculum* 71 (1996): 897–99 [884–906].

36. Eugene Vance, "Style and Value: From Soldier to Pilgrim in the *Song of Roland*," *Yale French Studies* 80 (1991): 78, 80 [75–96].

37. In his commentary on Wordsworth's *Essays upon Epitaphs*, Geoffrey Hartman calls inscription "any verse conscious of the place on which it was written." Hartman, *The Unremarkable Wordsworth* (Minneapolis: University of Minnesota Press, 1987), p. 32. Although this notion of the "conscious[ness]" of verse is a particularly Romantic and post-Romantic one, the idea that writing associated with commemoration contains within itself a meeting point between language and the material world is useful for thinking about the nature of an object such as the "A" reliquary.

38. Vance, "Style and Value," 90. He refers to the line "Les colps Rollant conut en treis perruns" (l. 2875); I have cited Frederick Goldin's translation of lines 2874–75 (*The Song of Roland*, trans. Frederick Goldin [New York: W.W. Norton, 1978], p. 132).

39. James A. Rushing, Jr., "Images at the Interface: Orality, Literacy, and the Pictorialization of the Roland Material," in *Visual Culture and the German Middle Ages*, ed. Kathryn Starkey and Horst Wenzel (New York: Palgrave Macmillan, 2005), pp. 123, 128 [115–34].

40. Jacques Derrida, "*Différance*," in *Margins of Philosophy*, trans. Alan Bass (Chicago: University of Chicago Press, 1982), p. 4 [1–28].

41. Remensnyder, "Legendary Treasure," 892.

42. Theodore K. Lerud, "Quick Images: Memory and the English Corpus Christi Drama," in *Moving Subjects: Processional Performance in the Middle Ages and the Renaissance*, ed. Kathleen Ashley and Wim Hüsken (Atlanta, GA: Rodopi, 2001), p. 213 [213–38].

43. As Judson Boyce Allen has shown, much of what medieval people wrote explicitly about poetry was rhetorical or ethical in its force. "Grammar, Poetic Form, and the Lyric Ego: A Medieval *A Priori*," in *Vernacular Poetics*, p. 204 [199–226].

44. See Geoffrey of Vinsauf, *Poetria Nova*, in *Three Medieval Rhetorical Arts*, ed. and trans. James Jerome Murphy (Berkeley: University of California Press, 1971), p. 37.

45. Jody Enders, "Visions with Voices: The Rhetoric of Memory and Music in Liturgical Drama," *Comparative Drama* 24.1 (1990): 45 [34–54].

46. Paul Zumthor, *Toward a Medieval Poetics*, trans. Philip Bennett (Minneapolis: University of Minnesota Press, 1992), p. 359.

47. John Ganim, *Chaucerian Theatricality* (Princeton: Princeton University Press, 1990), pp. 4–5, 34, 41, and 93. Ganim also makes the important point, relevant to the present study, that although the prevailing critical metaphor in Chaucer studies was for a long time Gothic art and architecture, the theatrical metaphor can encompass both "artifact and performance" (5).

48. Carol Symes, "The Appearance of Early Vernacular Plays: Forms, Functions, and the Future of Medieval Theater," *Speculum* 77.3 (2002): 779 [778–831]. See also Symes's book-length study *A Common Stage: Theater and Public Life in Medieval Arras* (Ithaca, NY: Cornell University Press, 2007).

49. We might turn to a later play tradition to reinforce some of these points, because some aspects of early modern theater actually illuminate a semiotics of medieval drama capable of being only implied during the Middle Ages themselves. Drama's tendency to be self-referential about its own representational practices became increasingly explicit after certain reformist measures had come to pass. One of John Bale's lost plays deals with the shrine of Saint Thomas Becket, and the existence of such a play demonstrates with particular clarity the possibilities for performance to critique its own representational systems. If, as has been speculated, this play contained a critical portrayal of Becket's own scene of martyrdom, then such a play would have been making an argument about the role of performance aesthetics themselves in the constitution of the shrine's authenticity, what Peter Roberts refers to as the "theatrical nature of the cult" (see Roberts, "Politics, Drama, and the Cult of Thomas Becket," in *Pilgrimage: The English Experience*, pp. 225–26 [199–237]). More specifically, the pageant of Saint Thomas called attention to his miraculous blood and other relics (it took place on the eve of the Translation of the Relics into the 1530s), and so in this way as well a play critiquing the cult might have found at its center a relic whose meaning was constituted by the conventions of spectacle and audience interaction. At this stage the play could become a means of critiquing the authenticity of the relics, their status as signs, because dramatic expression had already established itself as a vehicle for discourse on the structure of the object's connection to its mimetic representation.

50. Brantley, *Reading in the Wilderness*, p. 9.

51. Steiner, *Documentary Culture*, p. 48.

52. O'Keeffe, *Visible Song*, pp. 4, 138.

53. O'Keeffe, *Visible Song*, p. 22. See also her discussion of Isidore of Seville's perception of pointing and punctuation as a "visual phenomenon" (pp. 145–46).

54. Ardis Butterfield, *Poetry and Music in Medieval France: From Jean Renart to Guillaume de Machaut* (New York: Cambridge University Press, 2002), p. 171.

55. Calvin B. Kendall, "The Gate of Heaven and the Fountain of Life: Speech-Act Theory and Portal Inscriptions," *Essays in Medieval Studies* 10 (1993): 112–18 [111–25]. See also Kendall's book-length study on Romanesque church inscription, which traces the Christian architectural adoption of inscriptional embellishment to communicate the physical church's allegorical meaning. Kendall, *The Allegory of the Church: Romanesque Portals and Their Verse Inscriptions* (Toronto: University of Toronto Press, 1998).

56. Ernestus Duemmler, rec. *Poetae latini aevi carolini* 2 (Munich, Germany: Germaniae Historica, 1978), p. 665. Translated in William J. Diebold, *Word and Image: An Introduction to Early Medieval Art* (Boulder, CO: Westview, 2000), p. 130.

57. Jeffrey F. Hamburger, "Introduction," in *The Mind's Eye*, pp. 4–5 [3–10]. In a later essay in this volume, Hamburger raises the specific issue of inscriptions on devotional objects, but then returns to his focus on iconography, arguing that "for all their recourse to the word, however, medieval images have something to say over and against the texts that claim to speak for them" (Hamburger, "The Medieval Work of Art," in *The Mind's Eye*, p. 376). His refusal to privilege textual over visual expression provides an important model for this study.

58. "The image is not the reflection of some external view of the world but the beginning and foundation of a process of thought." See Michael Camille, "Before the Gaze: The Internal Senses and Late Medieval Practices of Seeing," in *Visuality Before and Beyond the Renaissance: Seeing as Others Saw*, ed. Robert S. Nelson (New York: Cambridge University Press, 2000), p. 216 [197–223].

59. See, for instance, Harvey Stahl, "Heaven in View: The Place of the Elect in an Illuminated Book of Hours," in *Last Things: Death and the Apocalypse in the Middle Ages*, ed. Caroline Walker Bynum and Paul Freedman (Philadelphia: University of Pennsylvania Press, 2000), pp. 205–6 [205–32]; and Linda Seidel, *Legends in Limestone: Lazarus, Gislebertus, and the Cathedral of Autun* (Chicago: University of Chicago Press, 1999).

60. Hamburger, "Introduction," p. 5.

61. Ann R. Meyer makes a related claim that architectural forms exerted an influence on literary productions in the late Middle Ages in Meyer, *Medieval Allegory*, p. 158. While she sees these artistic manifestations as "respon[ding]" to each other, and in particular the text as the "poetic

descendant" of the architectural construction (p. 140), the present study instead makes the case that the visual provides a language for articulating a process occurring in the verbal realm.

62. On the late-medieval "incarnational aesthetic," see Gibson, *Theater of Devotion*, pp. 1–18.

63. Saint Augustine, *De vera relig.* 22.42. I draw here upon Eugene Vance's discussion of Augustine's doctrine in *Mervelous Signals: Poetics and Sign Theory in the Middle Ages* (Lincoln: University of Nebraska Press, 1986), pp. 45–47. See also Lawrence Rothfield, "Autobiography and Perspective in the *Confessions* of St. Augustine," *Comparative Literature* 33.3 (1981): 211 [209–23], on Augustine's use of the "verbalized epistemology" of the Incarnation as a way of understanding language's capacity for representing the temporality and spatiality of autobiographical experience.

64. Chap. 3's perspective on a play text as performed poetic occasion will elaborate further on this point.

65. Saint Augustine, *De Doctrina Christiana*, ed. and trans. R.P.H. Green (Oxford: Clarendon, 1995), 2.2, p. 56. On Augustine's sense of signs as things, which, "in addition to being things themselves, also refer to other things," see Marcia L. Colish, *The Mirror of Language: A Study in the Medieval Theory of Knowledge* (New Haven, CT: Yale University Press, 1968), pp. 59–60.

66. On the reliquary's function as memorial in literate culture, see Brian Stock's discussion of Bernard of Angers and Sainte Foy of Conques in *The Implications of Literacy: Written Language and Models of Interpretation in the Eleventh and Twelfth Centuries* (Princeton: Princeton University Press, 1983), p. 70: "St. Foy's statue, however it appeared to the literate, was not merely an oracle which one consulted blindly or an idol to which one made sacrifices. It was a likeness whose purpose was to keep alive the remembered record of a martyr (*ob memoriam reverende martyris. . .simulacrum*)."

67. See, for instance, Yrjö Hirn, *The Sacred Shrine: A Study of the Poetry and Art of the Catholic Church* (London: Macmillan, 1912), p. 44.

68. Hans Belting, *Likeness and Presence: A History of the Image before the Era of Art*, trans. Edmund Jephcott (Chicago: University of Chicago Press, 1994), pp. 301–2.

69. Belting, *Likeness and Presence*, pp. 8–9. Belting specifies that his study deals with the image as the likeness of a person (p. xxi).

70. Jeffrey F. Hamburger, "The Place of Theology in Medieval Art History: Problems, Positions, Possibilities," in *The Mind's Eye*, pp. 23–24 [11–31].

71. Bruce Holsinger points out that Derrida's interest in the trace has its foundation in an intellectual tradition surrounding liturgy: "Derrida directly credits Levinas's recent writings, and this liturgical essay in particular ['On the Trail of the Other'], for inspiring his own notion of the *trace*, the 'absent present' or 'empty fullness' of the signifier that has constituted one of the central terms in the lexicon of deconstruction." See Holsinger,

The Premodern Condition: Medievalism and the Making of Theory (Chicago: University of Chicago Press, 2005), p. 131.

72. On late-medieval England as a particular locus for the establishment and development of cycle drama, see, for instance, V.A. Kolve, *The Play Called Corpus Christi* (Stanford: Stanford University Press, 1966), pp. 37–38.

73. Burt Kimmelman, "Ockham, Chaucer, and the Emergence of a Modern Poetics," in *The Rhetorical Poetics of the Middle Ages: Reconstructive Polyphony: Essays in Honor of Robert O. Payne*, ed. John M. Hill and Deborah M. Sinnreich-Levi (Madison, NJ: Fairleigh Dickinson University Press, 2000), pp. 179–81 [177–205]. "The connection between philosophy and poetry was abundant and provocative in Chaucer's time, as is typified by the development of the persona in fourteenth-century England, which could but only have been influenced by the Ockhamist debate" (pp. 182–83).

74. Edmund Reiss, "Ambiguous Signs and Authorial Deceptions in Fourteenth-Century Fictions," in *Sign, Sentence, Discourse*, p. 114 [113–37].

75. Stanbury, *The Visual Object*, pp. 101–2.

76. Geoffrey Chaucer, *The Book of the Duchess*, ll. 321–27; ll. 332–34, in *The Riverside Chaucer*, ed. Larry D. Benson (Boston, MA: Houghton Mifflin, 1987), p. 334; all subsequent passages will be cited in the text.

77. On the Sainte-Chapelle as a reliquary, see n. 1 in the introduction.

78. On Chaucerian ecphrasis in these texts, see Margaret Bridges, "The Picture in the Text: Ecphrasis as Self-Reflectivity in Chaucer's *Parliament of Fowls, Book of the Duchess*, and *House of Fame*," *Word and Image* 5 (1989): 151–58.

79. Eugene Vance, "Chaucer's Pardoner: Relics, Discourse, and Frames of Propriety," *New Literary History* 20 (1989): 726 [723–45].

80. See, for instance, Fiona Somerset and Nicholas Watson, eds., *The Vulgar Tongue: Medieval and Postmedieval Vernacularity* (University Park, PA: Penn State University Press, 2003); Christopher Cannon, *The Grounds of English Literature* (New York: Oxford University Press, 2004); and Jocelyn Wogan-Brown, Nicholas Watson, Andrew Taylor, and Ruth Evans, eds., *The Idea of the Vernacular: An Anthology of Middle English Literary Theory, 1280–1520* (University Park, PA: Penn State University Press, 1999).

81. Chap. 4, which discusses the dream vision *Pearl*, will elaborate on the potential of dream visions, as well as visionary literature more generally, to accommodate what poetic language as performative brings into being.

82. On dreaming's role in language's ability to create new realities, and on the ways that dreaming and language complicate the meaning of visuality, see Elaine Scarry, *Dreaming by the Book* (New York: Farrar, Straus and Giroux, 1999), p. 34. As Scarry explains, both dreaming (daydreaming, in her instance) and literary language "bring into being things not previously existing in the world." But they differ in that the "verbal arts" also attempt to replace the "faintness" of dream vision with the "solidity...of the perceptible world." In this difference, we can

see writing's inclusion of "procedures for reproducing the deep structure of perception," which "themselves have an instructional character that duplicates the 'givenness' of perception."

83. A.C. Spearing, *Medieval Dream Poetry* (Cambridge: Cambridge University Press, 1976), pp. 4–5.

84. Dream theory from the classical period and the Middle Ages is familiar to most medievalists mainly because of Chaucer's frequent and varied explorations of the dream vision. Dreams in the Middle Ages were understood to occupy a number of different categories, such as Macrobius's nightmares, his oracular and prophetic dreams, and his more enigmatic visions (Michael St. John, *Chaucer's Dream Visions: Courtliness and Individual Identity* [Burlington, VT: Ashgate, 2000], p. 6).

85. Peter Brown, "On the Borders of Middle English Dream Vision," in *Reading Dreams: The Interpretation of Dreams from Chaucer to Shakespeare*, ed. Peter Brown (New York: Oxford University Press, 1999), p. 44 [22–50].

86. Brown, "On the Borders," in *Reading Dreams*, p. 25.

87. Steven F. Kruger, *Dreaming in the Middle Ages* (Cambridge: Cambridge University Press, 1992), pp. 129–30, 13–14.

88. Kathryn Lynch, "Baring Bottom: Shakespeare and the Chaucerian Dream Vision," in *Reading Dreams*, pp. 118, 100 [99–124].

89. As John Ganim points out, performance as a defining aesthetic in Chaucer's work problematizes the distinction between voiced and inscribed expression. Ganim, *Chaucerian Theatricality*, p. 122.

90. Suzanne Akbari discusses this interpretation of the knight's self-characterization, and argues further that the white wall refers not simply to a surface of inscription, but instead to "the receptive imagination in the act of seeing." In this sense as well, the knight's body signifies not through voice but through image. Akbari, *Seeing through the Veil: Optical Theory and Medieval Allegory* (Toronto: University of Toronto Press, 2004), p. 191.

91. Vincent Gillespie, "Medieval Hypertext: Image and Text from York Minster," in *Of the Making of Books: Medieval Manuscripts, Their Scribes and Readers. Essays Presented to M.B. Parkes* (Brookfield, VT: Ashgate, 1997), p. 207 [206–29].

92. Mary Carruthers, *The Book of Memory: A Study of Memory in Medieval Culture* (Cambridge: Cambridge University Press, 1990), p. 229.

93. Carruthers, *Book of Memory*, p. 225.

2   Silent Inscription, Spoken Ceremony: *Saint Erkenwald* and the Enshrined Judge

1. See, for instance, D.W. Robertson, *Essays in Medieval Culture* (Princeton: Princeton University Press, 1980).

2. Stanbury, *The Visual Object*, pp. 127–28.

3. Monika Otter, " 'New Werke': *St. Erkenwald*, St. Albans, and the Medieval Sense of the Past," *Journal of Medieval and Renaissance Studies* 24.3 (1994): 413 [387–414].

4. For a reading of the pagan judge as a figure onto whom the associations of Ricardian monarchy have been displaced, see Ruth Nissé, " 'A Coroun Ful Riche': The Rule of History in *Saint Erkenwald*," *ELH* 65 (1998): 282 [277–95].

5. E. Gordon Whatley, ed. and trans., *The Saint of London: The Life and Miracles of Saint Erkenwald* (Binghamton, NY: Medieval and Renaissance Texts and Studies, 1989), p. 153.

6. On the interpenetrability of "devotional" and "liturgical" in understanding the actual uses of objects in public and private ceremonial contexts, see Beth Williamson, "Liturgical Image or Devotional Image? The London *Madonna of the Firescreen*," in *Objects, Images, and the Word*, p. 313 [298–318]: "The possibility ought surely to be acknowledged that a devotional image might be interpreted in the light of the liturgy and the sacraments, and that it might proceed from liturgical and sacramental cues and references in the various ways in which it engages the viewer." See also Thomas Lentes's characterization of a "liturgicization of the private realm" in the fifteenth century. Lentes, "Rituals of Gazing in the Late Middle Ages," in *The Mind's Eye*, p. 364 [360–73].

7. See Whatley, *Saint of London*, p. 69.

8. Nowhere among the many miracles attributed to the saint appears the pagan baptism described in the poem *Saint Erkenwald*. See Sandra Cairns, "Fact and Fiction in the Middle English *De Erkenwaldo*," *Neuphilologische Mitteilungen* 83 (1982): 437 [430–38].

9. E. Gordon Whatley, "The Middle English *Saint Erkenwald* and Its Liturgical Context," *Mediaevalia* 8 (1992): 284 [277–306].

10. Holsinger, *The Premodern Condition*, p. 131: "Liturgy defeats synchrony just as it swallows diachrony."

11. Nissé, "A Coroun Ful Riche," 270, 280.

12. *Saint Erkenwald*, ll. 129–42, ed. Clifford Peterson (Philadelphia: University of Pennsylvania Press, 1977), pp. 328, 330. All subsequent line numbers will appear in the text.

13. John M. Howe, "The Conversion of the Physical World: The Creation of a Christian Landscape," in *Varieties of Religious Conversion in the Middle Ages*, ed. James Muldoon (Gainesville: University Press of Florida, 1997), p. 70 [63–78].

14. On the Austinian idea of object as event, see Shoshana Felman, *The Literary Speech Act: Don Juan with J.L. Austin, or Seduction in Two Languages*, trans. Catherine Porter (Ithaca, NY: Cornell University Press, 1983), pp. 106–8. On Derrida's performative making of the truth versus the definition of the event, see Derrida, "Composing 'Circumfession,' " in *Augustine and Postmodernism*, p. 23.

15. Mark Franko, "Given Movement: Dance and the Event," in *Ritual and Event: Interdisciplinary Perspectives*, ed. Mark Franko (New York: Routledge,

2007), p. 129 [125–37]. Franko is discussing Jean-François Lyotard's essay "March 23."

16. Nilson, *Cathedral Shrines*, pp. 33, 97–98. Beyond the Middle Ages, relic shrines also became sites of political significance, developing further their involvement in ceremony and pageantry. On Henry VII's request in the early sixteenth century for a silver gilt statue of himself to be placed by Becket's shrine, for instance, see Ronald C. Finucane, *Miracles and Pilgrims: Popular Beliefs in Medieval England* (Totowa, NJ: Rowman and Littlefield, 1977), p. 201.

17. See Nilson, *Cathedral Shrines*, pp. 83–86; and Tim Tatton-Brown, "Canterbury and the Architecture of Pilgrimage Shrines in England," in *Pilgrimage: The English Experience*, p. 99 [90–107].

18. Nilson, *Cathedral Shrines*, p. 91.

19. Frank Grady, "*Piers Plowman, Saint Erkenwald*, and the Rule of Exceptional Salvations," *Yearbook of Langland Studies* 6 (1992): 85 [61–88].

20. For accounts of relic thefts and other forms of *translatio*, see Patrick Geary, *Furta Sacra: Thefts of Relics in the Central Middle Ages*, rev. edn. (Princeton: Princeton University Press, 1990). See also Nicole Herrmann-Mascard, *Les reliques des saints: formation coutumière d'un droit* (Paris: Klincksieck, 1975), pp. 323–35, on the ways that relics changed meaning and value by moving through space. Herrmann-Mascard looks at relics in their economic capacity, examining the implications of the donations, gifts, and revenues that relics generated. She points out that princes and other political figures began to use relics as a form of compensation for those who had rendered them a service, introducing them into a market economy, yet another kind of space.

21. Geary, *Furta Sacra*, p. 56.

22. Geary, *Furta Sacra*, p. 114.

23. Nilson, *Cathedral Shrines*, p. 33.

24. Paul Strohm, "The Trouble with Richard: The Reburial of Richard II and Lancastrian Symbolic Strategy," *Speculum* 71 (1996): 104–5 [87–111].

25. Nilson, *Cathedral Shrines*, p. 66.

26. Whatley, *Saint of London*, p. 60.

27. Whatley, *Saint of London*, p. 64.

28. Whatley, *Saint of London*, p. 153.

29. Steiner, *Documentary Culture*, p. 2.

30. Nilson, *Cathedral Shrines*, p. 37.

31. This dynamic is visible in the Chaucerian dream vision as well; see chap. 1.

32. Kolve, *The Play Called Corpus Christi*, p. 32.

33. Hamburger, "The Place of Theology," in *The Mind's Eye*, p. 23.

34. Kessler, "Turning a Blind Eye," in *The Mind's Eye*, p. 433.

35. Francis Wormald, "The Rood of Bromholm," *Journal of the Warburg Institute* 1.1 (1937): 32–34 [31–45]. See also the description of this page in M.R. James and Claude Jenkins, eds., *A Descriptive Catalogue of Manuscripts in the Library of Lambeth Palace: The Mediaeval Manuscripts*

(Cambridge: Cambridge University Press, 1932), p. 749. James adds, "A very similar but larger picture is in MS. Fitzwilliam 55 with the same inscriptions.... It may well have been produced at Bromholm Priory for sale to pilgrims" (pp. 749–50).

36. Lentes, "Rituals of Gazing in the Late Middle Ages," in *The Mind's Eye*, pp. 363–64.

37. The superimposition of the cross on the words suggests that the latter might not have been completely and actually legible. In this sense, the card behaves in a manner that Emily Steiner describes as pertaining to documents, whereby the visual aspect of the object signifies independently of the linguistic signifiers themselves. Steiner, *Documentary Culture*, p. 3.

38. Caroline Walker Bynum, "Seeing and Seeing Beyond: The Mass of Saint Gregory in the Fifteenth Century," in *The Mind's Eye*, p. 209 [208–40].

39. Bynum, "Seeing and Seeing Beyond," in *The Mind's Eye*, p. 223.

40. Don DeLillo, *White Noise* (New York: Viking, 1985), pp. 12–13.

41. Ann W. Astell also invokes Walter Benjamin in the context of studying medieval religious culture. She focuses on Benjamin's response to Hegel, pointing out Benjamin's perception that Hegel did not distinguish between cult and exhibition value, but on the other hand did seem to be aware of this distinction in some of his writings. As Hegel puts it in *Aesthetics*, "We are beyond the stage of reverence for works of art as divine and objects deserving our worship." Astell's study uses these modernist perspectives on cult value and aesthetics to argue that "medieval formulations of Eucharistic doctrine are…strikingly aesthetic." *Eating Beauty*, pp. 8–9, 19.

42. Walter Benjamin, "The Work of Art in the Age of Mechanical Reproduction," in *Illuminations*, ed. Hannah Arendt, trans. Harry Zohn (New York: Schocken Books, 1986), pp. 243, 224.

43. Benjamin, "The Work of Art," in *Illuminations*, pp. 220–21.

44. As Katherine H. Tachau has suggested, medieval theories of visual perception, as influenced by Graeco-Arabic thought, also imagine the possibility of an actively constituted space between object and viewer, one that participates vitally in the perceptual experience. See, for instance, her account of Grosseteste's interactions between "visible species" and "visible spirit," as well as the later Baconian notion of "bi-directional action and reception" between the viewer's eye and celestial bodies. Katherine H. Tachau, "Seeing as Action and Passion in the Thirteenth and Fourteenth Centuries," in *The Mind's Eye*, pp. 339–40, 351 [336–59].

45. Benjamin, "The Work of Art," in *Illuminations*, pp. 228–29.

46. See Miller, for example, on "the power of inscription, once it is inscribed, to continue working in the complete absence of the intentional structure that originally inhabited it" (Miller, *Speech Acts in Literature*, p. 106).

47. Ruth Nissé, for instance, reads the text's reflection on the English vernacular as related to the project of "an accurate and irreparable history of the foreign invasions and perversions," Nissé, "A Coroun Ful Riche," 289. See also Patricia Gillies, "What Happened When the Normans

Arrived?" in Beowulf *and Other Stories: A New Introduction to Old English, Old Icelandic and Anglo-Norman Literatures,* ed. Richard North and Joe Allard (London: Longman, 2007), pp. 482–83, on *Saint Erkenwald* and the late-medieval interest in Anglo-Saxon culture. See Bruce Mitchell and Fred C. Robinson, *A Guide to Old English,* 5th edn. (Cambridge: Blackwell, 1992), p. 233, for a transcription of this riddle.

48. Ann R. Meyer's description of these runes as at once "a revelation of divine presence, and a concealment of God's will" represents another way of thinking about absent presence through these illegible inscriptions (Meyer, *Medieval Allegory,* p. 165).

49. See also Nissé's discussion of alliterative technique as involved in the way that "the *Erkenwald*-poet problematizes the prior exchange of idols for saints" (Nissé, "A Coroun Ful Riche," 277).

50. See Otter, " 'New Werke,' " 413, on the poem's uses of vestigial buildings and objects in its presentation of historical narrative. *Saint Erkenwald's* opening, with its conception of history specifically as a narrative of the vestigial, adds to Otter's point the notion that the poem is concerned not only with its relationship to history, but also with the particular ways in which poetry itself, through its incorporation of monumental imagery, can convey this model of the past as a pattern of vestiges.

51. Jennifer L. Sisk, "The Uneasy Orthodoxy of *St. Erkenwald,*" *ELH* 74.1 (2007): 102 [89–115]. See also William Kamowski, "*Saint Erkenwald* and the Inadvertent Baptism: An Orthodox Response to Heterodox Ecclesiology," *Religion and Literature* 27.3 (1995): 5–27.

52. E. Gordon Whatley, "Heathens and Saints: *St. Erkenwald* in Its Legendary Context," *Speculum* 61.2 (1986): 341–42 [330–63].

53. See n. 26, introduction.

54. Jacques Derrida, *Of Grammatology,* trans. Gayatri Chakravorty Spivak (Baltimore, MD: Johns Hopkins University Press, 1974), p. 46.

55. Holsinger, *The Premodern Condition,* p. 148.

3   The N-Town *Assumption*'s Impossible Reliquary

1. George Riley Kernodle, *From Art to Theatre: Form and Convention in the Renaissance* (Chicago: University of Chicago Press, 1944), p. 2.

2. See, for instance, Meg Twycross and Sarah Carpenter, eds., *Masks and Masking in Medieval and Early Tudor England* (Burlington, VT: Ashgate, 2002); Kolve, *The Play Called Corpus Christi*; Clifford Davidson, *Drama and Art: An Introduction to the Use of Evidence from the Visual Arts for the Study of Drama* (Kalamazoo, MI: Medieval Institute Publications, 1977); Pamela Sheingorn, "On Using Medieval Art in the Study of Medieval Drama," *Research Opportunities in Renaissance Drama* 22 (1979): 101–9; Theresa Coletti, "Devotional Iconography in the N-Town Marian Plays," *Comparative Drama* 11 (1977): 22–44; Gibson, *The Theater of Devotion*; and Sarah Beckwith, *Signifying God.*

3. On the dangers of the positivist approach, see Richard K. Emmerson, "Eliding the 'Medieval': Renaissance 'New Historicism' and Sixteenth-Century Drama," in *The Performance of Middle English Culture: Essays on Chaucer and the Drama in Honor of Martin Stevens*. Ed. James J. Paxson, Lawrence M. Clopper, and Sylvia Tomasch (Cambridge, UK: D.S. Brewer, 1998), pp. 25–41.

4. In one sense, what Derek Pearsall calls the "workaday" nature of certain kinds of verse during this period restricts our ability to imagine too expansively the aesthetic decisions and rationales that might have gone into choosing to express something in poetry rather than prose. But by virtue of their formal features, poetic texts necessarily engage in different kinds of representational claims and strategies than prose texts do, and thus even the most mechanized forms of poetry must in some sense be subject to interpretive practices that take into account the concerns of poetics. On the status of poetry within the context of other forms of late-medieval writing, see Derek Pearsall, "Towards a Poetic of Chaucerian Narrative," in *Drama, Narrative, and Poetry in the* Canterbury Tales (Toulouse, France: Presses Universitaires du Mirail, 2003), p. 100 [99–112]; and Elizabeth Salter, *Fourteenth-Century English Poetry: Contexts and Readings* (Oxford: Clarendon Press, 1984).

5. Charles Bernstein, "Introduction," in *Close Listening: Poetry and the Performed Word*, ed. Charles Bernstein (New York: Oxford University Press, 1998), p. 8 [3–28].

6. Kathleen Ashley, "Image and Ideology: Saint Anne in Late Medieval Drama and Narrative," in *Interpreting Cultural Symbols: Saint Anne in Late Medieval Society*, ed. Kathleen Ashley and Pamela Sheingorn (Athens: University of Georgia Press, 1990), pp. 113, 125 [111–30].

7. Jody Enders, *Rhetoric and the Origins of Medieval Drama* (Ithaca, NY: Cornell University Press, 1992), p. 9.

8. O.B. Hardison, *Christian Rite and Christian Drama in the Middle Ages: Essays in the Origin and Early History of Modern Drama* (Baltimore, MD: Johns Hopkins University Press, 1965), pp. 230–31.

9. Ogden, *Staging of Drama*, p. 17.

10. Lawrence M. Clopper, *Drama, Play, and Game: English Festive Culture in the Medieval and Early Modern Period* (Chicago: University of Chicago Press, 2001), pp. 3–6.

11. Stanton Garner, *Bodied Spaces: Phenomenology and Performance in Contemporary Drama* (Ithaca, NY: Cornell University Press, 1994), pp. 216–17.

12. Gibson, *Theater of Devotion*, p. 144.

13. Niklaus Largier, "Scripture, Vision, Performance: Visionary Texts and Medieval Religious Drama," in *Visual Culture and the German Middle Ages*, p. 212 [207–19].

14. Claire Sponsler, "The Culture of the Spectator: Conformity and Resistances to Medieval Performances," *Theater Journal* 44 (1992): 17 [15–29].

15. Davidson, *Drama and Art*, p. 11.

16. Gibson, *Theater of Devotion*, p. 10.

17. On the English girdle relic, see Jocelyn Perkins, *Westminster Abbey: Its Worship and Ornaments*, 2 vols. (London: Oxford University Press, 1938–52), p. 2:57; and Richard Firth Green, "Sir Gawain and the *Sacra Cintola*," *English Studies in Canada* 11 (1985): 3–4 [1–11]. Green discusses late-medieval English stories about the *sacra cintola* in circulation: "Whether or not there was a vernacular version of the story of the *sacra cintola* circulating in England before the end of the thirteenth century, there were at least two by the end of the fourteenth: a stanzaic poem on the Assumption, which appears in the Auchinleck manuscript (1330–40), and another couplet version, preserved in three mss of the northern homily collection....Finally, we might also notice that the Weavers' Pageant (XLVI) in the York Plays gives a further version of this story" (4). Brendan Cassidy traces the English veneration of the Virgin Mary's belt as far as 1610 in "A Relic, Some Pictures, and the Mothers of Florence," *Gesta* 30.2 (1991): 97 [91–99].

18. Gabriela Signori, "La bienheureuse polysémie Miracles et pèlerinages à la Vierge: pouvoir thaumaturgique et modèles pastoraux (Xe–XIIe siècles)," in *Marie: le culte de la Vierge dans la société médiévale*, ed. Dominique Iogna-Prat, Éric Palazzo, Daniel Russo (Paris: Beauchesne, 1996), p. 593 [591–617].

19. Hilda Graef, *Mary: A History of Doctrine and Devotion* (New York: Sheed and Ward, 1963), pp. 138–39.

20. Éric Palazzo, "Marie et l'élaboration d'un espace ecclésial au haut Moyen Âge," in *Marie: le culte de la Vierge*, p. 322 [313–25].

21. Marina Warner, *Alone of All Her Sex: The Myth and Cult of the Virgin Mary* (London: Weidenfeld and Nicholson, 1976), pp. 291–92.

22. Gibson, *Theater of Devotion*, pp. 139–43.

23. Donald Duclow, "The Virgin's 'Good Death,'" *Fifteenth-Century Studies* 21 (1994): 61 [55–86].

24. Duclow, "Good Death," 61.

25. Duclow, "Good Death," 63.

26. Donna Spivey Ellington, *From Sacred Body to Angelic Soul: Understanding Mary in Late Medieval and Early Modern Europe* (Washington, DC: Catholic University of America Press, 2001), p. 81.

27. Duclow, "Good Death," 60.

28. Stephen J. Shoemaker, "'Let Us Go and Burn Her Body': The Image of the Jews in the Early Dormition Traditions," *Church History* 68.4 (1999): 802–4 [775–823].

29. Shoemaker, "Let Us Go," 803.

30. Shoemaker, "Let Us Go," 802–3.

31. Belting, *Likeness and Presence*, p. 302.

32. Beckwith, *Signifying God*, p. 88. The Corpus Christi cycle, as Leah Sinanoglou has argued, deals with the issue of Christ's body through its liturgical associations, implicating itself in the bodily sacrifice of the Mass (Sinanoglou, "The Christ Child as Sacrifice: A Medieval Tradition and the Corpus Christi Plays," *Speculum* 48.3 [1973]: 500–502 [491–509]).

33. Gibson, *Theater of Devotion*, p. 1, Chaps. 1 and 6.

34. Gibson, *Theater of Devotion*, pp. 137, 6.

35. Anthropological discourses have traditionally understood theatrical performance as containing the potential to bring realities into being. See, for instance, Clifford Geertz's description of ritual and "metaphysical theatre": "theatre designed to present an ontology and, by presenting it, to make it happen—make it actual." In Geertz, *Negara: The Theater State in Nineteenth-Century Bali* (Princeton: Princeton University Press, 1980), p. 104. Gordon Kipling brings this concept into a late-medieval context in his examination of the effects of civic triumphs. See Kipling, *Enter the King: Theatre, Liturgy, and Ritual in the Medieval Civic Triumph* (New York: Oxford University Press, 1998), pp. 46–47.

36. Patrice Pavis, "From Text to Performance," in *Performing Texts*, pp. 90–93 [86–100]. See also Stanton Garner's characterization of mise-en-scène as an element of theatrical language that dynamically competes with reality: "In the theater, the mise-en-scène of language can exert such a powerful phenomenal impression that it will compete with or even eclipse the actuality of the visual present." Garner, *Bodied Spaces*, p. 141.

37. Stephen Spector, ed., *The Assumption of Mary*, in *The N-Town Play: Cotton MS Vespasian D.8*, Early English Text Society s.s. 11–12 (New York: Oxford University Press, 1991), 11:390, ll. 83–85. All subsequent play citations are from this edition; line numbers will appear in the text.

38. Ann Eljenholm Nichols, "The Hierosphthitic Topos, or the Fate of Fergus: Notes on the N-Town *Assumption*," *Comparative Drama* 25.1 (1991): 37 [29–41].

39. Shoemaker, "Let Us Go," 801–2.

40. Victor I. Scherb, *Staging Faith: East Anglian Drama in the Middle Ages* (Madison, NJ: Fairleigh Dickinson University Press, 2001), p. 38.

41. Clifford Davidson has noted that the image of the Virgin Mary with candles appears in several forms of devotional art and ceremony in the late Middle Ages. Examples include a servant of Mary's holding a candle in stained glass windows at Fairford and Great Malvern; an alabaster of Mary and other figures carrying candles; and the Purification feast day in February, Candlemas (*Drama and Art*, p. 114).

42. Coletti, "Devotional Iconography," 26.

43. Gibson, *Theater of Devotion*, p. 174.

44. Jacobus de Voragine, "The Assumption of the Virgin," in *The Golden Legend*, ed. and trans. William Granger Ryan, 2 vols. (Princeton: Princeton University Press, 1995), pp. 2:77–97.

45. On the artifact metaphors used to describe Mary in this play and their casting of Mary as an image-artifact, see Matthew Kinservik, "The Struggle over Mary's Body: Theological and Dramatic Resolution in the N-Town *Assumption* Play," *JEGP* 95.2 (1996): 190–204.

46. Sylvia Tomasch, "Breaking the Frame: Medieval Art and Drama," in *Early Drama to 1600*, ed. Albert H. Tricomi (Binghamton, NY: Center for Medieval and Early Renaissance Studies, 1987), p. 87 [81–93].

47. Peter Brown, *The Cult of the Saints: It's Rise and Function in Latin Christianity* (Chicago: University of Chicago Press), p. 4. Coletti, "Devotional Iconography," 38; see the plate she reproduces of the funeral of the Virgin (Fouquet). On the development of Mary as a mediating figure, see also Pietre Sevret, "Le Personnage de la Vierge dans les Mystères," in *Imagines Mariae: représentations du personnage de la Vierge dans la poésie, le théâtre, et l'éloquence entre le XIIe et le XVI siècles.* Ed. Christian Mouchel et al. (Lyon, France: Presses Universitaires de Lyon, 1999), p. 97.

48. Coletti, "Devotional Iconography," 38–39.

49. J.A. Tasioulas, "Between Doctrine and Domesticity: The Portrayal of Mary in the N-Town Plays," in *Medieval Women in Their Communities*, ed. Diane Watt (Toronto: University of Toronto Press, 1997), p. 235 [222–45]. See also J. Vriend, *The Blessed Virgin Mary in the Medieval Drama of England* (Purmerend, Holland: J. Muisse, 1928), p. 48.

50. Nicholas Watson, "The Methods and Objectives of Thirteenth-Century Anchoritic Devotion," in *The Medieval Mystical Tradition in England*, ed. Marion Glasscoe (Cambridge, UK: D.S. Brewer, 1987), p. 138 [132–53].

51. Watson, "Methods and Objectives," in *Medieval Mystical Tradition*, p. 140.

52. Christopher Cannon, "Enclosure," in *The Cambridge Companion to Medieval Women's Writing*, ed. Carolyn Dinshaw and David Wallace (New York: Cambridge University Press, 2003), pp. 113–14 [109–23].

53. Sarah Beckwith, "Passionate Regulation: Enclosure, Ascesis, and the Feminist Imaginary," *South Atlantic Quarterly* 93.4 (1995): 808 [803–24].

54. Beckwith, "Passionate Regulation," 811.

55. Sharon Elkins, *Holy Women of Twelfth-Century England* (Chapel Hill: University of North Carolina Press, 1988), p. 151.

56. Elizabeth A. Robertson, *Early English Devotional Prose and the Female Audience* (Knoxville: University of Tennessee Press, 1990), p. 59.

57. Robertson, *Devotional Prose*, pp. 49–57.

58. William Fitzhenry, "The N-Town Plays and the Politics of Metatheater," *Studies in Philology* 100.1 (2003): 23 [22–43]. For Fitzhenry, this performed introspection mainly involves political questions concerning the nature of image worship within the context of Lollard debate. See also Kathleen Ashley's argument about the social self-reflexivity apparent in the York Cycle plays in Ashley, "Sponsorship, Reflexivity, and Resistance: Cultural Readings of the York Cycle Plays," in *The Performance of Middle English Culture*, p. 9 [9–24].

59. Jacobus de Voragine, "The Assumption of the Virgin," in *The Golden Legend*, p. 2: 90.

60. Ashley, "Image and Ideology," in *Interpreting Cultural Symbols*, p. 115.

61. Rosemary Woolf, *The English Mystery Plays* (Berkeley: University of California Press, 1972), p. 287.

62. See Janette Dillon, *Language and Stage in Medieval and Renaissance England* (Cambridge: Cambridge University Press, 1998), pp. 31–38; and Zumthor, *Toward a Medieval Poetics*, p. 360. Dillon sees the insertion of Latin dialogue as a means of exalting the material and also emphasizing the fluctuation in which these plays engage between the audience's lived experience and a spiritual world beyond this one. Zumthor uses this characterization of medieval dramatic verse to make the case that medieval theatre more than modern required "an absolute predominance of extralinguistic factors."

63. See, for instance, Caroline Walker Bynum, *Resurrection*; Brown, *Cult of the Saints*; and Patrick Geary, *Furta Sacra*.

64. Cited in Frantisek Deak, "Structuralism in Theatre: The Prague School Contribution," *The Drama Review* 20.4 (1976): 88 [83–94].

65. Keir Elam, *The Semiotics of Theatre and Drama* (New York: Routledge, 2002), p. 8.

66. Elam, *Semiotics*, p. 9.

67. Bert O. States, "The Phenomenological Attitude," in *Critical Theory and Performance*, ed. Janelle G. Reinelt and Joseph R. Roach (Ann Arbor: University of Michigan Press, 1992), pp. 375–78 [369–79]. For a helpful overview of some of these terms of performance theory in their specific interactions with the traditions of late-medieval drama, see Beckwith, *Signifying God*, pp. 62–69.

68. W.J.T. Mitchell, *Iconology: Image, Text, Ideology* (Chicago: University of Chicago Press, 1986), p. 43; quoted in Scherb, *Staging Faith*, p. 48.

69. As Pamela M. King argues, "What the use of space in theatre depends upon and what the audience responds to is...a series of figurally inspired signals." King, "Spatial Semantics and the Medieval Theatre," in *The Theatrical Space*, Themes in Drama 9 (New York: Cambridge University Press, 1987), p. 47 [45–58].

70. Green, "Sir Gawain and the *Sacra Cintola*," 7.

71. Perkins, *Westminster Abbey*, pp. 2:49–50. See also Gibson's description of the decorative art at Holy Trinity Church. Long Melford, and the ways that it weaves together inscriptions of Lydgate's verse (with the command "Emprente thes thynges in thyn inward thought") with images of the Virgin Mary and Christ (*Theater of Devotion*, pp. 87–90).

72. In discussing the *Assumption* within the context of the rest of the cycle, however, it is important to remember that the text of the N-Town *Assumption* play was copied as a separate booklet by an unknown scribe and then inserted into the main text of the N-Town manuscript, which was written down by another scribe. Thus its relationship to the rest of the cycle is somewhat unclear and contested, and it is also not included in the banns for the play. See Alan J. Fletcher, "The N-Town Plays," in *The Cambridge Companion to Medieval English Theatre*, ed. Richard Beadle (Cambridge: Cambridge University Press, 1994), pp. 164, 171 [163–88].

73. Gibson, *Theater of Devotion*, p. 14.

4   Enshrining Form: *Pearl* as Inscriptional Object and Devotional Event

1. See the Cotton Nero A.x. project (http://www.ucalgary.ca/~scriptor/ cotton/, accessed April 25, 2008), which will eventually provide digital photographs, transcriptions, and editions of all the poems in the manuscript.
2. Gabrielle M. Spiegel, "History, Historicism, and the Social Logic of the Text in the Middle Ages," *Speculum* 65.1 (1990): 84 [59–86].
3. For views on the relationship between *Saint Erkenwald* and the other poems, see, for instance, Larry D. Benson, "The Authorship of *Saint Erkenwald*," *Journal of English and Germanic Philology* 64 (1965): 393–405.
4. For speculation on the identities of both the poet and the maiden, see Oscar Cargill and Margaret Schlauch, "The *Pearl* and Its Jeweller," *PMLA* 43 (1928): 105–23. More recently, Lynn Staley has speculated about Thomas of Woodstock's possible role as a patron of this poet. Staley, "*Pearl* and the Contingencies of Love and Piety," in *Medieval Literature and Historical Inquiry: Essays in Honour of Derek Pearsall*, ed. David Aers (Cambridge, UK: D.S. Brewer, 2000), pp. 83–114.
5. Paul F. Reichardt, "'Several Illuminations, Coarsely Executed': The Illustrations of the *Pearl* Manuscript," *Studies in Iconography* 18 (1997): 130 [119–42].
6. Jennifer A. Lee, "The Illuminating Critic: The Illustrator of Cotton Nero A.x.," *Studies in Iconography* 3 (1997): 40 [17–46].
7. Robert J. Blanch and Julian Wasserman, *From* Pearl *to* Gawain: *Form to Fynisment* (Gainesville: University Press of Florida, 1995), pp. 65–110.
8. Jessica Brantley, "*Pearl* and the Pictures of Cotton Nero A.x." (paper presented at the Thirty-third International Congress on Medieval Studies, Kalamazoo, MI, May 1998), p. 8; I am indebted to Professor Brantley for sharing this unpublished work with me.
9. Brantley, *Reading in the Wilderness*, p. 94.
10. Michael Camille, "Seeing and Reading: Some Visual Implications of Medieval Literacy and Illiteracy," *Art History* 8 (1985): 42–43 [26–94].
11. Nicholas Watson, "The Gawain-Poet as a Vernacular Theologian," in *A Companion to the* Gawain-*Poet*, ed. Derek Brewer and Jonathan Gibson (Cambridge, UK: D.S. Brewer, 1997), p. 299 [293–313].
12. Stanbury, *Seeing the* Gawain-*Poet*, pp. 3–5.
13. Eugene Vance, e.g., perceives in *Pearl* what he terms a "poetics of participation," through which the poet asks "how *multiple* individuals might be said to share in the being of a *single* Idea or Form" in order to produce in the poem a language that successfully conveys how "a universally shared love is essential to Christianity as a religion where human love is a valid, however incomplete, mode of participating in the reciprocated love of God." See Vance, "*Pearl*: Love and the Poetics of Participation," in *Poetics: Theory and Practice in Medieval English Literature*, ed. Piero Boitani and

Anna Torti (Cambridge, UK: D.S. Brewer, 1991), pp. 131–32, 146–47 [131–47]. Anne Howland Schotter examines the poem's impulse toward the divine from another perspective, noting that the *Pearl*-poet uses "the gap between the high and low elements in his own alliterative poetic tradition" to comment on the fallibility of human language, creating a "*sermo humilis* in which to achieve a poetic incarnation of the Word of God." See Schotter, "Vernacular Style and the Word of God: The Incarnational Art of *Pearl*," in *Ineffability: Naming the Unnamable from Dante to Beckett*, ed. Peter S. Hawkins and Anne Howland Schotter (New York: AMS Press, 1984), p. 24 [23–34].

14. "His movement toward spiritual love is manifested in the dreamer's efforts to replace a literal sense of words with an allegorical one. Once the dreamer begins to live and think allegorically, he will have applied the lessons of Easter morning; do not touch me, for I am not yet ascended to my Father." See Lynn Staley Johnson, *The Voice of the Gawain-Poet* (Madison: University of Wisconsin Press, 1984), p. 167.

15. Sandra Pierson Prior, *The Fayre Formez of the Pearl Poet* (East Lansing: Michigan State University Press, 1996), p. 16.

16. Elizabeth Schirmer, "Genre Trouble: Spiritual Reading in the Vernacular and the Literary Project of the *Pearl*-Poet" (Ph.D. diss., University of California, Berkeley, 2002), p. 97.

17. Stanbury, *The Visual Object*, pp. 23–25.

18. Anne Hudson, ed., *Two Wycliffite Texts: The Sermon of William Taylor 1406; The Testimony of William Thorpe 1407* (Oxford: Oxford University Press, 1993), p. 18. See also Stanbury's discussion of this Wycliffite context in *The Visual Object*, pp. 8–9 and Chap. 1, esp. pp. 62–66.

19. Felicity Riddy, "Jewels in *Pearl*," in *Companion to the Gawain-Poet*, p. 148 [143–55]. See also, for example, Marie Borroff, "The Many and the One: Contrasts and Complementarities in the Design of *Pearl*," in *Traditions and Renewals: Chaucer, the Gawain-Poet, and Beyond* (New Haven, CT: Yale University Press, 2003), pp. 124–62; Theodore Bogdanos, *Pearl: Image of the Ineffable: A Study in Medieval Poetic Symbolism* (University Park: Pennsylvania State University Press, 1983), pp. 18–23; and Kevin Marti, *Body, Heart, and Text in the Pearl-Poet* (Lewiston, NY: Edwin Mellen, 1991), p. 43.

20. Felicity Riddy, "Jewels in *Pearl*," in *Companion to the Gawain-Poet*, p. 148.

21. Marian Campbell, "White Harts and Coronets: The Jewellery and Plate of Richard II," in *The Regal Image of Richard II and the Wilton Diptych*, ed. Dillian Gordon, Lisa Monnas, and Caroline Elam (London: Harvey Miller, 1997), pp. 99, 106 [95–114]. For another perspective on the connection between *Pearl* and high courtly culture, see John M. Bowers, "*Pearl* in Its Royal Setting: Ricardian Poetry Revisited," *Studies in the Age of Chaucer* 17 (1995): 115 [111–55]. Bowers argues that the imagery of *Pearl* alludes to Ricardian symbols of political power (such as crowns and badges), and that the poem can be associated with "Richard II's Cheshire [c]onnection." Bowers elaborates further on this connection in

his book-length study *The Politics of* Pearl: *Court Poetry in the Age of Richard II* (Cambridge, UK: D.S. Brewer, 2001).

22. Campbell, "White Harts," in *Regal Image*, pp. 100–101.

23. Paul Binski, *Westminster Abbey and the Plantagenets* (New Haven, CT: Yale University Press, 1995), p. 179: "In England in the 1330s, these relationships were expressed by mixing stones of white, grey or black, as on the tomb of Edward II, that of Archbishop Meopham (d. 1333) at Canterbury cathedral, possibly from the same workshop, William Ramsey's cloister formerly at St. Paul's cathedral, and John XXII's tomb at Avignon. An analogous draining of colour was typical of contemporary illuminations from the London based *Queen Mary Psalter* workshop and in manuscripts, executed in *grisaille* by the group of Parisian illuminators around Jean Pucelle (d. 1334)." See also Kamerick, *Popular Piety and Art*, p. 73, on the popularity of alabaster carving in the late Middle Ages.

24. On the term *notional ekphrasis* as designating a poem about a work of art that does not necessarily exist, see John Hollander, "The Poetics of Ekphrasis," *Word & Image: A Journal of Verbal/Visual Enquiry* 4 (1988): 209 [209–19].

25. Meyer, *Medieval Allegory*, p. 157.

26. Meyer, *Medieval Allegory*, pp. 140–47.

27. Nilson, *Cathedral Shrines*, pp. 54–55.

28. Stock, *Implications of Literacy*, p. 71.

29. Brown, *Cult of the Saints*, pp. 69–71.

30. Ellert Dahl, "Heavenly Images: The Statue of St. Foy of Conques and the Signification of the Medieval 'Cult-Image' in the West," *Acta ad archaeologiam et artium historiam pertinentiae* 8 (1979): 189 [180–94]: "the *live* reaction of the image should not be seen in isolation as a kind of one-way activity. It needs to be understood as part of the mutual relationship with the worshipper."

31. Dahl discusses both the "identification...between statue and saint" and the statue's ability to represent her as "a living person, glorified through martyrdom; and the power of the statue's rich materials to signify the heavenly Jerusalem ("Heavenly Images," 178–82). He continues, "the eye of the saint is resplendent with grace and power, his glance has an inner fire, terrifying the beholder, penetrating the secret recesses of the heart" (187).

32. *Pearl*, ed. E.V. Gordon (Oxford: Clarendon, 1953), l. 179. All subsequent citations are from this edition, with line numbers appearing in the text. Translations are my own, with assistance from the published translations and editions of Marie Borroff, trans., *Pearl: A New Verse Translation* (New York: W.W. Norton, 1977); Casey Finch, trans., *The Complete Works of the* Pearl *Poet* (Berkeley: University of California Press, 1993); and A.C. Cawley and J.J. Anderson, eds., *Pearl, Cleanness, Patience, Sir Gawain and the Green Knight* (New York: E.P. Dutton, 1976).

33. Bogdanos, *Image of the Ineffable*, p. 72; P.M. Kean, *The Pearl: An Interpretation* (New York: Barnes & Noble, 1967), p. 120.

34. Bynum, *Resurrection*, caption accompanying plate 21; see also pp. 202–3 for a further discussion of this idea.

35. Bynum, *Resurrection*, p. 179.

36. Kevin Marti, "Traditional Characteristics of the Resurrected Body in *Pearl*," *Viator* 24 (1993): 334 [311–35]; see also Ian Bishop, Pearl *in Its Setting* (New York: Barnes & Noble, 1968), p. 101.

37. Ann W. Astell sees the *Pearl*-poet here as drawing upon Saint Bernard's use of "the enduring hardness and brightness of metals, gems, and stars" in his commentary on the bride figure in the Song of Songs as an "image of eternity." See Astell, *The Song of Songs in the Middle Ages* (Ithaca, NY: Cornell University Press, 1990), p. 127.

38. Kevin Marti associates these images of enclosure with the many "altar vessels," including reliquaries, that appeared in cathedrals and reminded the viewer of the building's role as a container for Christ's body. See Marti, *Body, Heart, and Text*, p. 43. As Casey Finch points out, the *Pearl*-poet exhibits an interest in the signifying potential of enclosures throughout his work: "enclosures, whether gravelike or protective, secure or precarious, form a recurring motif in the five poems [*Pearl, Patience, Cleanness, Sir Gawain and the Green Knight*, and, according to Finch's contention, *Saint Erkenwald*]. In *Patience*, the whale's belly in which Jonah is immured is perhaps the most elaborately and concretely realized of these gravelike enclosures." He sees such spaces as "the locus of a moral test" (Finch, "Introduction," in *Complete Works of the* Pearl-*Poet*, p. 8 [1–42]).

39. Borroff, trans., *Pearl*, p. xix.

40. Priscilla Martin, "Allegory and Symbolism," in *Companion to the* Gawain-*Poet*, p. 324 [315–28].

41. In the *Legenda aurea*, a dreamer sees three gold baskets and a fourth one of silver.

> One of the first three was filled with red roses, the other two with white roses; the fourth was filled with saffron. "These baskets are our coffins," Gamaliel said, "and the roses are our relics. The one with the red roses is Saint Stephen's, since he was the only one of us who merited the crown of martyrdom." (de Voragine, *The Golden Legend*, p. 2:41).

In this text, the gold and silver baskets constitute elaborate artifacts of enclosure that allow the roses to take on their metaphoric identity as relics. (The differences between the baskets also introduce the theme of authentication, which often attends textual examinations of relics.) Theodore Bogdanos points out the parallel imagery of the enclosed rose in *Pearl*, but does not discuss the identification between roses and relics. Bogdanos, *Image of the Ineffable*, p. 79.

42. Marti, *Body, Heart, and Text*, pp. 16–18.

43. Readers of *Pearl* have found other critical and theological contexts for the poem's conception of space. A.C. Spearing discusses *Pearl*'s creation of "three-dimensional space" as related to the Italian Renaissance's use of such space in the visual arts (Spearing, *The Gawain-Poet: A Critical Study* [Cambridge: Cambridge University Press, 1970], p. 37). Cary

Nelson argues that *Pearl* embodies a sphere that reflects "the common medieval conception—God is a sphere whose center is everywhere and whose circumference is nowhere." At another point in the argument, Nelson asserts that the circular aspects of the poem "become figures for man's return to a state of grace in a new Eden" (Nelson, *The Incarnate Word: Literature as Verbal Space* [Urbana: University of Illinois Press, 1973], pp. 49, 31).

44. Kean, *An Interpretation*, p. 52. Kean provides a survey of some of the medieval poetic and ideological traditions that may have influenced the *Pearl*-poet's conception of his garden. She cites St. Bernard discussing the Passion as "the fruits of the last harvest" and connects the poet's setting of the poem during harvest time to "calendar illustrations in which the corn harvest is shown.... The foreground is always filled by the figures of the reapers, whose sickles make a sharp accent against the background of the uncut corn.... The same iconography was, in fact, used both for the calendar pictures and for the illustration of the symbolical corn and grape-harvest of the Apocalypse" (p. 51). Here Kean's words indicate another possibility for reading *Pearl* in a visual artistic context.

45. English verse included a tradition of grave poetry, which emphasized the darkness and sense of entrapment that physical death entailed. "The Grave," a thirteenth-century addition to a twelfth-century manuscript of homilies, describes the grave as a hell of terrifying closeness and anticipates *Pearl*'s own conception of physical death and burial:

> Ne bith thin hus healice itinbred;
> Hit bith unheh and lah, thonne thu list therinne....
> Swa thu scealt on molde wunian ful calde,
> Dimme and deorcæ....
> Thær thu bist feste bidytt, and death hefth tha cæȝe.
>
> (Thorlac Turville-Petre, *The Alliterative Revival*
> [Cambridge, UK: D.S. Brewer, 1977], p. 9.)

46. O.D. Macrae-Gibson assigns the terms "refrain-line," "refrain-word," and "link-word" (54) in a systematic analysis that confirms Dorothy Everett's "suggestion that the link-words can form a key to the whole structure" (64). Macrae-Gibson points out that the refrain-line of this stanza group plays on the different senses of "spot" in order to emphasize the idea that "if the pearl is to be rediscovered it must, then, be by leaving the spot to which the poet's human mourning would confine him"; this assertion creates a transition to the next stanza, which picks up the word "spot." See Macrae-Gibson, "*Pearl*: The Link-Words and the Thematic Structure," *Neophilologus* 52.1 (1968): 55 [54–64].

47. Gregory Roper, "*Pearl*, Penitence, and the Recovery of the Self," *The Chaucer Review* 28.2 (1993): 169 [164–86]. Sarah Stanbury understands *Pearl*'s perception of natural cycles differently, explaining that the dreamer's sense of the "cosmic dimension" of the scene is somewhat flawed. Stanbury interprets his misperception as part of a too-narrowly perceived set of boundaries in the dreamer's own awareness of place. See Stanbury,

"Visions of Space: Acts of Perception in *Pearl* and in Some Late Medieval Illustrated Apocalypses," *Mediaevalia: A Journal of Mediaeval Studies* 10 (1988): 148–51 [133–58]. On the reliquary's use of artifice to gesture toward the heavenly and eternal, see Bynum, *Resurrection*, p. 209.

48. For an alternate reading of this line, with *fede* meaning "feed" rather than "fade," see Edward Vasta, "*Pearl*: Immortal Flowers and the Pearl's Decay," *Journal of English and Germanic Philology* 66 (1967): 519–31. In this argument, the line states that growing flowers and fruit must not feed on the lost pearl; it expresses a desire to preserve the pearl in its uncorrupted state.

49. The word *grayn* can signify "jewel" as well as "seed," as in the Harley lyric line "A greyn in golde that goodly shone." Thomas G. Duncan, ed., *Medieval English Lyrics 1200–1400* (New York: Penguin, 1995), p. 5.

50. "The *Pearl*-poet and the producers of thirteenth- and fourteenth-century Apocalypses shared an aesthetic theory which made rich and sophisticated patterns of imagery not merely decoration but the chief means of fulfilling the artist's function—the transmission and application of truth." Muriel A. Whitaker, "*Pearl* and Some Illustrated Apocalypse Manuscripts," *Viator: Medieval and Renaissance Studies* 12 (1981): 194 [183–96].

51. Stanbury, *Seeing the* Gawain-*Poet*, p. 7. Stanbury's reading of this poem makes the important point that "the method of the dreamer's visionary process is vision itself" (p. 17), clarifying the important role that visuality, as a way of both constituting and interpreting meaning, plays in the text. Stanbury uses shifts in the text's perceptual strategies (a "pattern of upward and downward gazes" on p. 20) and its references to directional space and sight to make her case. My approach takes up the question of *how* these visually related effects are represented in a verbal medium, and what kind of potential the language of the poem has to signify visually as well as verbally.

52. Stahl, "Heaven in View," in *Death and the Apocalypse*, pp. 229, 205.

53. V.A. Kolve, *Chaucer and the Imagery of Narrative: The First Five* Canterbury Tales (Stanford: Stanford University Press, 1984), p. 1. Kolve's strategy instead, one to which I am indebted, is to think in terms of "context" and how visual traditions might contribute to our understanding of medieval reading and cognitive practices.

54. Hamburger, *The Visual and the Visionary*, p. 29.

55. J. Allen Mitchell makes a related claim, arguing that *Pearl* resists typological reading. See Mitchell, "The Middle English *Pearl*: Figuring the Unfigurable," *The Chaucer Review* 35.1 (2000): 88 [86–111].

56. Roger Ellis, "The Word in Religious Art," in *Word, Picture, and Spectacle*, ed. Clifford Davidson (Kalamazoo, MI: Medieval Institute Publications, 1984), p. 23 [pp. 21–38].

57. Stanbury, *Seeing the* Gawain-*Poet*, pp. 36, 13; also "Critics have often condemned the description of the City, especially the first part with the catalogue of gems, for its simple recapitulation of the biblical text, yet they have not sufficiently recognized the originality of this section,

detailing as it does a city that is most often cited as a spiritual abstraction" (*Seeing the* Gawain-*Poet*, p. 24).

58. Suzannah Biernoff, *Sight and Embodiment in the Middle Ages* (New York: Palgrave Macmillan, 2002), p. 162.

59. Barbara Newman, "What Did It Mean to Say 'I Saw'?: The Clash between Theory and Practice in Medieval Visionary Culture," *Speculum* 80.1 (2005): 17–18 [1–43]. Newman also writes specifically about *Pearl's* heavenly Jerusalem vision in "The Artifice of Eternity: Speaking of Heaven in Three Medieval Poems," in *Envisaging Heaven in the Middle Ages*, ed. Carolyn Muessig and Ad Putter (New York: Routledge, 2007), pp. 185–206, arguing that "the celestial poetics of the Middle Ages reveled in its artificiality" (p. 186).

60. Newman, "What Did It Mean," 28–29.

61. On the poem's reference to Saint John's vision as a dream, see Constance B. Hieatt, *The Realism of Dream Visions: The Poetic Exploitation of the Dream-Experience in Chaucer and His Contemporaries* (Paris: Mouton, 1967), pp. 44–45.

62. Brigitte Bedos-Rezak, "Civic Liturgies and the Urban Records," in *City and Spectacle in Medieval Europe*, ed. Barbara Hanawalt and Kathryn L. Reyerson (Minneapolis: University of Minnesota Press, 1994), p. 46 [34–55].

63. Wendy Scase, "Writing and the 'Poetics of Spectacle': Political Epiphanies in *The Arrivall of Edward IV* and Some Contemporary and Lancastrian Texts," in *Images, Idolatry, and Iconoclasm in Late Medieval England: Textuality and the Visual Image*, ed. Jeremy Dimmick, James Simpson, and Nicolette Zeeman (New York: Oxford University Press, 2002), p. 180 [172–84].

64. Kipling, *Enter the King*, p. 15.

65. See Bowers, *The Politics of* Pearl, p. 156. In demonstrating potential connections between the *Pearl*-poet and the mainstream courtly and social life of London, Bowers continues work begun by Michael Bennett and others to remove the *Pearl*-poet from what were once believed to be his exclusively provincial West Midlands surroundings. See Michael J. Bennett, *Community, Class, and Careerism: Cheshire and Lancashire Society in the Age of* Sir Gawain and the Green Knight (New York: Cambridge University Press, 1982).

66. Bowers, *The Politics of* Pearl, pp. 154, 183.

67. Staley, "Contingencies of Love," in *Medieval Literature and Historical Inquiry*, p. 99.

68. For an explanation of the translation of line 1050, see Gordon, ed., *Pearl*, p. 83, note to line 1050.

69. On the processional role of such statuary, see Hamburger, *The Visual and the Visionary*, p. 84.

70. Ivan Illich, *In the Vineyard of the Text* (Chicago: University of Chicago Press, 1993), p. 118.

71. Herbert L. Kessler, *Seeing Medieval Art* (Orchard Park, NY: Broadview, 2004), p. 174.

72. In the context of media studies, Marshall McLuhan takes up the characterization of light in his statement that it "is the medium that shapes and controls the scale of human form and association." See McLuhan, *Understanding Media: The Extensions of Man*, critical edn. (Corte Madera, CA: Gingko, 2003), p. 20.
73. Cited in Illich, *Vineyard*, p. 18 n. 32.
74. Felman, *The Literary Speech Act*, p. 107. She elaborates here upon J.L. Austin's question about whether fire is an object or an event, and how it might elucidate the "myth," as Austin puts it, of the verb itself.
75. Kathryn L. Lynch, *The High Medieval Dream Vision: Poetry, Philosophy, and Literary Form* (Stanford: Stanford University Press, 1988), p. 16.
76. Brantley, *Reading in the Wilderness*, p. 2.
77. Nigel Morgan, *Early Gothic Manuscripts* (London: Harvey Miller, 1982–88), no. 101. Kessler mentions this image on p. 155 of *Seeing Medieval Art*.
78. Christopher Collins, *The Poetics of the Mind's Eye: Literature and the Psychology of the Imagination* (Philadelphia: University of Pennsylvania Press, 1991), pp. 6–7.
79. Newman, "What Did It Mean," 32–36.

5 Reliquaries of the Mind: Figuration, Enshrinement, and Performance in *The Pardoner's Tale*

1. Benson, ed., *The Canterbury Tales*, in *The Riverside Chaucer*, VI. 911, p. 201; all subsequent citations will appear in the text.
2. As Stanbury notes, Chaucer's use of relics in *The Pardoner's Tale* indicates his double consciousness of both the importance and the deeply problematic nature of devotional objects. Stanbury, *The Visual Object*, p. 120.
3. Cannon, *The Grounds of English Literature*, p. 9.
4. For Marx, the physical object as commodity "transcends sensuousness... and evolves out of its wooden brain grotesque ideas, far more wonderful than if it were to begin dancing of its own free will." In reading this passage as part of his larger argument about spectrality and memorial, Derrida points out the necessity of a "recourse to theatrical language" in order to characterize the commodity. See Derrida, *Specters of Marx: The State of the Debt, the Work of Mourning, and the New International*, trans. Peggy Kamuf (New York: Routledge, 1994), pp. 151–52. The reliquary of the mind, in turn, functions as a form derived not only from material culture, but also, in the specific context of *The Pardoner's Tale*, from a commodity culture. As a form, it contains the imaginative work of figuration; this work happens through its material form and not purely through imagination itself. The table as commodity reveals different possibilities for the reliquary of the mind. It can be mind as reliquary, or reliquary as mind, and this chapter explores both possibilities.
5. Eugene Vance, "Relics, Discourse," 742. See also Paul Beekman Taylor, "Peynted Confessiouns: Boccaccio and Chaucer," *Comparative*

Literature 34 (1982): 116 [116–29], on the medieval world' s "great interest" in "the discontinuity of mental concept and its physical sign." In addition, John Michael Crafton sees *The Pardoner's Tale*'s strategy in defining the relationship between language and reality as one that opposes exaggerated forms of realism and nominalism (Crafton, "Paradoxicum Semiotica: Signs, Comedy, and Mystery in Fragment VI of the *Canterbury Tales*," in *Chaucer's Humor: Critical Essays*, ed. Jean E. Jost [New York: Garland, 1994], p. 176 [163–86]).

6. Vance, "Relics, Discourse," 738–39.

7. G.R. Owst provides another way of thinking about the Pardoner's associations with relics by observing a connection between preaching and the anxieties about idolatry attendant upon relic worship and saint worship. Owst points out that sermons often depicted saints as "toil-stained flesh and blood" (p. 124). Pulpit preachers were often so successful in creating figures of saints that were vividly mystical, "a new race of deities and heroes," that it was inevitable that the unlearned people who listened to these sermons would grow credulous about miraculous relics, and eager to worship them even when such behavior met with disapproval from the church. The act of preaching itself magnified the dangers of false relics. See Owst, *Literature and Pulpit in Medieval England* (New York: Barnes & Noble, 1961).

8. Lee Patterson, "Chaucer's Pardoner on the Couch: Psyche and Clio in Medieval Literary Studies," *Speculum* 76.3 (2001): 676–77.

9. Anne Hudson, *The Premature Reformation: Wycliffite Text and Lollard History* (New York: Oxford University Press, 1988), p. 307.

10. Pamela Gradon, "Langland and the Ideology of Dissent," *Proceedings of the British Academy* 66 (1980): 194 [179–205].

11. Anne Hudson, ed., *Selections from English Wycliffite Writings* (New York: Cambridge University Press, 1978), p. 84.

12. Hudson, ed., *English Wycliffite Writings*, p. 27.

13. Hudson, ed., *English Wycliffite Writings*, pp. 83, 84–85.

14. Carolyn Dinshaw, "Eunuch Hermeneutics," in *Chaucer's Sexual Poetics* (Madison: University of Wisconsin Press, 1989), pp. 156–84.

15. On transpositions and parallels in the use of relics and the Eucharist, see G.J.C. Snoek, *Medieval Piety from Relics to the Eucharist: A Process of Mutual Interaction* (New York: E.J. Brill, 1995), pp. 382–86.

16. See Timothy Husband and Julien Chapuis, *The Treasury of Basel Cathedral* (New York: Metropolitan Museum of Art and Yale University Press, 2001), pp. 166–73, for a discussion of the late-medieval tower monstrance.

17. Michael Camille, "Before the Gaze," in *Visuality Before and Beyond the Renaissance*, p. 204.

18. In the fifteenth century, cadaver tombs would come to stage in a different way the process of transformation as related to the understanding of death. For discussions of cadaver tombs, see Eamon Duffy, *The Stripping of the Altars: Traditional Religion in England c. 1400–c. 1580* (New Haven, CT: Yale University Press, 1992), pp. 306–8, 329; and Gibson, *Theater*

of Devotion, which analyzes in particular the East Anglian tomb of John Baret (pp. 72–79).

19. Ann W. Astell, "The *Translatio* of Chaucer's Pardoner," *Exemplaria* 4.2 (1992): 424–27 [411–28].

20. For a discussion of the image of the face in relation to the tale's debt to Fals Semblant, see Jane Chance, " 'Disfigured Is Thy Face': Chaucer's Pardoner and the Protean Shape-Shifter Fals-Semblant (A Response to Britton Harwood)," *Philological Quarterly* 67.4 (1988): 423–37.

21. Paul Ricoeur, "The Metaphorical Process as Cognition, Imagination, and Feeling," in *On Metaphor,* ed. Sheldon Sacks (Chicago: University of Chicago Press, 1978), p. 142 [141–58].

22. Erich Auerbach, *"Figura,"* in *Scenes from the Drama of European Literature* (Minneapolis: University of Minnesota Press, 1984), p. 72 [11–76].

23. See also R.A. Shoaf's discussion of the Pardoner's own conflation and exchange of the concrete and symbolic as a "stew of metaphor and letter"; the text uses the Pardoner's body to figure a "literalism which kills." In *Dante, Chaucer, and the Currency of the Word: Money, Images, and Reference in Late-Medieval Poetry* (Norman, OK: Pilgrim Books, 1983), pp. 219–22.

24. On the "shades of meaning between model and copy" and "changing form and deceptive likenesses that walk in dreams," see Auerbach, *"Figura,"* in *Scenes from the Drama,* p. 21. See also the recent *Literary History and the Challenge of Philology: The Legacy of Erich Auerbach,* ed. Seth Lerer (Stanford: Stanford University Press, 1996) for a substantive revisiting of Auerbach's work, most particularly Jesse Gellrich's *"Figura,* Allegory, and the Question of History," which suggests a historicized and autobiographical motivation for Auerbach's privileging of the figural above the allegorical (p. 111 [107–23]). This argument suggests that *figura* contains the potential for a kind of concrete historicity as part of its representational work. Steven Justice has also brought a thoughtful medievalist perspective to bear on Auerbach's work in "The Authority of Ritual in the *Jeu d'Adam,*" *Speculum* 62.4 (1987): 851–64.

25. Maggie Kilgour, *From Communion to Cannibalism: An Anatomy of Metaphors of Incorporation* (Princeton: Princeton University Press, 1990), p. 28. Medieval conceptions of rhetoric borrowed from the Ciceronian notion of metaphor as *translatio,* a figure that comes into being through placing a term *in alieno loco.* Copeland prudently cautions against a haphazard conflation of metaphor and translation, something that critics have often been "teased" into puzzling over (Rita Copeland, *Rhetoric, Hermeneutics, and Translation in the Middle Ages: Academic Traditions and Vernacular Texts* [New York: Cambridge University Press, 1991], p. 235 n. 74).

26. John M. Steadman, "Old Age and *Contemptus Mundi* in the *Pardoner's Tale,*" in *Twentieth Century Interpretations of the* Pardoner's Tale: *A Collection of Critical Essays,* ed. Dewey R. Faulkner (Englewood Cliffs, NJ: Prentice-Hall, 1973), p. 73 [70–82].

27. L.O. Purdon, "The Pardoner's Old Man and the Second Death," *Studies in Philology* 89.3 (1992): 337 [334–49].

28. Rita Copeland, "The Pardoner's Body and the Disciplining of Rhetoric," in *Framing Medieval Bodies*, ed. Sarah Kay and Miri Rubin (New York: Manchester University Press, 1994), p. 141 [139–59].

29. Rita Copeland, "Rhetoric and the Politics of Literal Sense in Medieval Literary Theory: Aquinas, Wyclif, and the Lollards," in *Rhetoric and Hermeneutics in Our Time: A Reader*, ed. Walter Jost and Michael J. Hyde (New Haven, CT: Yale University Press, 1997), p. 343 [335–57].

30. Benson, ed., *Riverside Chaucer*, p. 909.

31. Carleton Brown, ed., *English Lyrics of the Thirteenth Century* (Oxford: Clarendon Press, 1932), pp. 92–100; W.F. Bryan and Germaine Dempster, eds., *Sources and Analogues of Chaucer's* Canterbury Tales (New York: Humanities Press, 1958), p. 437. Britton Harwood points out the unusual nature of the many references to containers throughout the tale, attached not only to the old man but also to the Pardoner. "Rare containers," he proposes, "proliferate about the Pardoner because the dialectical relationship between the inside and the outside of a 'boyste' is the *foyer* that produces him, perhaps in a more fundamental way than any tradition of ecclesiastical satire or any conception of the *vetus homo*." See Harwood, "Chaucer's Pardoner: The Dialectics of Inside and Outside," *Philological Quarterly* 67.4 (1988): 411 [409–22]. For Harwood, speech act theory helps to define the Pardoner's condition (p. 415).

32. Harwood contends that the gloss for cheste as "strongbox" is not necessarily a common meaning for the term, although Chaucer does employ the term in this capacity in the *Wife of Bath's Prologue*, the *Friar's Tale*, and the *Clerk's Prologue* as well. John Steadman argues that the emblem of the "cheste," and specifically the old man's willingness to give it up, is part of the old man's identity as a contrast to the worldly rioters ("Old Age," 82).

33. *Middle English Dictionary*, http://ets.umdl.umich.edu/m/med/, accessed April 26, 2008, s.v. "chaunge."

34. Shoaf, *Currency of the Word*, pp. 13, 171.

35. Death, despair, and greed have all been offered at various points as concepts for which the old man stands. See, for instance, Lee Patterson, "Chaucer's Pardoner on the Couch," 676–77; Alexandra Hennessey Olsen, "They Shul Desiren to Dye, and Deeth Shal Flee fro Hem: A Reconsideration of the Pardoner's Old Man," *Neuphilologische Mitteilungen* 84.3 (1983): 367 [367–71]; and F.N. Robinson, ed., *The Complete Works of Geoffrey Chaucer* (Boston, MA: Houghton Mifflin, 1933), p. 731. On the old man's association with avarice, see Astell, "*Translatio*," 419–21.

36. On the spatiality of metaphor in Quintilian's definition, and its characterization as a figure that "should always either occupy a place already vacant" or "should be more impressive than that which it displaces," see Astell, "*Translatio*," 422.

37. Ricoeur, "Metaphorical Process," in *On Metaphor*, p. 145.

38. Brown, *Cult of the Saints*, pp. 87–88.

39. *Middle English Dictionary*, s.v. "rollen."

40. On the problematics of the dead metaphor, see, for instance, Jacques Derrida, "White Mythology: Metaphor in the Text of Philosophy," in *Margins of Philosophy*, trans. Alan Bass (Chicago: University of Chicago Press, 1982), pp. 207–71.

41. Shoaf, *Currency of the Word*, p. 222.

42. Lerud, "Quick Images," in *Moving Subjects*, pp. 221–22.

43. Akbari, *Seeing through the Veil*, p. 3.

44. Akbari, *Seeing through the Veil*, pp. 6, 30.

45. Akbari, *Seeing through the Veil*, p. 41. See also Carruthers, *Book of Memory*, chap. 7, on the envisioning of memory as a spatialized activity that uses the visual tropes of inscriptionality and manuscript page layout. In addition, see Chaucer's own use of visual imagery to describe processes of signification in his Boethius translation, cited in Vance, "Relics, Discourse," 726.

46. John Michael Crafton suggests that "coins would be better understood by a medieval audience as connected to sign theory than by a modern audience, so the idea of coins functioning to signify death" would have been a viable one, at least to a medieval realist. See Crafton, "Paradoxicum Semiotica," in *Chaucer's Humor*, p. 182.

47. Thomas M. Greene, "Poetry as Invocation," *New Literary History* 24.3 (1993): 496–505 [495–517].

48. For a discussion of this moment's implication in various thematic and semantic inversions, see Marijane Osborn, "Transgressive Word and Image in Chaucer's Enshrined *Coillons* Passage," *The Chaucer Review* 37.4 (2003): 369, 377 [365–84]. She cites the associated passage in the *Roman de la rose*, in which the "couilles" are enshrined "en argent" (371).

49. Benson, ed., *Riverside Chaucer*, p. 910. See also Seeta Chaganti, "'A Form as Grecian Goldsmiths Make': Enshrining Narrative in Chrétien de Troyes's *Cligés* and the Stavelot Triptych," *New Medieval Literatures* 7 (2005): 183 [163–201].

50. Richard Firth Green, "The Pardoner's Pants and Why They Matter," *Studies in the Age of Chaucer* 15 (1993): 140 [131–45].

51. Paul Strohm proposes that this structure defines the place of Lollardy in *The Pardoner's Tale* as well. In Strohm's formulation the "Lollard joke" of the tale creates a dynamic in which what is enclosed also encloses. The tale's framework, as Strohm describes it, simultaneously contains and is contained by its correspondences with Lollard polemic. Strohm argues that *The Pardoner's Tale*'s incorporation of historical matter, even if the tale leaves this context unstated, is defined by a "constant instability of relations between what frames and what is framed"; this reversibility is ultimately reflected in the relationship between history and theory themselves ("Chaucer's Lollard Joke: History and the Textual Unconscious," *Studies in the Age of Chaucer* 19 [1995]: 42 [23–42]). Strohm's analysis proceeds from a contention that the Pardoner's reference to substance and accident (ll. 534–40) constitutes a joke that "enters a period of social unrest that complements its own restless textual center" (Strohm, "Lollard Joke," 27). The joke functions as a container for the Lollard

polemic within, but at the same time the passage's Lollard connotations "functio[n] protectively, diverting attention from a center" that is perhaps even more unruly and blasphemous (41). The term *seintuarie* and its companion *shryned* at the end of the tale thus play an important role in organizing not only narrative structure but also critical readings of the tale.

52. Richard Rambuss, "Devotion and Defilement: The Blessed Virgin Mary and the Corporeal Hagiographics of Chaucer's *Prioress's Tale*," in *Textual Bodies: Changing Boundaries of Literary Representation*, ed. Lori Hope Lefkovitz (Albany: State University of New York Press, 1993), p. 78 [75–99].

53. Osborn refers to the caricaturing effect of the passage as the "transgressive inversion" of parody ("Transgressive Word," 378).

54. This strategy recalls the dreamer's manipulation of time in the "maynful mone" simile discussed in chap. 4.

55. "In the world of the symbol it would be possible for the image to coincide with the substance, since the substance and its representation do not differ in their being but only in their extension; they are part and whole of the same categories. Their relationship is one of simultaneity, which, in truth, is spatial in kind, and in which the intervention of time is merely a matter of contingency, whereas, in the world of allegory, time is the originary constitutive category....[I]t remains necessary, if there is to be allegory, that the allegorical sign refer to another sign that precedes it" (Paul de Man, "The Rhetoric of Temporality," in *Critical Theory since 1965*, ed. Hazard Adams and Leroy Searle [Tallahassee: Florida State University Press, 1986], p. 209 [199–221]).

56. Melvin Storm, "The Pardoner's Invitation: Quaestor's Bag or Becket's Shrine?" *PMLA* 97.5 (1982): 815 [810–818].

57. H. Leith Spencer, *English Preaching in the Late Middle Ages* (Oxford: Clarendon Press, 1993), pp. 113–17. See also Siegfried Wenzel, "Chaucer and the Language of Contemporary Preaching," *Studies in Philology* 73 (1976): 138–61; and R.P. Merrix, "Sermon Structure in the *Pardoner's Tale*," *The Chaucer Review* 17 (1983): 235–49.

58. Alan J. Fletcher, *Preaching, Politics, and Poetry in Late Medieval England* (Dublin: Four Courts Press, 1998), pp. 264–65.

59. Spencer, *English Preaching*, p. 12.

60. Fletcher, *Preaching, Politics*, pp. 256–57.

61. Glenn Burger, "Kissing the Pardoner," *PMLA* 107.5 (1992): 1150 [1143–56]. Another view of the place of paradox in this tale appears in John Michael Crafton's essay on humor in the *Canterbury Tales* (Crafton, "Paradoxicum Semiotica," in *Chaucer's Humor*, p. 169).

62. Lee Patterson, *Chaucer and the Subject of History* (Madison: University of Wisconsin Press, 1991), p. 418.

63. On the status of the Pardoner's body in relation to the performative occasion of preaching, see Claire M. Waters, *Angels and Earthly Creatures: Preaching, Performance, and Gender in the Later Middle Ages* (Philadelphia: University of Pennsylvania Press, 2004), pp. 41–56.

64. Harwood, "Dialectics," 415.

Conclusion: A Lyric Poetics of Enshrinement

1. Olson, "Toward a Poetics," in *Vernacular Poetics*, p. 227.

2. Gregory Roper, "The Middle English Lyric 'I,' Penitential Poetics, and Medieval Selfhood," *Poetica* 42 (1994): 71–72 [71–103].

3. See, for instance, Ann Astell's reading of the Song of Songs as a basis for understanding the secular components of religious lyrics. Astell, *Song of Songs*, p. 139.

4. On Froissart's use of lyric in this context, see, for example, Julia Boffey, "The Lyrics in Chaucer's Longer Poems," *Poetica* 37 (1992): 30 [15–37]. See also Glending Olson's discussion of the late-medieval authorial tendency to juxtapose secular and sacred modes in Olson, "Toward a Poetics," in *Vernacular Poetics*, p. 237.

5. Siegfried Wenzel, *Preachers, Poets, and the Early English Lyric* (Princeton: Princeton University Press, 1986), p. 99.

6. Waters, *Angels and Earthly Creatures*, pp. 39–40.

7. Wenzel, *Preachers, Poets*, pp. 13, 99–100.

8. Wenzel, *Preachers, Poets*, p. 84. Wenzel addresses the performative potential of this work in his comment that while the act of preaching differs from the meditative context Rosemary Woolf associates with lyric, "the subject matter and ultimate purpose of both are entirely the same" (p. 13).

9. Wenzel, *Preachers, Poets*, p. 116.

10. Alan J. Fletcher, "The Lyric in the Sermon," in *A Companion to the Middle English Lyric*, ed. Thomas G. Duncan (Woodbridge, UK: D.S. Brewer, 2005), p. 197 [189–209].

11. Brantley, *Reading in the Wilderness*, pp. 122–23.

12. Brantley, *Reading in the Wilderness*, p. 134.

13. Christiania Whitehead, "Middle English Religious Lyrics," in *A Companion to the Middle English Lyric*, p. 102 [96–119].

14. Whitehead, "Religious Lyrics," in *A Companion to the Middle English Lyric*, pp. 103, 108.

15. Steiner, *Documentary Culture*, p. 80.

16. Bodleian MS Douce 326, fol. 14r. Indexed in Carleton Brown and R.H. Robbins, *The Index of Middle English Verse* (New York: Columbia University Press, 1943), index no. 927. Printed in R.T. Davies, ed., *Medieval English Lyrics* (London: Northwestern University Press, 1964), p. 201.

17. Brown and Robbins, *Index*, index no. 1761. According to Davies, this lyric exists in ten manuscripts; for a fuller discussion see *Medieval English Lyrics*, pp. 120, 324–25.

18. Julia Boffey, "Middle English Lyrics and Manuscripts," in *A Companion to the Middle English Lyric*, p. 2 [2–18].

19. Boffey, "Middle English Lyrics," in *A Companion to the Middle English Lyric*, p. 14; Wenzel, *Preachers, Poets*, p. 84.

20. As Brantley points out, "the division of English poems into visible metrical lines dates from the Middle English period" (*Reading in the Wilderness*, p. 122).

21. Wenzel, *Preachers, Poets*, pp. 167–69.
22. Brown and Robbins, *Index*, index no. 717. Printed in Maxwell Luria and Richard L. Hoffman, eds., *Middle English Lyrics* (New York: Norton, 1974), p. 121. A digital image of this manuscript page appears at http://www. diamm.ac.uk/diamm/apps/DisplayImage.jsp?imageKey=8444, accessed April 25, 2008. The DIAMM (Digital Image Archive of Medieval Music) Web site provides useful resources not only for musicologists, but also for literary scholars and historians of the Middle Ages.
23. Rosamond McKitterick and Richard Beadle, *Catalogue of the Pepys Library at Magdalene College, Cambridge V: Manuscripts I. Medieval* (Cambridge, UK: D.S. Brewer, 1993), p. 13.
24. I thank Barbara Zimbalist for her analysis of this manuscript page's musical content.
25. On other uses of the IHC monogram in conjunction with lyric, in addition to the crossed transverse as a way of suggesting a cruciform shape, see Brantley, *Reading in the Wilderness*, p. 142, and Figures 4.6 and 4.9.
26. As Brantley has argued, monograms contained the kind of talismanic power that would allow them to transcend their textual identity and subsume it: "holy words become 'objects' meaningful beyond their transparent, grammatical sense, and their manifestation in monograms and pictures, often unvoiceable, is imbued with the power to work miracles" (*Reading in the Wilderness*, p. 179).
27. See n. 9, Introduction.
28. Miller, *Speech Acts in Literature*, pp. 89–90.
29. W.J.T. Mitchell, *Picture Theory* (Chicago: University of Chicago Press, 1994), p. 154.
30. As a number of critics have pointed out, this phrase does not necessarily derive from a hortatory statement about a necessary parallel between the two art forms. See, for instance, Jean Hagstrum, *The Sister Arts: The Tradition of Literary Pictorialism and English Poetry from Dryden to Gray* (Chicago: University of Chicago Press, 1958), p. 9. For a discussion of early modern interactions between text and classical art, see Leonard Barkan, *Unearthing the Past: Archaeology and Aesthetics in the Making of Renaissance Culture* (New Haven, CT: Yale University Press, 1999). As Barkan argues, "The conjunction of text and object raises questions about textual authority itself by exposing the rhetoricity of the text. The solution to these uncertainties is to find truth in the object rather than in the text" (pp. 6–7).
31. On Leonardo, see Rensselaer W. Lee, *Ut Pictura Poesis: The Humanistic Theory of Painting* (New York: W.W. Norton, 1967), p. 6; on Lessing, see Norman Bryson, "Intertextuality and Visual Poetics," *Critical Texts* 4.2 (1987): 1 [1–6].
32. See in particular E.H. Gombrich, *Art and Illusion: A Study in the Psychology of Pictorial Representation* (New York: Bollingen Foundation, 1961). For a discussion of the ways in which Gombrich himself ultimately reestablished some of these more traditional boundaries and the reaction of art critics

and semioticians to his work, see Murray Krieger, "The Ambiguities of Representation and Illusion: An E.H. Gombrich Retrospective," *Critical Inquiry* 11 (1984): 184–87 [181–94].

33. Henryk Markiewicz, "Ut Pictura Poesis...A History of the Topos and the Problem," *New Literary History* 18.3 (1987): 542 [535–58].

34. Murray Krieger, "Ekphrasis and the Still Moment of Poetry: Or, *Laokoön* Revisited," in *Perspectives on Poetry*, ed. James L. Calderwood and Harold E. Toliver (New York: Oxford University Press, 1968), p. 325 [323–48]; Michael Davidson, "Ekphrasis and the Postmodern Painter Poem," *Journal of Aesthetics and Art Criticism* 42.1 (1983): 72 [69–79]. See also Fred Moramarco, "John Ashbery and Frank O'Hara: The Painterly Poets," *Journal of Modern Literature* 5.3 (1976): 436–62.

35. Davidson, "Postmodern Painter Poem," 77. As he puts it, O'Hara and Ashbery are both "acutely aware of how the painting offers a variety of formal solutions to their own compositional interests."

36. Leo Spitzer, "A Note on the Poetic and Empirical 'I' in Medieval Authors," *Traditio* 4 (1946): 415 [414–22].

37. Spitzer, "A Note," 418–21.

38. Allen, "Grammar, Poetic Form," in *Vernacular Poetics*, p. 208. See also Rita Copeland, "The Middle English 'Candet Nudatum Pectus' and Norms of Early Vernacular Translation Practice," *Leeds Studies in English* 15 (1984): 64–65 [57–81], on the shifting of voice and speaker as part of the process of translating meditative traditions into vernacular lyric. In addition, Sarah Stanbury makes the case that the lyric speaker in the Middle English Passion lyric often sustains a complicated relationship to the Marian gaze that this "I" portrays, demonstrating another way in which the lyric speaker locates itself variously. Stanbury, "The Virgin's Gaze: Spectacle and Transgression in Middle English Lyrics of the Passion," *PMLA* 106.5 (1991): 1085, 1089 [1083–93].

39. Roper, "The Middle English Lyric 'I,'" 77; emphases in original.

40. David L. Jeffrey, *Early English Lyric and Franciscan Spirituality* (Lincoln: University of Nebraska Press, 1975), p. 2.

41. Louise Fradenburg, "'Voice Memorial': Loss and Reparation in Chaucer's Poetry," *Exemplaria* 2 (1990): 169–202.

42. On the numbering of these lines, see Benson, ed., *Riverside Chaucer*, p. 1137. Line 480 is skipped to preserve the traditional numbering while omitting a line added in William Thynne's edition. Thynne's emendations attempt to replicate the rhyme scheme found in the knight's lyric at lines 1175–80.

43. Derrida, *Limited Inc*, p. 12; Miller, *Speech Acts in Literature*, p. 106.

44. On the "functional structure of the mark," see Derrida, *Limited Inc*, p. 48.

45. Arthur Bahr, "The Rhetorical Construction of Narrator and Narrative in Chaucer's the *Book of the Duchess*," *The Chaucer Review* 35.1 (2000): 55 [43–59].

46. Bahr, "Rhetorical Construction," 50.

47. Robert A. Watson, "Dialogue and Invention in the *Book of the Duchess*," *Modern Philology* 98.4 (2001): 545 [543–76].

48. Lois Ebin, "Poetics and Style," in *Vernacular Poetics in the Middle Ages*, p. 267 [263–93].

49. Robert J. Meyer-Lee, *Poets and Power from Chaucer to Wyatt* (New York: Cambridge University Press, 2007), pp. 3, 10. As Meyer-Lee points out, lyric tradition itself in the fifteenth century, even when centered around historically specific figures such as Charles d'Orléans, functions as part of a courtly mode that does not participate in these same poetics of authorial self-construction and self-designation (p. 9).

50. Marjorie Perloff, "Language Poetry and the Lyric Subject: Ron Silliman's *Albany*, Susan Howe's *Buffalo*," *Critical Inquiry* 25 (1999): 405–7 [405–34].

51. Michael Greer, "Ideology and Theory in Recent Experimental Writing, or the Naming of 'Language Poetry,' " *boundary 2* 16.2/3 (1989): 336, 343 [335–55].

52. Oren Izenberg, "Language Poetry and the Collective Life," *Critical Inquiry* 30 (2003): 148 [132–59].

53. Cited in Perloff, "Language Poetry and the Lyric Subject," 405.

54. Ron Silliman, "Who Speaks: Ventriloquism and the Self in the Poetry Reading," in *Close Listening*, p. 362.

55. Bob Perelman, ed. *Writing/Talks* (Carbondale: Southern Illinois University Press), 1985.

56. Greer, "Ideology and Theory," 345.

57. Izenberg, "Collective Life," 156.

58. Michael Palmer, "Sun," in *Sun* (San Francisco: North Point Press, 1988), p. 84.

59. In a sense, this move simply forms part of a larger tendency to turn toward specific elements of postmodern culture—particularly its means of disseminating information—to understand more completely medieval epistemologies, aesthetics, and ways of organizing information. See, for instance, Gillespie, "Medieval Hypertext," in *Of the Making of Books*, and Ruth Evans, "Chaucer in Cyberspace: Medieval Technologies of Memory and the *House of Fame*," *Studies in the Age of Chaucer* 23 (2001): 43–69. Somewhat tellingly, the Derridean theoretical foundations on which this study relies have been characterized as endemic to a culture that has moved beyond print, that is something other than print culture (Miller, *Speech Acts in Literature*, p. 88). And this idea of an electronic alternative to print culture carries, as the two essays cited suggest, many analogies to the information culture that existed before print. I have, however, been interested less in methods of categorizing and communicating information than in finding new languages for describing medieval representational practices themselves. Thus while thinking of Derrida's work as applicable to an information culture similar to that of the Middle Ages might motivate certain connections and relevances, I have wished

to focus more upon ways of describing the medieval mind's approach to artistic creation.

60. See for instance, the 2008 New Chaucer Society Congress session on "Form," as well as a 2008 symposium in honor of Anne Middleton at the University of California, Berkeley, entitled "The State of the Literary: Form after Historicism."

61. Greer, "Ideology and Theory," 342.

BIBLIOGRAPHY

Primary Texts

Andrew, Malcolm, and Ronald Waldron, eds. *The Poems of the Pearl Manuscript*. Exeter, UK: University of Exeter Press, 2002.

The Assumption of Mary. In *The N-Town Play: Cotton MS Vespasian D.8*. Ed. Stephen Spector, vol. 1, EETS s.s. 11. New York: Oxford University Press, 1991.

Brown, Carleton, ed. *English Lyrics of the Thirteenth Century*. Oxford: Clarendon, 1932.

Chaucer, Geoffrey. *The Riverside Chaucer*. Ed. Larry D. Benson. Boston, MA: Houghton Mifflin, 1987.

Davidson, Clifford, ed. *A Tretise of Miraclis Pleyinge*. Kalamazoo, MI: Medieval Institute Publications, 1993.

Davies, R.T., ed. *Medieval English Lyrics*. London: Northwestern University Press, 1964.

de Voragine, Jacobus. "The Assumption of the Virgin." In *The Golden Legend*, vol. 2. Ed. and trans. William Granger Ryan. Princeton: Princeton University Press, 1995.

Duemmler, Ernestus, rec. *Poetae latini aevi carolini*, vol. 2. Munich, Germany: Monumenta Germaniae Historica, 1978.

Duncan, Thomas G., ed. *Medieval English Lyrics 1200–1400*. New York: Penguin, 1995.

Geoffrey of Vinsauf. *Poetria Nova*. In *Three Medieval Rhetorical Arts*. Ed and trans. James Jerome Murphy. Berkeley: University of California Press, 1971.

Goldin, Frederick, ed. and trans. *The Song of Roland*. New York: W.W. Norton, 1978.

Gordon, E.V., ed. *Pearl*. Oxford: Clarendon, 1953.

Luria, Maxwell, and Richard L. Hoffman, eds. *Middle English Lyrics*. New York: Norton, 1974.

Lydgate, John. *Troy Book*. Ed. Henry Bergen. London: Kegan Paul, 1906–20.

Peterson, Clifford, ed. *Saint Erkenwald*. Philadelphia: University of Pennsylvania Press, 1977.

Robinson, F.N., ed. *The Complete Works of Geoffrey Chaucer*. Boston, MA: Houghton Mifflin, 1933.

Saint Augustine. *De Doctrina Christiana*. Ed. and trans. R.P.H. Green. Oxford: Clarendon, 1995.

Steward, Aubrey, trans. *The Epitome of S. Eucherius about Certain Holy Places*. London: Palestine Pilgrims' Text Society, 1971.

Secondary Texts

Abou-el-Haj, Barbara. "The Audiences for the Medieval Cult of Saints." *Gesta* 30 (1991): 3–15.

Aers, David. *Chaucer, Langland, and the Creative Imagination*. Boston, MA: Routledge and Kegan Paul, 1980.

Akbari, Suzanne. *Seeing through the Veil: Optical Theory and Medieval Allegory*. Toronto: University of Toronto Press, 2004.

Allen, Judson Boyce. *The Ethical Poetic of the Later Middle Ages*. Toronto: University of Toronto Press, 1982.

———. "Grammar, Poetic Form, and the Lyric Ego." In *Vernacular Poetics in the Middle Ages*. Ed. Lois Ebin. Kalamazoo, MI: Medieval Institute Publications, 1984.

Ashley, Kathleen. "Image and Ideology: Saint Anne in Late Medieval Drama and Narrative." In *Interpreting Cultural Symbols: Saint Anne in Late Medieval Society*. Ed. Kathleen Ashley and Pamela Sheingorn. Athens: University of Georgia Press, 1990.

———. "Sponsorship, Reflexivity, and Resistance: Cultural Readings of the York Cycle Plays." In *The Performance of Middle English Culture: Essays on Chaucer and the Drama in Honor of Martin Stevens*. Ed. James J. Paxson, Lawrence M. Clopper, and Sylvia Tomasch. Rochester, NY: D.S. Brewer, 1998.

Astell, Ann W. *Eating Beauty: The Eucharist and the Spiritual Arts of the Middle Ages*. Ithaca, NY: Cornell University Press, 2006.

———. *The Song of Songs in the Middle Ages*. Ithaca, NY: Cornell University Press, 1990.

———. "The *Translatio* of Chaucer's Pardoner." *Exemplaria* 4, no. 2 (1992): 411–28.

Auerbach, Erich. "*Figura*." In *Scenes from the Drama of European Literature*. Minneapolis: University of Minnesota Press, 1984.

Bahr, Arthur. "The Rhetorical Construction of Narrator and Narrative in Chaucer's the *Book of the Duchess*." *Chaucer Review* 35, no. 1 (2000): 43–59.

Barkan, Leonard. *Unearthing the Past: Archaeology and Aesthetics in the Making of Renaissance Culture*. New Haven, CT: Yale University Press, 1999.

Beckwith, Sarah. "Passionate Regulation: Enclosure, Ascesis, and the Feminist Imaginary." *South Atlantic Quarterly* 93, no. 4 (1995): 803–24.

———. *Signifying God: Social Relation and Symbolic Act in the York Corpus Christi Plays*. Chicago: University of Chicago Press, 2001.

Bedos-Rezak, Brigitte. "Civic Liturgies and the Urban Records." In *City and Spectacle in Medieval Europe*. Ed. Barbara Hanawalt and Kathryn L. Reyerson. Minneapolis: University of Minnesota Press, 1994.

Belting, Hans. *Likeness and Presence: A History of the Image before the Era of Art*. Trans. Edmund Jephcott. Chicago: University of Chicago Press, 1994.

Benjamin, Walter. "The Work of Art in the Age of Mechanical Reproduction." In *Illuminations*. Ed. Hannah Arendt. Trans. Harry Zohn. New York: Schocken Books, 1986.

Bennett, Michael J. *Community, Class, and Careerism: Cheshire and Lancashire Society in the Age of* Sir Gawain and the Green Knight. New York: Cambridge University Press, 1982.

Benson, Larry D. "The Authorship of *Saint Erkenwald*." *Journal of English and Germanic Philology* 64 (1965): 393–405.

Bernstein, Charles. "Introduction." In *Close Listening: Poetry and the Performed Word*. Ed. Charles Bernstein. New York: Oxford University Press, 1998.

Biernoff, Suzannah. *Sight and Embodiment in the Middle Ages*. New York: Palgrave Macmillan, 2002.

Binski, Paul. *Becket's Crown: Art and Imagination in Gothic England, 1170–1300*. New Haven, CT: Yale University Press, 2004.

———. "The English Parish Church and Its Art in the Later Middle Ages: A Review of the Problem." *Studies in Iconography* 20 (1999): 1–25.

———. "Liturgy and Local Knowledge: English Perspectives on Trondheim Cathedral." In *The Medieval Cathedral of Trondheim: Architectural and Ritual Constructions in Their European Context*. Ed. Margrete Syrstad Andås, Øystein Ekroll, Andreas Haug, and Nils Holger. Turnhout, Belgium: Brepols, 2007.

———. *Westminster Abbey and the Plantagenets*. New Haven, CT: Yale University Press, 1995.

Bishop, Ian. *Pearl in Its Setting*. New York: Barnes & Noble, 1968.

Blanch, Robert J., and Julian Wasserman. *From Pearl to Gawain: Form to Fynisment*. Gainesville: University Press of Florida, 1995.

Boehm, Barbara Drake. "Body-Part Reliquaries: The State of Research." *Gesta* 36 (1997): 8–19.

Boffey, Julia. "The Lyrics in Chaucer's Longer Poems." *Poetica* 37 (1992): 15–37.

———. "Middle English Lyrics and Manuscripts." In *A Companion to the Middle English Lyric*. Ed. Thomas G. Duncan. Woodbridge, UK: D.S. Brewer, 2005.

Bogdanos, Theodore. Pearl: *Image of the Ineffable: A Study in Medieval Poetic Symbolism*. University Park: Pennsylvania State University Press, 1983.

Bolter, Jay David, and Richard Grusin. *Remediation: Understanding New Media*. Cambridge, MA: MIT Press, 1999.

Borroff, Marie, trans. *Pearl: A New Verse Translation*. New York: W.W. Norton, 1977.

———. *Traditions and Renewals: Chaucer, the* Gawain-*Poet, and Beyond*. New Haven, CT: Yale University Press, 2003.

Bowers, John M. "*Pearl* in Its Royal Setting: Ricardian Poetry Revisited." *Studies in the Age of Chaucer* 17 (1995): 111–55.

———. *The Politics of* Pearl: *Court Poetry in the Age of Richard II*. Cambridge, UK: D.S. Brewer, 2001.

Brantley, Jessica. "*Pearl* and the Pictures of Cotton Nero A.x." Paper presented at the Thirty-Third International Congress on Medieval Studies, Kalamazoo, MI, May 1998.

Brantley, Jessica. *Reading in the Wilderness: Private Devotion and Public Performance in Late Medieval England.* Chicago: University of Chicago Press, 2007.

Bridges, Margaret. "The Picture in the Text: Ecphrasis as Self-Reflectivity in Chaucer's *Parliament of Fowls, Book of the Duchess,* and *House of Fame.*" *Word and Image* 5 (1989): 151–58.

Brodsky, Joyce. "Le groupe du triptyque Stavelot: notes sur un atelier mosan et sur les rapports avec Saint-Denis." *Cahiers de civilisation médiévale* 21 (1978): 103–20.

Brown, Carleton, and R.H. Robbins. *The Index of Middle English Verse.* New York: Columbia University Press, 1943.

Brown, Elizabeth A.R. "Death and the Human Body in the Later Middle Ages: The Legislation of Boniface VIII on the Division of the Corpse." *Viator: Medieval and Renaissance Studies* 12 (1981): 221–70.

Brown, Peter. *The Cult of the Saints: Its Rise and Function in Latin Christianity.* Chicago: University of Chicago Press, 1982.

Brown, Peter. "On the Borders of Middle English Dream Vision." In *Reading Dreams: The Interpretation of Dreams from Chaucer to Shakespeare.* Ed. Peter Brown. New York: Oxford University Press, 1999.

Bryan, W.F., and Germaine Dempster, eds. *Sources and Analogues of Chaucer's Canterbury Tales.* New York: Humanities Press, 1958.

Bryson, Norman. "Intertextuality and Visual Poetics." *Critical Texts* 4, no. 2 (1987): 1–6.

Burger, Glenn. "Kissing the Pardoner." *PMLA* 107, no. 5 (1992): 1143–56.

Butterfield, Ardis. *Poetry and Music in Medieval France: From Jean Renart to Guillaume de Machaut.* New York: Cambridge University Press, 2002.

Bynum, Caroline Walker. *Fragmentation and Redemption: Essays on Gender and the Human Body in Medieval Religion.* New York: Zone, 1991.

———. *The Resurrection of the Body in Western Christianity, 200–1336.* New York: Columbia University Press, 1995.

———. "Seeing and Seeing Beyond: The Mass of Saint Gregory in the Fifteenth Century." In *The Mind's Eye: Art and Theological Argument in the Middle Ages.* Ed. Jeffrey F. Hamburger and Anne-Marie Bouché. Princeton: Princeton University Press, 2006.

Bynum, Caroline Walker, and Paula Gerson. "Body-Part Reliquaries and Body Parts in the Middle Ages." *Gesta* 36 (1997): 3–7.

Cairns, Sandra. "Fact and Fiction in the Middle English *De Erkenwaldo.*" *Neuphilologische Mitteilungen* 83 (1982): 430–38.

Camille, Michael. "Before the Gaze: The Internal Senses and Late Medieval Practices of Seeing." In *Visuality Before and Beyond the Renaissance.* Ed. Robert S. Nelson. New York: Cambridge University Press, 2000.

———. *The Gothic Idol: Ideology and Image-making in Medieval Art.* New York: Cambridge University Press, 1989.

———. "Seeing and Reading: Some Visual Implications of Medieval Literacy and Illiteracy." *Art History* 8 (1985): 26–94.

Campbell, Marian. "Metalwork in England, c. 1200–1400." In *The Age of Chivalry: Art in Plantagenet England, 1200–1400.* Ed. Jonathan Alexander and Paul Binski. London: Royal Academy of Arts. 1987.

————. "White Harts and Coronets: The Jewellery and Plate of Richard II." In *The Regal Image of Richard II and the Wilton Diptych*. Ed. Dillian Gordon, Lisa Monnas, and Caroline Elam. London: Harvey Miller, 1997.

Cannon, Christopher. "Enclosure." In *The Cambridge Companion to Medieval Women's Writing*. Ed. Carolyn Dinshaw and David Wallace. New York: Cambridge University Press, 2003.

————. *The Grounds of English Literature*. New York: Oxford University Press, 2004.

Caputo, John D. "Shedding Tears Beyond Being: Derrida's Confession of Prayer." In *Augustine and Postmodernism: Confessions and Circumfession*. Ed. John D. Caputo and Michael J. Scanlon. Bloomington: Indiana University Press, 2005.

Cargill, Oscar, and Margaret Schlauch. "The *Pearl* and Its Jeweller." *PMLA* 43 (1928): 105–23.

Carruthers, Mary. *The Book of Memory: A Study of Memory in Medieval Culture*. Cambridge: Cambridge University Press, 1990.

————. "Reading with Attitude, Remembering the Book." In *The Book and the Body*. Ed. Dolores Warwick Frese and Katherine O'Brien O'Keeffe. Notre Dame, IN: University of Notre Dame Press, 1997.

Cassidy, Brendan. "A Relic, Some Pictures, and the Mothers of Florence." *Gesta* 30, no. 2 (1991): 91–99.

Cawley, A.C., and J.J. Anderson, eds. *Pearl, Cleanness, Patience, Sir Gawain and the Green Knight*. New York: E.P. Dutton, 1976.

Chaganti, Seeta. "'A Form as Grecian Goldsmiths Make': Enshrining Narrative in Chrétien de Troyes's *Cligés* and the Stavelot Triptych." *New Medieval Literatures* 7 (2005): 163–201.

Chance, Jane. "'Disfigured Is Thy Face': Chaucer's Pardoner and the Protean Shape-Shifter Fals-Semblant (A Response to Britton Harwood)." *Philological Quarterly* 67, no. 4 (1988): 423–37.

Ciresi, Lisa Victoria. "A Liturgical Study of the Shrine of the Three Kings at Cologne." In *Objects, Images, and the Word: Art in the Service of the Liturgy*. Ed. Colum Hourihane. Princeton: Princeton University Press, 2003.

Clopper, Lawrence M. *Drama, Play, and Game: English Festive Culture in the Medieval and Early Modern Period*. Chicago: University of Chicago Press, 2001.

Coldstream, Nicola. "The Kingdom of Heaven: Its Architectural Setting." In *The Age of Chivalry: Art in Plantagenet England, 1200–1400*. Ed. Jonathan Alexander and Paul Binski. London: Royal Academy of Arts, 1987.

Coletti, Theresa. "Devotional Iconography in the N-Town Marian Plays." *Comparative Drama* 11 (1977): 22–44.

————. *Naming the Rose: Eco, Medieval Signs, and Modern Theory*. Ithaca, NY: Cornell University Press, 1988.

Colish, Marcia L. *The Mirror of Language: A Study in the Medieval Theory of Knowledge*. New Haven. CT: Yale University Press, 1968.

Collette, Carolyn P. "'Ubi Peccaverant, Ibi Punirenturn': The Oak Tree and the *Pardoner's Tale*." *The Chaucer Review* 19 (1984): 39–45.

Collins, Christopher. *The Poetics of the Mind's Eye: Literature and the Psychology of the Imagination.* Philadelphia: University of Pennsylvania Press, 1991.

Connor, Steven. "Postmodern Performance." In *Analysing Performance: A Critical Reader.* Ed. Patrick Campbell. New York: Manchester University Press, 1996.

Cooper, Helen. "Generic Variations on the Theme of Poetic and Civil Authority." In *Poetics: Theory and Practice in Medieval English Literature. The J.A.W. Bennett Memorial Lectures.* Ed. Piero Boitani and Anna Torti. Woodbridge, UK: D.S. Brewer, 1991.

Copeland, Rita. "The Middle English 'Candet Nudatum Pectus' and Norms of Early Vernacular Translation Practice." *Leeds Studies in English* 15 (1984): 157–81.

———. "The Pardoner's Body and the Disciplining of Rhetoric." In *Framing Medieval Bodies.* Ed. Sarah Kay and Miri Rubin. New York: Manchester University Press, 1994.

———. "Rhetoric and the Politics of Literal Sense in Medieval Literary Theory: Aquinas, Wyclif, and the Lollards." In *Rhetoric and Hermeneutics in Our Time: A Reader.* Ed. Walter Jost and Michael J. Hyde. New Haven, CT: Yale University Press, 1997.

———. *Rhetoric, Hermeneutics, and Translation in the Middle Ages: Academic Traditions and Vernacular Texts.* New York: Cambridge University Press, 1991.

Crafton, John Michael. "Paradoxicum Semiotica: Signs, Comedy, and Mystery in Fragment VI of the *Canterbury Tales*." In *Chaucer's Humor: Critical Essays.* Ed. Jean E. Jost. New York: Garland, 1994.

Dahl, Ellert. "Heavenly Images: The Statue of St. Foy of Conques and the Signification of the Medieval 'Cult-Image' in the West." *Acta ad archaeologiam et artium historiam pertinentiae* 8 (1979): 180–94.

Davidson, Clifford. *Drama and Art: An Introduction to the Use of Evidence from the Visual Arts for the Study of Drama.* Kalamazoo, MI: Medieval Institute Publications, 1977.

Davidson, Michael. "Ekphrasis and the Postmodern Painter Poem," *Journal of Aesthetics and Art Criticism* 42, no. 1 (1983): 69–79.

Deak, Frantisek. "Structuralism in Theatre: The Prague School Contribution." *The Drama Review* 20, no. 4 (1976): 83–94.

de Man, Paul. "The Rhetoric of Temporality." In *Critical Theory since 1965.* Ed. Hazard Adams and Leroy Searle. Tallahassee: Florida State University Press, 1986.

DeLillo, Don. *White Noise.* New York: Viking, 1985.

Derrida, Jacques. "Composing 'Circumfession.'" In *Augustine and Postmodernism: Confessions and Circumfession.* Ed. John D. Caputo and Michael J. Scanlon. Bloomington: Indiana University Press, 2005.

———. *Of Grammatology.* Trans. Gayatri Chakravorty Spivak. Baltimore, MD: Johns Hopkins University Press, 1974.

———. *Limited Inc.* Trans. Samuel Weber and Jeffrey Mehlman. Evanston, IL: Northwestern University Press, 1988.

———. *Margins of Philosophy.* Trans. Alan Bass. Chicago: University of Chicago Press, 1982.

————. *Memoires: For Paul de Man.* Trans. Cecile Lindsay, Jonathan Culler, and Eduardo Cadava. New York: Columbia University Press, 1986.

————. *Specters of Marx: The State of the Debt, the Work of Mourning, and the New International.* Trans. Peggy Kamuf. New York: Routledge, 1994.

Diebold, William. *Word and Image: An Introduction to Early Medieval Art.* Boulder, CO: Westview, 2000.

Dillenberger, John. *Images and Relics: Theological Perceptions and Visual Images in Sixteenth-Century Europe.* New York: Oxford University Press, 1999.

Dillon, Janette. *Language and Stage in Medieval and Renaissance England.* Cambridge: Cambridge University Press, 1998.

Dinshaw, Carolyn. *Chaucer's Sexual Poetics.* Madison: University of Wisconsin Press, 1989.

Draper, Peter. "Architecture and Liturgy." In *The Age of Chivalry: Art in Plantagenet England, 1200–1400.* Ed. Jonathan Alexander and Paul Binski. London: Royal Academy of Arts, 1987.

Duclow, Donald. "The Virgin's 'Good Death.'" *Fifteenth-Century Studies* 21 (1994): 55–86.

Duffy, Eamon. "The Dynamics of Pilgrimage in Late Medieval England." In *Pilgrimage: The English Experience from Becket to Bunyan.* Ed. Colin Morris and Peter Roberts. New York: Cambridge University Press, 2002.

————. *The Stripping of the Altars: Traditional Religion in England c. 1400–c. 1580.* New Haven, CT: Yale University Press, 1992.

Ebin, Lois. "Poetics and Style in Late Medieval Literature." In *Vernacular Poetics in the Middle Ages.* Ed. Lois Ebin. Kalamazoo, MI: Medieval Institute Publications, 1984.

Edwards, A.S.G. "Chaucer and the Poetics of Utterance." In *Poetics: Theory and Practice in Medieval English Literature. The J.A.W. Bennett Memorial Lectures.* Ed. Piero Boitani and Anna Torti. Woodbridge, UK: D.S. Brewer, 1991.

Ehresmann, Donald L. "Some Observations on the Role of Liturgy in the Early Winged Altarpiece." *Art Bulletin* 64, no. 3 (1982): 359–69.

Elam, Keir. *The Semiotics of Theatre and Drama.* New York: Routledge, 2002.

Eliade, Mircea. *The Encyclopedia of Religion.* Vol. 12. New York: Macmillan, 1987.

————. *Images et symboles.* Paris: Gallimard, 1952.

Elkins, Sharon. *Holy Women of Twelfth-Century England.* Chapel Hill: University of North Carolina Press, 1988.

Ellington, Donna Spivey. *From Sacred Body to Angelic Soul: Understanding Mary in Late Medieval and Early Modern Europe.* Washington, DC: Catholic University of America Press, 2001.

Ellis, Roger. "The Word in Religious Art." In *Word, Picture, and Spectacle.* Ed. Clifford Davidson. Kalamazoo, MI: Medieval Institute Publications, 1984.

Emmerson, Richard K. "Eliding the 'Medieval': Renaissance 'New Historicism' and Sixteenth-Century Drama." In *The Performance of Middle English Culture: Essays on Chaucer and the Drama in Honor of Martin Stevens.* Cambridge: D.S. Brewer, 1998.

Enders, Jody. *Rhetoric and the Origins of Medieval Drama.* Ithaca, NY: Cornell University Press, 1992.

Enders, Jody. "Visions with Voices: The Rhetoric of Memory and Music in Liturgical Drama." *Comparative Drama* 24, no. 1 (1990): 34–54.

Evans, Ruth. "Chaucer in Cyberspace: Medieval Technologies of Memory and the *House of Fame*." *Studies in the Age of Chaucer* 23 (2001): 43–69.

Felman, Shoshana. *The Literary Speech Act: Don Juan with J.L. Austin, or Seduction in Two Languages.* Trans. Catherine Porter. Ithaca, NY: Cornell University Press, 1983.

Finch, Casey, trans. *The Complete Works of the Pearl Poet.* Berkeley: University of California Press, 1993.

Finucane, Ronald C. *Miracles and Pilgrims: Popular Beliefs in Medieval England.* Totowa, NJ: Rowman and Littlefield, 1977.

———. "Sacred Corpse, Profane Carrion: Social Ideals and Death Rituals in the Later Middle Ages." In *Mirrors of Mortality: Studies in the Social History of Death.* Ed. Joachim Whaley. London: Europa, 1981.

Fitzhenry, William. "The N-Town Plays and the Politics of Metatheater." *Studies in Philology* 100, no. 1 (2003): 22–43.

Fletcher, Alan J. "The Lyric in the Sermon." In *A Companion to the Middle English Lyric.* Ed. Thomas G. Duncan. Woodbridge, UK: D.S. Brewer, 2005.

———. "The N-Town Plays." In *The Cambridge Companion to Medieval English Theatre.* Ed. Richard Beadle. Cambridge: Cambridge University Press, 1994.

———. *Preaching, Politics, and Poetry in Late Medieval England.* Dublin: Four Courts Press, 1998.

Fradenburg, Louise. "'Voice Memorial': Loss and Reparation in Chaucer's Poetry." *Exemplaria* 2 (1990): 169–202.

Franko, Mark. "Given Movement: Dance and the Event." In *Ritual and Event: Interdisciplinary Perspectives.* Ed. Mark Franko. New York: Routledge, 2007.

Fulton, Rachel. *From Judgment to Passion: Devotion to Christ and the Virgin Mary, 800–1200.* New York: Columbia University Press, 2002.

Gaborit-Chopin, Danielle. "L'Ordre du Saint-Esprit: Les anges d'Anne de Bretagne." *La revue du Louvre et des musées de France* 44 (1994): 17–28.

Ganim, John. *Chaucerian Theatricality.* Princeton: Princeton University Press, 1990.

Garner, Stanton. *Bodied Spaces: Phenomenology and Performance in Contemporary Drama.* Ithaca, NY: Cornell University Press, 1994.

Geary, Patrick. *Furta Sacra: Thefts of Relics in the Central Middle Ages.* Rev. edn. Princeton: Princeton University Press, 1990.

Geertz, Clifford. *Negara: The Theater State in Nineteenth-Century Bali.* Princeton: Princeton University Press, 1980.

Gellrich, Jesse M. "*Figura*, Allegory, and the Question of History." In *Literary History and the Challenge of Philology: The Legacy of Erich Auerbach.* Ed. Seth Lerer. Stanford: Stanford University Press, 1996.

———. *The Idea of the Book in the Middle Ages.* Ithaca, NY: Cornell University Press, 1985.

Gibson, Gail McMurray. *The Theater of Devotion: East Anglian Drama and Society in the Late Middle Ages.* Chicago: University of Chicago Press, 1989.

Gillespie, Vincent. "Medieval Hypertext: Image and Text from York Minster." In *Of the Making of Books: Medieval Manuscripts, Their Scribes and Readers. Essays Presented to M.B. Parkes*. Ed. P.R. Robinson and Rivkah Zim. Brookfield, VT: Ashgate, 1997.

Gillies, Patricia. "What Happened When the Normans Arrived?" In *Beowulf and Other Stories: A New Introduction to Old English, Old Icelandic and Anglo-Norman Literatures*. Ed. Richard North and Joe Allard. London: Longman, 2007.

Gombrich, E.H. *Art and Illusion: A Study in the Psychology of Pictorial Representation*. New York: Bollingen Foundation, 1961.

Gradon, Pamela. "Langland and the Ideology of Dissent." *Proceedings of the British Academy* 66 (1980): 185–205.

Grady, Frank. "*Piers Plowman, Saint Erkenwald*, and the Rule of Exceptional Salvations." *Yearbook of Langland Studies* 6 (1992): 61–88.

Graef, Hilda. *Mary: A History of Doctrine and Devotion*. New York: Sheed and Ward, 1963.

Green, Richard Firth. "The Pardoner's Pants and Why They Matter." *Studies in the Age of Chaucer* 15 (1993): 131–45.

———. "Sir Gawain and the *Sacra Cintola*." *English Studies in Canada* 11 (1985): 1–11.

Greene, Thomas M. "Poetry as Invocation." *New Literary History* 24, no. 3 (1993): 495–517.

Greer, Michael. "Ideology and Theory in Recent Experimental Writing, or the Naming of 'Language Poetry.'" *boundary 2* 16, no. 2/3 (1989): 335–55.

Hagstrum, Jean. *The Sister Arts: The Tradition of Literary Pictorialism and English Poetry from Dryden to Gray*. Chicago: University of Chicago Press, 1958.

Hahn, Cynthia. "The Voices of the Saints: Speaking Reliquaries." *Gesta* 36, no. 1 (1997): 20–31.

Haidu, Peter. "Fragments in Search of Totalization: *Roland* and the Historical Text." In *Modernité au Moyen Âge: Le Défi du passé*. Ed. Brigitte Cazelles and Charles Méla. Geneva: Droz, 1990.

Hamburger, Jeffrey F. "The Medieval Work of Art: Wherein the 'Work'? Wherein the 'Art'?" In *The Mind's Eye: Art and Theological Argument in the Middle Ages*. Ed. Jeffrey F. Hamburger and Anne-Marie Bouché. Princeton: Princeton University Press, 2006.

———. "The Place of Theology in Medieval Art History: Problems, Positions, Possibilities." In *The Mind's Eye: Art and Theological Argument in the Middle Ages*. Ed. Jeffrey F. Hamburger and Anne-Marie Bouché. Princeton: Princeton University Press, 2006.

———. *The Visual and the Visionary: Art and Female Spirituality in Late-Medieval Germany*. New York: Zone Books, 1998.

Harbus, Antonina. "Text as Revelation: Constantine's Dream in *Elene*." *Neophilologus* 78, no. 4 (1994): 645–53.

Hardison, O.B. *Christian Rite and Christian Drama in the Middle Ages: Essays in the Origin and Early History of Modern Drama*. Baltimore, MD: Johns Hopkins University Press, 1965.

Hartman, Geoffrey. *The Unremarkable Wordsworth*. Minneapolis: University of Minnesota Press, 1987.

Harwood, Britton. "Chaucer's Pardoner: The Dialectics of Inside and Outside." *Philological Quarterly* 67, no. 4 (1988): 409–22.

Herrmann-Mascard, Nicole. *Les reliques des saints: formation coutumière d'un droit.* Paris: Klincksieck, 1975.

Hieatt, Constance B. *The Realism of Dream Visions: The Poetic Exploitation of the Dream-Experience in Chaucer and His Contemporaries.* Paris: Mouton, 1967.

Hirn, Yrjö. *The Sacred Shrine: A Study of the Poetry and Art of the Catholic Church.* London: Macmillan, 1912.

Hoerner, Fred. "Church Office, Routine, and Self-Exile in Chaucer's Pardoner." *Studies in the Age of Chaucer* 16 (1994): 69–98.

Holbert, Kelly McKay. "Mosan Reliquary Triptychs and the Cult of the True Cross in the Twelfth Century." Ph.D. diss., Yale University, 1995.

Hollander, John. "The Poetics of Ekphrasis." *Word & Image: A Journal of Verbal/Visual Enquiry* 4 (1988): 209–19.

Holloway, Julia Bolton. "*The Dream of the Rood* and Liturgical Drama." *Comparative Drama* 18, no. 1 (1984): 19–37.

Holsinger. Bruce. *The Premodern Condition: Medievalism and the Making of Theory.* Chicago: University of Chicago Press, 2005.

Howe, John M. "The Conversion of the Physical World: The Creation of a Christian Landscape." In *Varieties of Religious Conversion in the Middle Ages.* Ed. James Muldoon. Gainesville: University Press of Florida, 1997.

Hudson, Anne. *The Premature Reformation: Wycliffite Text and Lollard History.* New York: Oxford University Press, 1988.

———, ed. *Selections from English Wycliffite Writings.* New York: Cambridge University Press, 1978.

———, ed. *Two Wycliffite Texts: The Sermon of William Taylor 1406; The Testimony of William Thorpe 1407.* Oxford: Oxford University Press, 1993.

Husband, Timothy, and Julien Chapuis. *The Treasury of Basel Cathedral.* New York: The Metropolitan Museum of Art and Yale University Press, 2001.

Illich, Ivan. *In the Vineyard of the Text.* Chicago: University of Chicago Press, 1993.

Issacharoff, Michael, and Robin F. Jones, eds. *Performing Texts.* Philadelphia: University of Pennsylvania Press, 1988.

Izenberg, Oren. "Language Poetry and the Collective Life." *Critical Inquiry* 30 (2003): 132–59.

Jager, Eric. *The Book of the Heart.* Chicago: University of Chicago Press, 2000.

James, M.R., and Claude Jenkins, eds. *A Descriptive Catalogue of Manuscripts in the Library of Lambeth Palace: The Mediaeval Manuscripts.* Cambridge: Cambridge University Press, 1932.

Jeffrey, David L. *Early English Lyric and Franciscan Spirituality.* Lincoln: University of Nebraska Press, 1975.

Johnson, Lynn Staley. *The Voice of the Gawain-Poet.* Madison: University of Wisconsin Press, 1984.

Justice, Steven. "The Authority of Ritual in the *Jeu d'Adam.*" *Speculum* 62, no. 4 (1987): 851–64.

Kamerick, Kathleen. *Popular Piety and Art in the Late Middle Ages: Image Worship and Idolatry in England 1350–1500.* New York: Palgrave Macmillan, 2002.

Kamowski, William. "*Saint Erkenwald* and the Inadvertent Baptism: An Orthodox Response to Heterodox Ecclesiology." *Religion and Literature* 27, no.3 (1995): 5–27.

Kean, P.M. *The Pearl: An Interpretation.* New York: Barnes & Noble, 1967.

Kendall, Calvin B. *The Allegory of the Church: Romanesque Portals and Their Verse Inscriptions.* Toronto: University of Toronto Press, 1998.

———. "The Gate of Heaven and the Fountain of Life: Speech-Act Theory and Portal Inscriptions." *Essays in Medieval Studies* 10 (1993): 111–25.

Kernodle, George Riley. *From Art to Theatre: Form and Convention in the Renaissance.* Chicago: University of Chicago Press, 1944.

Kessler, Herbert L. *Seeing Medieval Art.* Orchard Park, NY: Broadview, 2004.

———. *Spiritual Seeing: Picturing God's Invisibility in Medieval Art.* Philadelphia: University of Pennsylvania Press, 2000.

———. "Turning a Blind Eye: Medieval Art and the Dynamics of Contemplation." In *The Mind's Eye: Art and Theological Argument in the Middle Ages.* Ed. Jeffrey F. Hamburger and Anne-Marie Bouché. Princeton: Princeton University Press, 2006.

Kilgour, Maggie. *From Communion to Cannibalism: An Anatomy of Metaphors of Incorporation.* Princeton: Princeton University Press, 1990.

Kimmelman, Burt. "Ockham, Chaucer, and the Emergence of a Modern Poetics." In *The Rhetorical Poetics of the Middle Ages: Reconstructive Polyphony: Essays in Honor of Robert O. Payne.* Ed. John M. Hill and Deborah M. Sinnreich-Levi. Madison, NJ: Fairleigh Dickinson University Press, 2000.

King, Pamela M. "Spatial Semantics and the Medieval Theatre." In *The Theatrical Space.* Themes in Drama, vol. 9. Gen. ed. James Redmond. New York: Cambridge University Press, 1987.

Kinservik, Matthew. "The Struggle over Mary's Body: Theological and Dramatic Resolution in the N-Town *Assumption* Play." *JEGP* 95, no. 2 (1996): 190–203.

Kipling, Gordon. *Enter the King: Theatre, Liturgy, and Ritual in the Medieval Civic Triumph.* New York: Oxford University Press, 1998.

Knopp, Sherron E. "Augustinian Poetic Theory and the Chaucerian Imagination." In *The Idea of Medieval Literature: New Essays on Chaucer in Honor of Donald R. Howard.* Ed. James M. Dean and Christian K. Zacher. Newark: University of Delaware Press, 1992.

Kolve, V.A. *Chaucer and the Imagery of Narrative: The First Five Canterbury Tales.* Stanford: Stanford University Press, 1984.

———. *The Play Called Corpus Christi.* Stanford: Stanford University Press, 1966.

Kowalik, Barbara. "Traces of Romance Textual Poetics in the Non-Romance Works Ascribed to the *Gawain*-Poet." In *From Medieval to Medievalism.* Ed. John Simons. London: Macmillan, 1992.

Krieger, Murray. "The Ambiguities of Representation and Illusion: An E.H. Gombrich Retrospective." *Critical Inquiry* 11 (1984): 181–94.

Krieger, Murray. "Ekphrasis and the Still Moment of Poetry: Or, *Laokoön* Revisited." In *Perspectives on Poetry*. Ed. James L. Calderwood and Harold E. Toliver. New York: Oxford University Press, 1968.

Kruger, Steven F. *Dreaming in the Middle Ages*. Cambridge: Cambridge University Press, 1992.

Largier, Niklaus, "Scripture, Vision, Performance: Visionary Texts and Medieval Religious Drama." In *Visual Culture and the German Middle Ages*. Ed. Kathryn Starkey and Horst Wenzel. New York: Palgrave Macmillan, 2005.

Lee, Jennifer A. "The Illuminating Critic: The Illustrator of Cotton Nero A.x." *Studies in Iconography* 3 (1997): 17–46.

Lee, Rensselaer W. *Ut Pictura Poesis: The Humanistic Theory of Painting*. New York: W.W. Norton, 1967.

Lentes, Thomas. "Rituals of Gazing in the Late Middle Ages." In *The Mind's Eye: Art and Theological Argument in the Middle Ages*. Ed. Jeffrey F. Hamburger and Anne-Marie Bouché. Princeton: Princeton University Press, 2006.

Lerud, Theodore K. "Quick Images: Memory and the English Corpus Christi Drama." In *Moving Subjects: Processional Performance in the Middle Ages and the Renaissance*. Ed. Kathleen Ashley and Wim Hüsken. Atlanta, GA: Rodopi, 2001.

Levillain, Léon. "Essai sur les origines du Lendit." *Révue Historique* 157 (1927): 241–76.

Lewis, Katherine J. "Pilgrimage and the Cult of St. Katherine." In *Pilgrimage Explored*. Ed. J. Stopford. Rochester, NY: York Medieval Press, 1999.

Litten, Julian. "The Funeral Effigy: Its Function and Purpose." In *The Funeral Effigies of Westminster Abbey*. Ed. Anthony Harvey and Richard Mortimer. Rochester, NY: Boydell Press, 1994.

Loerke, William. "'Real Presence' in Early Christian Art." In *Monasticism and the Arts*. Ed. Timothy Gregory Verdon. Syracuse, NY: Syracuse University Press, 1984.

Lupton, Julia Reinhard. *Afterlives of the Saints: Hagiography, Typology, and Renaissance Literature*. Stanford: Stanford University Press, 1996.

Lynch, Kathryn L. "Baring Bottom: Shakespeare and the Chaucerian Dream Vision." In *Reading Dreams: The Interpretation of Dreams from Chaucer to Shakespeare*. Ed. Peter Brown. New York: Oxford University Press, 1999.

———. *The High Medieval Dream Vision: Poetry, Philosophy, and Literary Form*. Stanford: Stanford University Press, 1988.

Macrae-Gibson, O.D. "*Pearl*: The Link-Words and the Thematic Structure." *Neophilologus* 52, no. 1 (1968): 54–64.

Markiewicz, Henryk. "Ut Pictura Poesis...A History of the Topos and the Problem." *New Literary History* 18, no. 3 (1987): 535–58.

Marti, Kevin. *Body, Heart, and Text in the* Pearl-*Poet*. Lewiston, NY: Edwin Mellen, 1991.

———. "Traditional Characteristics of the Resurrected Body in *Pearl*." *Viator* 24 (1993): 311–35.

Martin, Priscilla. "Allegory and Symbolism." In *A Companion to the Gawain-Poet*. Ed. Derek Brewer and Jonathan Gibson. Cambridge, UK: D. S. Brewer, 1997.

McAlindon, T. "Hagiography into Art: A Study of *St. Erkenwald*." *Studies in Philology* 67 (1970): 472–94.

McKitterick, Rosamond, and Richard Beadle. *Catalogue of the Pepys Library at Magdalene College, Cambridge V: Manuscripts I. Medieval*. Cambridge, UK: D.S. Brewer, 1993.

McLuhan, Marshall. *Understanding Media: The Extensions of Man*. Critical edn. Corte Madera, CA: Gingko, 2003.

Merleau-Ponty, Maurice. "Indirect Language and the Voices of Silence." In *Signs*. Trans. Richard C. McCleary. Evanston, IL: Northwestern University Press, 1964.

Merrix, R.P. "Sermon Structure in the *Pardoner's Tale*." *Chaucer Review* 17 (1983): 235–49.

Meyer, Ann R. *Medieval Allegory and the Building of the New Jerusalem*. Woodbridge, UK: D.S. Brewer, 2003.

Meyer-Lee, Robert J. *Poets and Power from Chaucer to Wyatt*. New York: Cambridge University Press, 2007.

Miller, J. Hillis. *Speech Acts in Literature*. Stanford: Stanford University Press, 2001.

Minnis, Alastair J. *Medieval Theory of Authorship: Scholastic Literary Attitudes in the Later Middle Ages*. 2nd edn. London: Scholar, 1988.

———. "The Author's Two Bodies? Authority and Fallibility in Late-Medieval Textual Theory." In *Of the Making of Books: Medieval Manuscripts, Their Scribes and Readers: Essays Presented to M.B. Parkes*. Ed. P.R. Robinson and Rivkah Zim. Brookfield, VT: Ashgate, 1997.

Mitchell, Bruce, and Fred C. Robinson, eds. *A Guide to Old English*. 5th edn. Cambridge: Blackwell, 1992.

Mitchell, J. Allen. "The Middle English *Pearl*: Figuring the Unfigurable." *Chaucer Review* 35, no. 1 (2000): 86–111.

Mitchell, W.J.T. *Iconology: Image, Text, Ideology*. Chicago: University of Chicago Press, 1986.

———. *Picture Theory*. Chicago: University of Chicago Press, 1994.

Moramarco, Fred. "John Ashbery and Frank O'Hara: The Painterly Poets," *Journal of Modern Literature* 5, no. 3 (1976): 436–62.

Morgan, Nigel. *Early Gothic Manuscripts*. London: Harvey Miller, 1982–88.

Nelson, Cary. *The Incarnate Word: Literature as Verbal Space*. Urbana: University of Illinois Press, 1973.

Newman, Barbara. *From Virile Woman to WomanChrist: Studies in Medieval Religion and Literature*. Philadelphia: University of Pennsylvania Press, 1995.

———. "What Did It Mean to Say 'I Saw'?: The Clash between Theory and Practice in Medieval Visionary Culture." *Speculum* 80, no. 1 (2005): 1–43.

Nichols, Ann Eljenholm. "The Hierosphthitic Topos, or the Fate of Fergus: Notes on the N-Town *Assumption*." *Comparative Drama* 25, no. 1 (1991): 29–41.

Nichols, Stephen G. "Ekphrasis, Iconoclasm, and Desire." In *Rethinking the Romance of the Rose: Text, Image, Reception.* Ed. Kevin Brownlee and Sylvia Huot. Philadelphia: University of Pennsylvania Press, 1992.

———. *Romanesque Signs: Early Medieval Narrative and Iconography.* New Haven, CT: Yale University Press, 1983.

Nilson, Benjamin. *Cathedral Shrines of Medieval England.* Rochester, NY: Boydell, 1998.

Nissé, Ruth. "'A Coroun Ful Riche': The Rule of History in *Saint Erkenwald.*" *ELH* 65 (1998): 277–95.

Ogden, Dunbar H. *The Staging of Drama in the Medieval Church.* London: Associated University Presses, 2002.

O'Keeffe, Katherine O'Brien. *Visible Song: Transitional Literacy in Old English Verse.* New York: Cambridge University Press, 1990.

Olsen, Alexandra Hennessey. "They Shul Desiren to Dye, and Deeth Shal Flee fro Hem: A Reconsideration of the Pardoner's Old Man." *Neuphilologische Mitteilungen* 84, no. 3 (1983): 367–71.

Olson, Glending. "Toward a Poetics of the Late Medieval Court Lyric." In *Vernacular Poetics in the Middle Ages.* Ed. Lois Ebin. Kalamazoo, MI: Medieval Institute Publications, 1984.

Ong, Walter. *Interfaces of the Word: Studies in the Evolution of Consciousness and Culture.* Ithaca, NY: Cornell University Press, 1977.

Osborn, Marijane. "Transgressive Word and Image in Chaucer's Enshrined *Coillons* Passage." *Chaucer Review* 37, no. 4 (2003): 365–84.

Otter, Monika. "'New Werke': *St. Erkenwald*, St. Albans, and the Medieval Sense of the Past." *Journal of Medieval and Renaissance Studies* 24, no. 3 (1994): 387–414.

Ousterhout, Robert. "Loca Sancta and the Architectural Response to Pilgrimage." In *The Blessings of Pilgrimage*, ed. Robert Ousterhout. Urbana and Chicago: University of Illinois Press, 1990.

Owst, G.R. *Literature and Pulpit in Medieval England.* New York: Barnes & Noble, 1961.

Palazzo, Éric. "Marie et l'élaboration d'un espace ecclesial au haut Moyen Âge." In *Marie: le culte de la Vierge dans la société médiévale.* Ed. Dominique Iogna-Prat, Éric Palazzo, Daniel Russo. Paris: Beauchesne, 1996.

Palmer, Michael. "Sun." In *Sun.* San Francisco: North Point Press, 1988.

Parker, Andrew, and Eve Kosofsky Sedgwick, eds. *Performativity and Performance.* New York: Routledge, 1995.

Patterson, Lee. *Chaucer and the Subject of History.* Madison: University of Wisconsin Press, 1991.

———. "Chaucer's Pardoner on the Couch: Psyche and Clio in Medieval Literary Studies," *Speculum* 76, no. 3 (2001): 638–80.

Pearsall, Derek. "Chaucer's Pardoner: The Death of a Salesman." *The Chaucer Review* 17 (1983–84): 358–65.

———. "Towards a Poetics of Chaucerian Narrative." In *Drama, Narrative, and Poetry in the* Canterbury Tales. Toulouse, France: Presses Universitaires du Mirail, 2003.

Perelman, Bob, ed. *Writing/Talks.* Carbondale: Southern Illinois University Press, 1985.

Perkins, Jocelyn. *Westminster Abbey: Its Worship and Ornaments.* 2 vols. London: Oxford University Press, 1938–52.

Perloff, Marjorie. "Language Poetry and the Lyric Subject: Ron Silliman's Albany, Susan Howe's Buffalo." *Critical Inquiry* 25 (1999): 405–34.

Prior, Sandra Pierson. *The Fayre Formez of the* Pearl *Poet.* East Lansing: Michigan State University Press, 1996.

Purdon, L.O. "The Pardoner's Old Man and the Second Death." *Studies in Philology* 89, no. 3 (1992): 334–49.

Quinn, William A. "The Psychology of *St. Erkenwald.*" *Medium Aevum* 53 (1984): 180–93.

Rambuss, Richard. "Devotion and Defilement: The Blessed Virgin Mary and the Corporeal Hagiographics of Chaucer's *Prioress's Tale.*" In *Textual Bodies: Changing Boundaries of Literary Representation.* Ed. Lori Hope Lefkovitz. Albany: State University of New York Press, 1993.

Read, Charles Hercules. "On a Triptych of the Twelfth Century from the Abbey of Stavelot in Belgium." *Archaeologia* 62 (1910): 21–30.

Reichardt, Paul F. " 'Several Illuminations, Coarsely Executed': The Illustrations of the *Pearl* Manuscript." *Studies in Iconography* 18 (1997): 119–42.

Reiss, Edmund. "Ambiguous Signs and Authorial Deceptions in Fourteenth-Century Fictions." In *Sign, Sentence, Discourse: Language in Medieval Thought and Literature.* Ed. Julian N. Wasserman and Lois Roney. Syracuse, NY: Syracuse University Press, 1989.

Remensnyder, Amy G. "Legendary Treasure at Conques: Reliquaries and Imaginative Memory." *Speculum* 71 (1996): 884–906.

Ricoeur, Paul. *La Métaphore vive.* Paris: Editions du Seuil, 1975.

———. "The Metaphorical Process as Cognition, Imagination, and Feeling." In *On Metaphor.* Ed. Sheldon Sacks. Chicago: University of Chicago Press, 1978.

Riddy, Felicity. "Jewels in *Pearl.*" In *A Companion to the* Gawain-*Poet.* Ed. Derek Brewer and Jonathan Gibson. Cambridge, UK: D.S. Brewer, 1997.

Ringbom, Sixten. *Icon to Narrative.* Acta Academiae Aboensis, ser. A, 31, no, 2. Åbo, Finland: Åbo Akademi, 1965.

Roberts, Peter. "Politics, Drama, and the Cult of Thomas Becket." In *Pilgrimage: The English Experience from Becket to Bunyan.* Ed. Colin Morris and Peter Roberts. New York: Cambridge University Press, 2002.

Robertson, D.W. *Essays in Medieval Culture.* Princeton: Princeton University Press, 1980.

Robertson, Elizabeth A. *Early English Devotional Prose and the Female Audience.* Knoxville: University of Tennessee Press, 1990.

Roper, Gregory. "*Pearl,* Penitence, and the Recovery of the Self." *The Chaucer Review* 28, no. 2 (1993): 164–86.

———. "The Middle English Lyric 'I,' Penitential Poetics, and Medieval Selfhood." *Poetica* 42 (1994): 71–103.

Rothfield, Lawrence. "Autobiography and Perspective in the *Confessions* of St. Augustine." *Comparative Literature* 33, no. 3 (1981): 209–23.

Rubin, Miri. *Corpus Christi: The Eucharist in Late Medieval Culture*. New York: Cambridge University Press, 1991.

———. "The Body, Whole and Vulnerable, in Fifteenth-Century England." In *Bodies and Disciplines: Intersections of Literature and History in Fifteenth-Century England*. Ed. Barbara A. Hanawalt and David Wallace. Minneapolis: University of Minnesota Press, 1996.

Rushing, James A., Jr. "Images at the Interface: Orality, Literacy, and the Pictorialization of the Roland Material." In *Visual Culture and the German Middle Ages*. Ed. Kathryn Starkey and Horst Wenzel. New York: Palgrave Macmillan, 2005.

Salter, Elizabeth. *Fourteenth-Century English Poetry: Contexts and Readings*. Oxford: Clarendon, 1984.

Scarry, Elaine. *Dreaming by the Book*. New York: Farrar, Straus and Giroux, 1999.

Scase, Wendy. "Writing and the 'Poetics of Spectacle': Political Epiphanies in *The Arrivall of Edward IV* and Some Contemporary and Lancastrian Texts." In *Images, Idolatry, and Iconoclasm in Late Medieval England: Textuality and the Visual Image*. Ed. Jeremy Dimmick, James Simpson, and Nicolette Zeeman. New York: Oxford University Press, 2002.

Scherb, Victor I. *Staging Faith: East Anglian Drama in the Middle Ages*. Madison, NJ: Fairleigh Dickinson University Press, 2001.

Schirmer, Elizabeth. "Genre Trouble: Spiritual Reading in the Vernacular and the Literary Project of the *Pearl*-Poet." Ph.D. diss. University of California, Berkeley, 2002.

Schotter, Anne Howland. "Vernacular Style and the Word of God: The Incarnational Art of *Pearl*." In *Ineffability: Naming the Unnamable from Dante to Beckett*. New York: AMS Press, 1984.

Seidel, Linda. *Legends in Limestone: Lazarus, Gislebertus, and the Cathedral of Autun*. Chicago: University of Chicago Press, 1999.

Sevret, Pierre. "Le Personnage de la Vierge dans les Mystères." In *Imagines Mariae: représentations du personnage de la Vierge dans la poésie, le théâtre, et l'éloquence entre le XIIe et le XVI siècles*. Ed. Christian Mouchel et al. Lyon, France: Presses Universitaires de Lyon, 1999.

Sheingorn, Pamela, trans. *The Book of Sainte Foy*. Philadelphia: University of Pennsylvania Press, 1995.

———. "On Using Medieval Art in the Study of Medieval Drama." *Research Opportunities in Renaissance Drama* 22 (1979): 101–9.

Shoaf, R.A. *Dante, Chaucer, and the Currency of the Word: Money, Images, and Reference in Late-Medieval Poetry*. Norman, OK: Pilgrim Books, 1983.

———. "Medieval Studies after Heidegger after Derrida." In *Sign, Sentence, Discourse: Language in Medieval Thought and Literature*. Ed. Julian N. Wasserman and Lois Roney. Syracuse, NY: Syracuse University Press, 1989.

Shoemaker, Stephen J. "'Let Us Go and Burn Her Body': The Image of the Jews in the Early Dormition Traditions." *Church History* 68, no. 4 (1999): 775–823.

Signori, Gabriela. "La bienheureuse polysémie Miracles et pèlerinages à la Vierge: pouvoir thaumaturgique et modèles pastoraux (Xe–XIIe siècles)." In

Marie: le culte de la Vierge dans la société médiévale. Ed. Dominique Iogna-Prat, Éric Palazzo, Daniel Russo. Paris: Beauchesne, 1996.

Silliman, Ron. "Who Speaks: Ventriloquism and the Self in the Poetry Reading." In *Close Listening: Poetry and the Performed Word.* Ed. Charles Bernstein. New York: Oxford University Press, 1998.

Sinanoglou, Leah. "The Christ Child as Sacrifice: A Medieval Tradition and the Corpus Christi Plays." *Speculum* 48, no. 3 (1973): 491–509.

Sisk, Jennifer L. "The Uneasy Orthodoxy of *St. Erkenwald.*" *ELH* 74, no. 1 (2007): 89–115.

Snoek, G.J.C. *Medieval Piety from Relics to the Eucharist: A Process of Mutual Interaction.* New York: E.J. Brill, 1995.

Somerset, Fiona, and Nicholas Watson, eds. *The Vulgar Tongue: Medieval and Postmedieval Vernacularity.* University Park, PA: Penn State University Press, 2003.

Soussloff, Catherine. "Like a Performance: Performativity and the Historicized Body, from Bellori to Mapplethorpe." In *Acting on the Past: Historical Performance across the Disciplines.* Ed. Mark Franko and Annette Richards. Hanover, NH: Wesleyan University Press, 2000.

Spearing, A.C. *The Gawain-Poet: A Critical Study.* Cambridge: Cambridge University Press, 1970.

———. *Medieval Dream Poetry.* Cambridge: Cambridge University Press, 1976.

Spencer, H. Leith. *English Preaching in the Late Middle Ages.* Oxford: Clarendon, 1993.

Spitzer, Leo. "A Note on the Poetic and Empirical 'I' in Medieval Authors." *Traditio* 4 (1946): 412–22.

Sponsler, Claire. "The Culture of the Spectator: Conformity and Resistances to Medieval Performances." *Theater Journal* 44 (1992): 15–29.

St. John, Michael. *Chaucer's Dream Visions: Courtliness and Individual Identity.* Burlington, VT: Ashgate, 2000.

Stahl, Harvey. "Heaven in View: The Place of the Elect in an Illuminated Book of Hours." In *Last Things: Death and the Apocalypse in the Middle Ages.* Ed. Caroline Walker Bynum and Paul Freedman. Philadelphia: University of Pennsylvania Press, 2000.

Staley, Lynn. "*Pearl* and the Contingencies of Love and Piety." In *Medieval Literature and Historical Inquiry: Essays in Honour of Derek Pearsall.* Ed. David Aers. Cambridge: D.S. Brewer, 2000.

Stanbury, Sarah. *Seeing the Gawain-Poet: Description and the Act of Perception.* Philadelphia: University of Pennsylvania Press, 1991.

———. "The Virgin's Gaze: Spectacle and Transgression in Middle English Lyrics of the Passion." *PMLA* 106, no. 5 (1991): 1083–93.

———. "Visions of Space: Acts of Perception in *Pearl* and in Some Late Medieval Illustrated Apocalypses." *Mediaevalia: A Journal of Mediaeval Studies* 10 (1988): 133–58.

———. *The Visual Object of Desire in Late Medieval England.* Philadelphia: University of Pennsylvania Press, 2007.

States, Bert O. "The Phenomenological Attitude." In *Critical Theory and Performance.* Ed. Janelle G. Reinelt and Joseph R. Roach. Ann Arbor: University of Michigan Press, 1992.

Steadman, John M. "Old Age and *Contemptus Mundi* in the *Pardoner's Tale*." In *Twentieth Century Interpretations of the* Pardoner's Tale: *A Collection of Critical Essays*. Ed. Dewey R. Faulkner. Englewood Cliffs, NJ: Prentice-Hall, 1973.

Steiner, Emily. *Documentary Culture and the Making of Medieval English Literature*. New York: Cambridge University Press, 2003.

Steiner, Wendy. *The Colors of Rhetoric: Problems in the Relation between Modern Literature and Painting*. Chicago: University of Chicago Press, 1982.

Stevens, Martin, and Kathleen Falvey. "Substance, Accident, and Transformations: A Reading of the *Pardoner's Tale*." *The Chaucer Review* 17 no. 2 (1982): 142–58.

Stewart, Aubrey, trans. *The Epitome of S. Eucherius About Certain Holy Places*. London: Palestine Pilgrims' Text Society, 1971.

Stock, Brian. *The Implications of Literacy: Written Language and Models of Interpretation in the Eleventh and Twelfth Centuries*. Princeton: Princeton University Press, 1983.

———. *Listening for the Text: On the Uses of the Past*. Baltimore, MD: Johns Hopkins University Press, 1990.

Storm, Melvin. "The Pardoner's Invitation: Quaestor's Bag or Becket's Shrine?" *PMLA* 97, no. 5 (1982): 810–18.

Strohm, Paul. "Chaucer's Lollard Joke: History and the Textual Unconscious." *Studies in the Age of Chaucer* 19 (1995): 23–42.

———. "The Trouble with Richard: The Reburial of Richard II and Lancastrian Symbolic Strategy." *Speculum* 71 (1996): 87–111.

Sumption, Jonathan. *Pilgrimage: An Image of Medieval Religion*. London: Faber & Faber, 1975.

Symes, Carol. "The Appearance of Early Vernacular Plays: Forms, Functions, and the Future of Medieval Theater." *Speculum* 77, no. 3 (2002): 778–831.

———. *A Common Stage: Theater and Public Life in Medieval Arras*. Ithaca, NY: Cornell University Press, 2007.

Szittya, Penn R. *The Antifraternal Tradition in Medieval Literature*. Princeton: Princeton University Press, 1986.

Tachau, Katherine H. "Seeing as Action and Passion in the Thirteenth and Fourteenth Centuries." In *The Mind's Eye: Art and Theological Argument in the Middle Ages*. Ed. Jeffrey F. Hamburger and Anne-Marie Bouché. Princeton: Princeton University Press, 2006.

Tasioulas, J.A. "Between Doctrine and Domesticity: The Portrayal of Mary in the N-Town Plays." In *Medieval Women in Their Communities*. Ed. Diane Watt. Toronto: University of Toronto Press, 1997.

Tatton-Brown, Tim. "Canterbury and the Architecture of Pilgrimage Shrines in England." In *Pilgrimage: The English Experience from Becket to Bunyan*. Ed. Colin Morris and Peter Roberts. New York: Cambridge University Press, 2002.

Taylor, Paul Beekman. "Peynted Confessiouns: Boccaccio and Chaucer." *Comparative Literature* 34 (1982): 116–29.

Tomasch, Sylvia. "Breaking the Frame: Medieval Art and Drama." In *Early Drama to 1600*. Ed. Albert H. Tricomi. Binghamton, NY: Center for Medieval and Early Renaissance Studies, 1987.

Townsend, Eleanor. "Pilgrimage." In *Gothic Art for England, 1400–1547*. Ed. Richard Marks and Paul Williamson, assisted by Eleanor Townsend. London: V&A Publications, 2003.

Turville-Petre, Thorlac. *The Alliterative Revival*. Cambridge, UK: D.S. Brewer, 1977.

Twycross, Meg, and Sarah Carpenter, eds. *Masks and Masking in Medieval and Early Tudor England*. Burlington, VT: Ashgate, 2002.

van Os, Henk. *The Way to Heaven: Relic Veneration in the Middle Ages*. Amsterdam: de Prom, 2001.

Vance, Eugene. "Chaucer's Pardoner: Relics, Discourse, and Frames of Propriety." *New Literary History* 20 (1989): 723–45.

———. *Mervelous Signals: Poetics and Sign Theory in the Middle Ages*. Lincoln: University of Nebraska Press, 1986.

———. "*Pearl*: Love and the Poetics of Participation." In *Poetics: Theory and Practice in Medieval English Literature*. Ed. Piero Boitani and Anna Torti. Cambridge, UK: D.S. Brewer, 1991.

———. "Semiotics and Power: Relics, Icons, and the *Voyage de Charlemagne à Jérusalem et à Constantinople*." *Romanic Review* 79, no. 1 (1988): 164–83.

———. "Style and Value: From Soldier to Pilgrim in the *Song of Roland*." *Yale French Studies* 80 (1991): 75–96.

Vasta, Edward. "*Pearl*: Immortal Flowers and the Pearl's Decay." *Journal of English and Germanic Philology* 66 (1967): 519–31.

Voelkle, William. *The Stavelot Triptych: Mosan Art and the Legend of the True Cross*. New York: Pierpont Morgan Library, 1980.

Vriend, J. *The Blessed Virgin Mary in the Medieval Drama of England*. Purmerend, Holland: J. Muisse, 1928.

Warner, Marina. *Alone of All Her Sex: The Myth and Cult of the Virgin Mary*. London: Weidenfeld and Nicholson, 1976.

Waters, Claire M. *Angels and Earthly Creatures*. Philadelphia: University of Pennsylvania Press, 2004.

Watson, Nicholas. "The Methods and Objectives of Thirteenth-Century Anchoritic Devotion." In *The Medieval Mystical Tradition in England*. Ed. Marion Glasscoe. Cambridge, UK: D.S. Brewer, 1987.

———. "The *Gawain*-Poet as a Vernacular Theologian." In *A Companion to the* Gawain-*Poet*. Ed. Derek Brewer and Jonathan Gibson. Cambridge, UK: D.S. Brewer, 1997.

Watson, Robert A. "Dialogue and Invention in the *Book of the Duchess*." *Modern Philology* 98, no. 4 (2001): 543–76.

Weiss, Daniel H. "Architectural Symbolism and the Decoration of the Sainte-Chapelle." *The Art Bulletin* 77 (1995): 308–20.

Wenzel, Siegfried. "Chaucer and the Language of Contemporary Preaching." *Studies in Philology* 73 (1976): 138–61.

———. *Preachers, Poets, and the Early English Lyric*. Princeton: Princeton University Press, 1986.

Whatley, E. Gordon. "Heathens and Saints: *St. Erkenwald* in Its Legendary Context." *Speculum* 61, no. 2 (1986): 330–63.

Whatley, E. Gordon. "The Middle English *St. Erkenwald* and Its Liturgical Context." *Mediaevalia* 8 (1992): 277–306.

———, ed. and trans. *The Saint of London: The Life and Miracles of Saint Erkenwald.* Binghamton, NY: Medieval and Renaissance Texts and Studies, 1989.

Whitaker, Muriel A. "*Pearl* and Some Illustrated Apocalypse Manuscripts." *Viator: Medieval and Renaissance Studies* 12 (1981): 183–96.

White, Hugh. "Blood in *Pearl*." *Review of English Studies* n.s. 38, no. 194 (1987): 1–13.

Whitehead, Christiania. "Middle English Religious Lyrics." In *A Companion to the Middle English Lyric*. Ed. Thomas G. Duncan. Woodbridge, UK: D.S. Brewer, 2005.

Williamson, Beth. "Liturgical Image or Devotional Image? The London *Madonna of the Firescreen*." In *Objects, Images, and the Word: Art in the Service of the Liturgy*. Ed. Colum Hourihane. Princeton: Princeton University Press, 2003.

Wogan-Brown, Jocelyn, Nicholas Watson, Andrew Taylor, and Ruth Evans, eds. *The Idea of the Vernacular: An Anthology of Middle English Literary Theory, 1280–1520*. University Park, PA: Penn State University Press, 1999.

Woolf, Rosemary. *The English Mystery Plays*. Berkeley: University of California Press, 1972.

Wormald, Francis. "The Rood of Bromholm." *Journal of the Warburg Institute* 1, no. 1 (1937): 31–45.

Zumthor, Paul. *Toward a Medieval Poetics*. Trans. Philip Bennet. Minneapolis: University of Minnesota Press, 1992.

INDEX

Note: *italicized* page numbers refer to illustrations.